MY DREAMS, MY INTERPRETATIONS:

Night Visions in My Head

Volume 1

God Revealing His Plan
for you and me through Dreams

Sarah A. Jones

WestBow
PRESS
A DIVISION OF THOMAS NELSON

ISBN: 978-1-4497-1927-2 (e)
ISBN: 978-1-4497-1928-9 (sc)
ISBN: 978-1-4497-1929-6 (hc)
Library of Congress Control Number: 2011931400

WestBow Press books may be ordered through booksellers or by contacting:

WestBow Press
A Division of Thomas Nelson
1663 Liberty Drive
Bloomington, IN 47403
www.westbowpress.com
1-(866) 928-1240

Printed in the United States of America

WestBow Press rev. date: 11/29/2011

For any information, prayer requests, comments about this book, permissions, author appearance, or book orders, please contact Author. For large book orders contact Publisher directly.

Sarah A. Jones
P.O. Box 260524
Brooklyn, NY 11226-0524

We would love to hear from you, and thank you for your sincere prayers and support.
My website is forthcoming.

In Loving Memory of My Parents

Elder and Assistant Pastor, Jesse Jones, my father, a man with great humility, love, faith, integrity, strength, and courage. A very hard worker, provided for his family, always there for us, and others who needed his aid. He was a loving husband and father. I always said (and believed), that he was the "best daddy in the whole world."

Mrs. Amanda Jones, my beloved mother, and best friend who always prayed for me, and always had an ear and heart to listen. She encouraged me to answer the call of God on my life, and to write this book; a woman of great faith, love, integrity, strength and courage; and a loving wife and mother.

Thank you for raising me in the admonition of God; for teaching, and nurturing me in the word of God at a very young age. Thanks for making me go to church, Sunday school and bible study even when I didn't want to. Thank you for your love and words of wisdom. Not only did you teach us (my brothers, sister, and me) to trust God, you showed us how to trust Him. I am so proud of you. If I had to choose my own parents, you would have been my choice. I miss you so very much, and even now I can see your loving smiles. I thank God for you.

GENERAL PREFACE

This book is about how God our Father, and Jesus Christ His Son, our Lord and Saviour, communicates with me through dreams (and a few visions); and my relationship and fellowship with Him. All of the dreams you read in this book are given by God (just as He gave them to me); and all of my interpretations are revealed and inspired by God, Jesus, and the Holy Spirit.

As you read this book, God may speak to you differently, or give you another interpretation from what I have written. If so, that's okay—it is all in His plan, and it's between you and Him. He wants to minister to you personally, one on one.

Allow God to visit and speak to you wherever you are in life right now. He knows everything about you; what you've done, what you're doing, where you've been, where you want to go; and where you are destined to go. He knows what you are thinking even at this very moment. Whatever you may be going through, and no matter what the problem is God will work it out for your good, if you love and trust Him.

God wants you to know that He knows, cares, and loves you so much that He gave His only Son Jesus Christ to die on the cross for you, and raised Him from the dead on the third day for your justification; so that you (we) who believe would have a chance to live forever with Him, in that place that Jesus has prepared for us. Jesus Christ is now seated at the right hand of God making intercession for us. He is saying to you: "If you do my will and abide in Me, and if you have faith and do not doubt; whatever things you ask (Me) in prayer (according to My word), believing, you will receive. Whatever you ask in My name, that I will do, that the Father may be glorified in the Son. But you must ask in faith and do not doubt." (Read Matthew 21:22; John 14:13, 14; James 1:6)

Don't be afraid to launch out on faith, see where God takes you, and do what He has called and ordained you to do. He's not going to tell you to do something that He hasn't already anointed, equipped, and given you the ability and authority to do it. Don't let fear, doubt, Satan, or even yourself keep you from obtaining all that God has for you; and from reaching that place He has planned and purposed for your life (from your mother's womb). God told me to write this book, and He said that it will be a blessing to all those who read it. This book is for you. Read, believe, receive, and be blessed.

ACKNOWLEDGMENTS

First and far most, I thank God our Father, and Jesus Christ His Son, our Lord and Saviour. I thank Him for salvation. I thank Him for His love, mercy, and grace. I thank Him for His presence, and guidance. I thank Him for communicating with me in such a real, marvelous, and fulfilling way. I thank Him for His longsuffering, for not giving up on me (in spite of me), His faithfulness, His favor, and for never leaving nor forsaking me. For in Him I live, move, and I have my being. For without Him you would not be reading this book right now. I thank the Holy Spirit for his guidance, revelations, encouragement, strength, comfort, and his awesome presence. It is also because of him this book is made possible. Glory to God!

I sincerely thank Michelle Riley, a true friend (and is like a sister to me) for her tireless dedication and aid with typing and proofing the manuscript. Not once did I ever hear you complain regardless of the time of day I asked for help, or the numerous times we went over the manuscript. A true friend indeed and I thank God for you. God bless and keep you always.

To my loving children: Rhonda, Ursula, and Tameeka. Thanks for always having my back, cheering me on, and encouraging me to write this book. Thank you for having such great love for me, respect for me, and faith in me. I always thank God for giving me such beautiful, wonderful, and obedient daughters. I am so proud of you for your: hard work, your achievements in life, respect, integrity, strength, faith, and your moral beliefs. For your love for God our heavenly Father, and Jesus Christ our Lord and Saviour; the love and respect you have for each other; and the way you live your lives. Stay with God and stay in His word. Continue therein what you have been taught. Allow God to use you, as He will for His glory. I want us to spend eternity together with Jesus. You were my joy delight from the day that you were born, and you still are. I love you all more than you will ever know; and more than words could ever say.

Rhonda, you have already published 2 wonderful books, and even with your hectic schedule as a Social Worker serving children and families so compassionately and faithfully; you still find the time to write, and have now almost completed your manuscript for a third book. You're an excellent writer and speaker. Thank you for everything that you have done for me.

Ursula, you always know what to do or say to make me smile (when I am feeling low). Keep writing your poetry and poems, which seems to be so easy for you to do. You are gifted and good at this, and you should compile enough poems to publish a book. I believe it will be a success. Thank you for everything that you have done for me.

Tameeka, you're a wonderful mother and wife, and I'm so happy, thankful, and grateful to God, to you, and Ricardo for giving me my grandchildren. Teach them the word, and ways of God, as you and their father were taught. God bless you and your family. Thank you for everything that you have done for me.

Finally, my dear children, I pray that the mercy and grace of our Lord Jesus Christ be with you always, and bless each of you abundantly, guide your footsteps, and protect you. I pray that Jesus Christ will use you for His glory according to His will, plan, and purpose for your lives. Amen. I thank God for you, and because of you my life has been filled with joy and happiness. If I had to choose my own children you (all) would have been my choice.

To my loving grandchildren, Elisa and Ricardo III: You are the apple of my eyes. I watched you grow from the time you were just a tiny spot on film in your mother's womb. And finally, on the day that you were born, I watched with awe and joy your entrance into this world. My eyes filled with tears of happiness, and my heart with joy unspeakable. Truly you are a gift from God, and your parents and I are so very thankful for you. God will bless you and prosper you in all that you do. God will always give His angels charge over you to guide, protect, and keep you from all harm (seen and unseen). No weapon formed against you shall prosper, and your enemies shall be your foot stool. Amen. You will always be Grandma Sarah's "baby girl," and "baby boy." I love you with every beat of my heart. God bless and use you for His glory.

Ricardo, you're the son-in-law that every mother desires for her daughter. Thank you for being such a loving, caring, giving, and patient husband and father to my daughter (Tameeka) and grandchildren (Elisa and Ricardo III). Thank you for being a hard worker providing the very best for your family. Thank you for always making me feel very welcome in your home. Thank you for all that you have done for me: the love, and the respect you've shown me, and for being supportive of me. I'm proud that you are my son-in-law, and to call you "son." God bless you.

Jessie, you are my miracle. Thanks for being my sister. I love you, God bless you. Shaquanna, my great-niece; and Trina, my niece, thanks for always being there for me, and the love and respect you have always shown me. I love you, God bless you.

To all my family and friends: I love you and you are truly in my prayers. God bless you.

Thanks to my Publisher, and to everyone who worked on this book. God bless you all individually and corporately. "The Lord gave the word: great was the company of those that published it." (Psalm 68:11 JKV) "The grace of the Lord Jesus Christ, and the love of God, and the communion of the Holy Spirit be with you all. Amen" (2 Corinthians 13:14).

A Personal Word
(To Me From The Lord Our God)

"But raise and stand on your feet! Do not fear. I will stand with you, and I will strengthen you so that the message I give you will be preached fully through you; so that all might hear, believe, receive, and adhere to. Cry loud, and do not spare, lift up your voice like a trumpet. Tell the people that Jesus saves, and He is coming. Open your mouth and I will fill it with My words. Do the work you are called to do. Fulfill your ministry. Trust Me, seek Me, ask Me, obey Me; do the work that I have called you to do, and I will bless you. Do not be afraid, but speak and do not keep silent. Do not be dismayed, but be encouraged, for I Am is with you. You did not choose Me, but I have chosen you, I have called you, and I have ordained you to go and do the work I've told you to do. Go! Go! Go! I say. Go! Go! Go! You will do what I've called you to do. Go! I say, (Saith the LORD God)."

"For I have appeared to you for this purpose, to make you a minister and a witness both of the things which you have seen (and heard) and of the things which I will yet reveal to you" (Acts 26:13). "Whatever I tell you in the dark, speak in the light; and what you hear in the ear, preach on the housetops" (Matthew 10:27). "Preach the word! Be ready in season and out of season. Convince, rebuke, exhort, with all longsuffering and teaching. Be watchful in all things, endure afflictions, do the work of an evangelist, fulfill your ministry" (2 Timothy 4:2, 5).

"Behold, the former things have come to pass, and new things I declare; before they spring forth I will tell you of them" (Isaiah 42:9). "And do not fear those who kill the body but cannot kill the soul. But rather fear Him who is able to destroy both soul and the body in hell" (Matthew 10:28). "He who receives you receives Me, and he who receives Me receives Him who sent Me" (Matthew 10:40). "Therefore whoever confesses Me before men, him will I confess before My Father who is in heaven. But whoever denies Me before men, him I will deny before My Father who is in heaven" (Matthew 10:32, 33).

Go now, and sound the trumpet! And whosoever will believe and obey will be saved. You fight a good fight; you finish the race; and you keep the faith.

I have held my peace a long time. I have been still and restrained myself. Now I will cry like a woman in labor, I will pant and gasp at once. (Isaiah 42:14—given to me in a dream)

I will not keep silent anymore. I will sound the trumpet as God commands me.

General Introduction

God uses different channels to speak to His people through pastors, preachers, teachers, His word, dreams, visions, songs, and any other way that He chooses. One of the ways He has chosen to speak to me is through dreams (and a few visions), and they have been a blessing to me. The events I experience in dreams are very vivid and cannot be ignored. For many years I paid little to no attention to my dreams, so, I don't remember many of them. In 1980, I began to keep a journal of many of my dreams. I knew that God was calling me, and preparing me for my ministry, but I wasn't ready to adhere to His call. I still wanted to do my own thing and do what pleased the flesh.

There are wide selections of books on this subject that will go into more detail of the theology of the various types of dreams and their interpretations. However, this book speaks of the dreams that God the Father, and Jesus Christ His Son, our Lord and Saviour, shared with me personally, and what I believe He is saying to me (and to you); thus my interpretation of those dreams by the revelation and divine inspiration of God, Jesus Christ, and the Holy Spirit. As you read my dreams, God may speak to you differently, or give you another interpretation; if so, that's okay—it is all in His plan, and it's between you and Him. He wants to minister to you personally, one on one.

Over the years, God has communicated with me through dreams (and a few visions). Through them, He has taught and shown me many things, some of which you will read about in this book. Through dreams, and visions, God can show His people what to do or say, show us where to go and act on His behalf, prepare us for our ministry, and reveal His plan and purpose for our lives. Through dreams and visions, God instructs and guides us, teach us His ways and precepts, and convey or confirm special messages to others from Him (at which time God would have already spoken to or shown the individual whom the message is being delivered to). Through dreams, and visions, God calls men and women to repent, to pray for certain situations, warn us of danger, make known to us Satan's plots and devices, and whatever else He wants to reveal to us.

There are people who may not think very much of spiritual dreams or visions, while others hold them highly in esteem, and may live by them because of their faith in God and Jesus Christ, our Saviour. You should

1

be aware that Satan (Lucifer, the devil) can also show you things. The Bible tells us that he (Satan) comes as an angel of light trying to deceive, mislead, and confuse us. (2 Corinthians 11:14) But the Holy Spirit (who dwells in us) will expose Satan, and you will be able to determine light from darkness. "For greater is He who is in you, than he who is in the world" (1 John 4:4). You can be assured that Satan isn't going to lead you to God, or tell you that Jesus Christ loves you, died for your sins, and rose for your justification. Neither is Satan going to tell you that Jesus is the Way, the Truth, and the Life. No, that would be against his nature, for he hates Jesus, God, you, and me. Satan even hates those people who foolishly worship and follow him.

Dreams are scriptural and the Bible places great emphasis on them. People of the Old and New Testament thought very highly of dreams (as well as visions). God spoke numerous times to prophets, preachers, and even ordinary people through dreams and visions. These dreams and visions were personal, religious, and some were even political. You do not have to have a special title or go to a certain church or denomination for God to visit you in dreams or visions. There were, and are now, people who can also interpret dreams. If you have not studied, or if God has not dealt with you in this area, then you may not fully understand the importance of receiving dreams and visions. It is truly a rewarding, amazing, and an awesome experience.

In the Bible you will find many Scriptures on dreams and visions, that you can read at your convenience, and I have listed a few of them at the end of this book. You will be fascinated by what you will discover. I am always elated and open to receive dreams and visions from God. And I'm greatly honored and humbled that He has chosen me to share in this wonderful experience. And yes, for those of you who may be wondering, I do have dreams unrelated to spiritual things, but such dreams are rarely retained in my memory.

God began to speak to me several years ago about writing this book, and said that people would be blessed as they read it. Pastors, ministers, prophets, and prophetesses also gave confirmation through prophecy, and the word of knowledge and wisdom to me. They too told me that God shows me dreams, and that He wants me to write a book, and people would be blessed as they read it.

It has not been an easy task, for Satan has fought me nearly every step of the way. He knows that people of all religions, races, colors, and genders, those who would dare to read, believe, and receive the words written in this book will be blessed by Jehovah God our Father; and Jesus

Christ, our Lord and Saviour. Satan knows that people will be saved and delivered (from him and any addiction), healed and strengthen (spiritually, physically, mentally, emotionally), encouraged, informed, restored, revived, and their lives will be transformed as they read this book. Satan knows that he would lose many souls as a result of people reading this book. He also knows that he will be exposed even the more for the liar, thief, destroyer, deceiver, conniver, accuser, and the devil that he is.

Satan also knows that as people read this book they will gain more insight and knowledge about the ways, and plans of God for their lives, and how He communicates with His children. Satan knows that their faith will come alive, and a spiritual change will take place in their hearts and lives, and he doesn't want this to happen. He doesn't want you to be free, or to be blessed; and he desires to keep you and your family in bondage, and in total darkness.

But thanks be unto God our Father, Jesus Christ our Saviour, and the Holy Spirit who stood with me, encouraged me, strengthened me, and anointed me, so that I could complete this book and make it available to you.

For God wants you to know that He loves you, He wants to bless you, and that He speaks to ordinary people (such as you and me). You don't have to have a college education or attend seminary. You don't have to be labeled as a bishop, pastor, priest, prophet, prophetess, evangelist, elder, or minister. You don't have to live in a big fancy house or drive fancy cars. You don't have to wear expensive clothing. You don't have to be rich or out of debt in order to hear from God. Although nothing is wrong with any of these things, none of them are required by God in order for you to hear from Him, and be in fellowship with Him.

What you do need is love, trust, and faith in Jesus Christ, the Son of God, Lord and Saviour of the world; and in God our Heavenly Father, creator of heaven and earth, and all that is in it. You must be born again of the Spirit of God. You must believe that Jesus Christ gave His life for your sins, and rose on the third day for your justification. You must be obedient to the call and will of God for your life. You must have love for all people. You must live a holy and righteous life. You must read and trust His word, activate it by faith, and let it work in your life. You must pray, and you must have an ear to hear, and a heart to believe and receive from the Holy Spirit. Satan was determined that this book wouldn't get published and into your hands. But God was determined to get this book get to you, and so was I. We got the victory!

Finally, by the grace of God Almighty (El-Shaddai), I have finished what Satan told me that I *could not* and *would not* finish. I have completed this part of my work that God has assigned, entrusted me with, and told me to do. All the praise and glory goes to God my heavenly Father, Jesus Christ, my Lord and Saviour, and the Holy Spirit, my teacher.

This book is not written with a particular group of people or denomination in mind, but it is written for those who have an ear to hear, and a heart to believe and receive what the Spirit of God is saying (to you), and what is written herein.

In this life, there will always be people in need of help, physically, spiritually, mentally, and emotionally. As I visit hospitals, nursing homes, and shelters, and converse with people I meet in the course of the day; I have discovered that people of all ages are searching for answers and seek hope today more than ever.

People of all ages, nationalities, genders, colors, and religions, are hurting and dying as they are confronted with enormous problems such as, HIV, AIDS, cancer, sexually transmitted diseases, drugs, gangs, peer pressure, women abuse, child abuse, men abuse, verbal abuse, child abduction, rape, loneliness, depression, anxiety, relationships, divorce, marital issues, singleness, racism, employment, unemployment, financial problems, health problems, and all the rest.

And if that isn't enough, then there are those everyday life disappointments when you're trying to make ends meet on one or two small salaries. Problems with the spouse, children, baby sitter (you can't trust), house work, this, that, and the other. Don't you think that it is time to cast your burdens and cares upon Jesus and trust Him? Trust Him to do what you and man cannot do. Trust Him to do the impossible in your life. Trust Him to give you love, joy, peace, and happiness. Trust God our Father, and Jesus our Saviour, to give you a new life with new meaning and purpose. Trust Him to lead and direct you in this life and give you eternal life.

I am so overwhelmed and very humbled to be used by God to share with you what He has imparted to me. My desire for you is that you be blessed as you read this book; that you move into that place God has designed just for you; that He reveals His plan and purpose for your life giving you hope and a wonderful future; and that your life will be spiritually changed, renewed, enriched, and transformed. May the Holy Spirit remove the scales from your eyes so that you can see, unstop your ears so that you can hear, and open your mind and your heart so that you can believe and receive, as you journey with me through *My Dreams, My Interpretations: Night Visions in My Head*. All of my dreams and interpretations are given, revealed, and divinely inspired by God, Jesus Christ, and the Holy Spirit.

VOLUME 1
Journey with me through
MY DREAMS, MY INTERPRETATIONS:
NIGHT VISIONS IN MY HEAD

And expect to be immensely blessed by God

Read in faith with expectation that God our Father, and Jesus Christ, our Lord and Saviour is going to do something exceedingly and abundantly in your life as you read this book. Allow Him to reveal His wonderful plan and purpose for your life.

> "For God may speak in one way or in another, Yet man does not perceive it. In a dream, in a vision of the night, When deep sleep falls upon men, While slumbering on their beds, Then He opens the ears of men, And seals their instruction" (Job 33:14-16).

> "Write the vision And make it plain on tablets, That he may run who reads it" (Habakkuk 2:2). "He who has ears to hear, let him hear (what the Spirit of God is saying to them)."(Matthew 11:15)

> "Then you will call upon Me and go and pray to Me, and I will listen to you. And you will seek Me and find Me, when you search for Me with all your heart. I will be found by you, says the LORD, and I will . . ." (Jeremiah 29:12-14).

> "For I know the thoughts that I think towards you, says the LORD, thoughts of peace and not of evil, to give you a future and a hope" (Jeremiah 29:11).

> "I know the plans that I have for you," declares the Lord, "plans to prosper you and not to harm you, plans to give you hope and a future" (Jeremiah 29:11 KJV).

REMINISCING

When I was sixteen years old God began showing me spiritual dreams. I have forgotten many of them especially those I had in my teenage years. In the beginning, the dreams were about fire and a house that I lived in when I was eight years old. My family and I lived in this house for four years. This house was very special to me. There were rumors of the house being haunted and anyone who moved into this house never stayed very long. There was a graveyard about one mile in the back of the house. Sometimes at night and during the day, strange noises could be heard inside the house and on top of the roof. My parents didn't seem to pay any attention to the noise, and they always thought of reassuring words to tell my sister, two brothers, and myself.

The house was white with pretty green vines growing in front of it and around the windows, and there were flowers of every kind. People driving by would often stop and admire the beautiful flowers. We also had a vegetable garden that was just as beautiful filled with all kinds of vegetables. My mother would always give vegetables to folks (friends, strangers, and relatives) and the rest was preserved in jars for the winter for the family to eat. She loved working with her flowers and in her vegetable garden. Mom could make anything grow.

Another house in my dreams was a house I lived in when I was twelve years old. I also enjoyed living in this house. Both of the houses were located in the country near a place called Joiner Cross Road about two miles from a small town. Two lanes lead to this house and it was a very large house with plenty of rooms and a big front and back yard. I was familiar with this house because we often visited my great-great uncle and his family who had also once lived in this house.

I was raised in church, and as far back as I can remember, my parents always attended church. My mother was a mother of the church, and my father an elder and assistant pastor. They both feared and reverence God. Countless times, I would lay awake in my bed at night listening to my mother pray. She would sometimes be on her knees by her bedside, or she would walk from room to room praying, giving praise unto God for all He had done, and for the things she was asking Him to do. My father would kneel by the bed (often with his right hand on his forehead bowed) and pray. Around the house, in the fields, in the yard, or in the car you could often hear them singing old hymns. My father's favorite song was "Oh Land of Rest," and my mother's was "Amazing Grace." They both love the song, *"Father I Sketch My Hands to Thee,"* and they both had very nice voices.

As long as my parents were present, I never worried about being sick, or where my next meal would come from. I never worried about anyone harming us, even after we found a cross burned in our backyard. I was never afraid when there were very bad thunderstorms with lightning so sharp it would light up the whole house, and with claps of thunder so loud, surely I thought it shook both heaven and earth. I believed that the God my parents served, believed, trusted, prayed to, sung to, and boasted about would take care of us. They trusted this God, this invisible being, who could do anything, is everywhere at the same time, and can see and hear everything that we do and say. So, I too, trusted and believed in this same God.

Our family attended church services on Saturdays and Sundays. Wednesday nights were prayer and bible study at a church member house. Weeknights including Sunday evening were prayer meetings at the home of the sick and shut-in at their request. Sometimes I grew tired of going to church, Sunday school, bible study, and prayer meetings. But today I am truly grateful to my parents for making me go to church, and for teaching me the way they felt that I should go according to the Word of God.

Between the ages of fourteen and fifteen years old while doing houses chores or relaxing in the cool of the day, I would play church, pray to God and pretend that I was preaching to a congregation. Sometimes JC, my brother, would join me and he would also preach. I did not know too much about the name of Jesus. My parents' denomination was Primitive Baptists. They always prayed to God in the name of the Father, Son, and Holy Ghost (Spirit). We loved and reverence all three. We believed in the Divine Trinity.

Summer 1966

I commenced having dreams and visions at the age of sixteen years old. I had countless dreams about fire. Many times the fires occurred at the two houses I lived in as a child. Both houses weren't too far from Joiners' Crossroad. The amazing thing was that the houses were never destroyed by the flames.

In one of my dreams, the fire literally opened. It became a burning wall of fire on my left and on my right, allowing me to walk through and bring my family out to safety one by one (my mother, two brothers, sister, and my father) and then the fire closed. I was reminded (in my dream) of God parting the waters for Moses, and the children of Israel at the Red Sea, so that they could cross over to safety from Pharaoh and his army. It was an awesome sight to behold.

My Interpretation

You may feel like your life is surrounded by fire, and that there's no way out. But whatever situation you're in, whatever you're going through right now – no matter what it is (for there is nothing too hard for God), do not allow the cares of this world overwhelm and smother you. God our Heavenly Father, and Jesus Christ, our Saviour, is right there with you to walk with you, or carry you through it all. He will shield, protect, deliver, heal, save, supply your need, and keep you. He will keep your life from destruction and from caving in on you. Don't you give in, for God is bringing you out of that thing that you thought there was just no way out of. Begin to praise and thank God right now for your victory!

"Then Moses stretched out his hand over the sea; and the LORD caused the sea to go back by a strong east wind all that night, and made the sea into dry land and the waters were divided. So the children of Israel went into the midst of the sea on the dry ground, and the waters were a wall to them on their right hand and on their left" (Exodus 14:21-22).

Winter 1966

I saw multitudes of people standing before the throne of God to be judged. The number "144,000" appeared before me. And then I saw a great multitude of people of every race, and from every nation. This multitude of people was too vast, and they could not be numbered.

My Interpretation

One day we all must appear before the judgment seat of Christ and give an account for all the things we've said or done; whether good or bad. (2 Corinthians 5:10) Jesus said for every idle word men may speak, we would give account of it in the Day of Judgment. "For by your words you will be justified, and by your words you will be condemned" (Matthew 12:36, 37). So, be careful of what you say and do, and be careful how you treat others, because one day you will stand before God in judgment. God is an excellent bookkeeper, His memory doesn't fail, and He doesn't make mistakes. Pray that your name has been written in the Book of Life, and that the record being kept on you will be a good report. For that record will determine your final and eternal destiny, as you will be evaluated and judged based on what is written therein.

"Then I saw a great white throne and Him who sat on it, from whose face the earth and the heaven fled away. And there was found no place for them. And I saw the dead, small and great, standing before God, and books were opened. And another book was opened, which is the Book of Life. And the dead were judged according to their works, the things which were written in the books. The sea gave up the dead who were in it, and Death and Hades delivered up the dead who were in them. And they were judged, each one according to his works. Then Death and Hades was cast into the lake of fire. This is the second death. And anyone not found written in the Book of Life was cast into the lake of fire" (Revelation 20:11-15).

The number 144,000 that I saw represents the children of Israel; twelve thousand from each of the twelve tribes (12 sons of Jacob), descendants of Abraham by faith, and heirs of God's promises. "And I heard the number of those who were sealed. One hundred and forty-four thousand of all the tribes of the children of Israel were sealed" (Revelation 7:4). Then it goes on and lists the name of each tribe and the number (twelve thousand each) that was to be sealed. (Revelation 7:5-8)

The great multitude that was innumerable of all nations, tribes, and people with different languages, standing before the Lamb (Jesus Christ) clothed with white robes, and with palms in their hands, are the ones who went through the tribulation, and accepted Jesus Christ as their Lord and Saviour. (They were saved through faith in the death of Jesus Christ, and they believed in Him for their salvation). They refused to take the mark of the beast (Satan), and decided to take the mark of Jesus instead, believing that if they suffered for Christ sake, they would soon reign with Him forever.

"Then one of the elders answered, saying to me, who are these arrayed in white robes, and where did they come from?" And I said to him, "Sir, you know." So he said to me, "These are the ones who come out of the great tribulation, and washed their robes and made them white in the blood of the Lamb. Therefore they are before the throne of God, and serve Him day and night in His temple. And He who sits on the throne will dwell among them" (Revelation 7:13-17).

Summer 1967

In another dream, I was standing looking towards heaven with my arms out stretched Saying, "Father, I stretch my hands to thee."

My Interpretation

This is a hymn that I use to hear my parents often sing at home and in church. Some of the lyrics are: Father, I stretch my hands to thee. No other help I know: If thou withdraw thyself from me, Ah! Whither shall I go? Sometimes I would sing along with them.

When you're feeling discourage, depressed, anxiety, lonely, friendless, unloved, unwanted, suicidal, stressed, and misunderstood. When bills are past due, not sure of your next meal, and you've been downsized from your job. When you're homeless with nowhere to lay your head, and you have no money in your pocket, low self-esteem, not happy with whom you are, or wish you were someone else. When you feel like you're too ugly, or not pretty enough, too short or too tall, too skinny or too fat, hair too long or too short, and your complexion is too dark or too light. And your family and so-called friends have forsaken you, and they are nowhere to be found.

When you've been abused, misused, and mistreated. When you feel unloved, useless, and like you're no longer needed by your love ones, or anyone. You have an alcohol or drug abuse problem, and you feel like no one (not even God) cares about you, or understand what you're going through. When you've lost all hope, and you feel like you just want to self-destruct.

Or, maybe you have everything going your way but you still feel this emptiness, and loneliness that you can't explain. You think you have everything; fame, beauty, money, a big house, fancy cars, social status, friends, and family, yet you're not truly happy. Your heart is aching for someone or something more. There is someone or something still missing in your life, and there's a void that needs to be fulfilled. But what or whom can fill it? Your spirit is troubled, you toss and turn with restlessness and sleep has deserted you.

Then, now is the time for you to throw your hands up toward heaven and cry out to God with your whole heart, and say: "Father, I stretch my hands to You, no other help I know. If You withdraw Yourself from me, where will I go? If You don't help me, if You turn Your face from me, there's no one else for me to turn to, and no place for me to go. In Your Word, You told me to cast all my cares (anxiety, hurt, pain, problems) upon You, because You care for me. (1 Peter 5:7) You said in Your word You would never leave nor forsake me. (Hebrews 13:5) You said in Your word that Jesus Christ was wounded for my transgressions, bruised for my iniquities; the chastisement for my peace is upon Him, and by His stripes I am healed. Surely Jesus has borne my griefs and pain, and carried all of my sorrows and sicknesses. (Isaiah 53:4, 5)

You said in Your word that if I would take Your yoke upon me, Your yoke would be easy and Your burdens would be light. (Matthew 11:29, 30) You said in Your word that if I would come to You, and accept You into my life, You would by no means turn me away. (John 6:37) You said in Your word, that if I would just open the door of my heart You would come in and dine with me; and that You would receive me and fellowship with me. (1 Peter 5:7: Revelation 3:20) Father, in the name of Jesus, here I am with my hands stretched out to You. I need Your help right now. Hear my cry, help me, and save me. Embrace me in Your love, mercy, and grace. I repent of my sins, and I ask for your forgiveness.

"I stretch forth my hands unto thee" (Psalm 143:6 KJV). "I spread out my hands to You; my soul *longs* for You like a thirsty land. Selah" (Psalm 143:6).

If you haven't already accepted Jesus Christ as your Lord and Saviour, and asked Him to forgive you of your sins, then right *now* is the time to do it. Jesus will then have access and your permission to reign in and over your life. He will lift every burden, mend your broken heart, and give you unspeakable joy, and peace that surpasses all understanding. Your life will never be the same again. I guarantee it. Just trust Him, and let Him be your compass. I'm not saying that there won't be some storms in your life, but you have the comfort of knowing that Jesus will never leave or forsake you; and that He can speak to any storm, and it must obey His voice.

Before reading any further, would you please say this short prayer with me and believe with your whole heart as you say it.

"Jesus, forgive me of all of my sins. I confess with my mouth and believe in my heart that you are the Son of God, You died on the cross for my sins, and that God raised You from the grave on the third day. Come into my life. I accept You as my Lord and Saviour." If you believe in your heart what you just said—you are saved!

As the Angels of God in heaven rejoice that you are now a child of God, adopted into the royal family of God, so do I. Welcome! Welcome! Glory to God! Converse with God through prayer, read the Bible and learn of His ways, and let Him speak to you through His written word. Allow the Holy Spirit to lead, guide, and direct you. Find a church that believes, preaches, and teaches the Bible—the full gospel of Jesus Christ. Draw near to God, and He will draw near to you.

"That if you confess with your mouth the Lord Jesus and believe in your heart that God raised Him from the dead, you will be saved. For with the heart one believes unto righteousness, and with the mouth confession is made unto salvation" (Romans 10:9, 10). "For, whoever calls upon the name of the Lord shall be saved" (Romans 10:13) "Blessed be the LORD, because He has heard the voice of my supplications! The LORD is my strength and my shield; my heart trusted in Him, and I am helped" (Psalm 28:7).

My prayer for you: Father God, help your people, save your people, heal your people, deliver your people, bless your people, encourage your people, shepherd your people, have mercy on your people, and bear them up. Show Yourself strong in their lives that they will know that Your almighty hand is at work; and that it was You (without a shadow of doubt), that helped them with whatever their need or problem had been. You visited them; You heard their cry and are mindful of them. You do care about them, and You do love them so very much. In Jesus name, the name that is above all names, I ask. Amen.

Summer 1968

I picked up the telephone to make a call (it seemed so real) and heard an evil voice on the phone. Immediately, I called on the name of Jesus to help me. The evil voice said to me, "He (Jesus) can't help you now." I replied with assurance and force, "Oh, yes He can!" Then I no longer heard the evil spirit voice.

Trance-like state: Another time, I was lying on my bed (in a trance-like state) and suddenly a very heavy sleep came over me, and I could barely keep my eyes open. Again, I would call on Jesus saying, "Jesus, Jesus." And Jesus always rescued me. However Satan always had something to say to try and make me doubt that Jesus heard me. I would respond by telling him that Jesus did hear me, and I would call Jesus a little bit louder. Jesus delivered me every time.

My Interpretation

When we're burdened by the cares of this world and things aren't going the way we would like; and when life seems to be smothering you and you just can't breathe, the devil (Satan) will always try to make us doubt God's love for us. Remember, Satan is a liar and he is the father of lies, so don't believe anything he tells you. (John 8:44) Resist him and he will flee from you. (James 4:7) Give him absolutely no place in your life. (Ephesians 4:27) His only goal in life is to keep you from believing in Jesus Christ (and from obeying and doing God's will); to kill, steal, and ultimately totally destroy you. And he wants your eternal soul to be tortured with him in hell.

Let Satan know boldly that Jesus told you to throw all of your cares upon Him because He cares, and is concerned about you. (2 Peter 5:7) Tell Satan, and his demons, that Jesus loves you so much that He gave His life for you, and shed His precious blood on the cross at Calvary for your sins, and you have eternal life with Him. And, that on the third day, God raised Jesus from the dead with the keys of life and death, and with all power in His hand. (John 3:16; Matthew 28:6, 18)

Remind Satan, again, that he is defeated and his destiny is hell. (Revelation 20:10) Tell the Satan that Jesus promised that He would never leave nor forsake you. (Hebrew 13:5) Tell the devil (Satan) boldly that Jesus is your Redeemer, Lord, Saviour, God, Bishop of your soul, Protector, Source, and the Rock of your salvation. Tell the devil that Jesus is everything to you. Now, you just call Jesus a little bit louder, and He will hear you. I know that He will because He hears me when I call. Also, because He promised that He will hear and answer us.

"Call upon Me in the day of trouble; I will deliver you, and you will glorify Me" (Psalms 50:15). "He will call upon Me, and I will answer him; I will be with him in trouble; I will deliver him and honor him" (Psalms 91:15).

The dreams did not cease. Many nights I laid awake wondering what could be the meaning of these dreams. Sometimes I went to church, prayed, and read the Bible. My parents taught me to fear God with a reverent fear; to love Him, respect Him and His works, and to obey and trust Him. They said that God would always take care of His children, and I believed them.

Spring 1968 (Vision)

I was lying on my bed looking out of the window at a couple in the next apartment building that appeared to have been arguing. Suddenly, I was in a trance, as a spirit came through my bedroom window and stood at the foot of my bed. I tried to look at it, but it was as bright as the sun. The spirit spoke to me and said, "In time you will change." I asked, "When?" He said, "I will come back and let you know." Again I asked, "When?" He replied, "I will come back to let you know," and he disappeared.

After this appearance the dreams ceased a great deal. I no longer spent hours and sleepless nights worrying about the dreams. I thank God for that visit, for now I was finally able to sleep, rest, and have some peace of mind.

"I will wait, Til my change comes. You shall call and I will answer You; For now You number my steps, But do not watch over my sin. My transgression is sealed up in a bag, And You cover my iniquity" (Job 14:14-17).

1970-1973

I didn't write down any of my dreams, or visions, even though I was told (by God) to do so in many of my dreams. Regrettably, I never kept a journal of them. A few of my dreams I shared with my mother in letters written to her when I was very troubled by some of the dreams.

The dreams commenced again quite heavily. I found myself once again spending sleepless nights pondering over these dreams. Now they were about clear water (whether it was an ocean, river, sea, or stream), fire, and the world coming to an end. The words fire and water are mentioned in the Bible numerous times literally and as a symbolism of the Holy Spirit.

"But the water that I shall give him will become in him a fountain of water springing up into everlasting life" (John 4:14).

January 27, 1973

I was traveling down a very narrow road, talking to a man who was driving a big truck. I was in a car in front of him with a relative who was driving. It seemed silly to me at first because I had my head out of the car window conversing with a man I had never seen before. He was telling me how he had been accused of reckless driving, and his license had been revoked. It hurt him because his accusers were lying. He went on to say that since he got his license back, he still tries to please the other driver. He always gives them the right-a-way. "They are the reckless drivers, not me, I have always driven with care," he said.

Suddenly a giant screen appeared (out of nowhere) showing that he drove very carefully. I watched and saw that this man gave all people the right-a-way even when it was in his favor. He had the right-a-way yet he allowed the other drivers to proceed. It was such a narrow road and I wondered how another car could pass, but that was the reason why one had to be so very careful on this road. The man said that he was never in a hurry like those other drivers. I was saddened by the fact that the man had been falsely accused and was treated so unfairly.

My Interpretation

The man accused in this dream reminds me of Jesus Christ. Jesus was and is still being falsely accused by those who do not know Him or God the Father. Christ was our licentiate. God gave Him an official and legal assignment, permission, and authority over 2000 years ago.

He came down from His heavenly throne to become flesh and live among men. Jesus freely and of His own will died on the cross at Calvary, and He shed His precious blood for the sins of every human being (that was born and would be born into this world). He then went down into hell and exposed Satan. Jesus took the keys of death from him and set the captives free. Victoriously, God raised Jesus from the grave on the third day for our justification, and with all power in His hands. Jesus holds the keys of life and death. He reconciled us to God, giving us a second chance (if we so choose) to spend our eternal life with Him and the Father.

Satan thought that he had revoked Jesus' license when He died on the cross. But Jesus took the keys of death from him, and thereby destroyed our last enemy which is death. Jesus has taken the sting out of death, and the grave no longer has victory over our lives. Glory to God!

Jesus said, "I am He who lives, and was dead, and behold, I am alive forever more. Amen. And I have the keys of Hades and of Death" (Revelations 1:18). And, on that Day when the trumpet of God sounds, we will be changed in a moment before we can blink our eyes. Jesus' last enemy which is "Death" has been swallowed up in victory. (I Corinthians 15:52-54)

"O Death, where is your sting? O Hades (grave), where is your victory?" (1 Corinthians 15:55).

We are the reckless drivers and are always in a hurry. We pay little or no attention to others. We always want to be first. We're licentiousness, unwilling to yield to the way, will, and word of God, and we turn our face and close our eyes to the need of others. We should have had our license revoked for the reason of lack of love and concern for others, and misusing our customary or legal right as a person and as a child of God.

However, Jesus Christ, in His infinite love, mercy, and grace still grants us the right-a-way. He still gives us a license, legal right, power of attorney, and authorization to officially use His name (His name is above every name, and has awesome power) here on earth; to walk in His word, teach His word, and to preach the Gospel. Jesus represents us before God. He is our High Priest, Intercessor, Mediator, Advocate, Redeemer, and Bishop of our souls. He is our Lord, Saviour, and King. He is our salvation.

He's always watching over us and protecting us from danger and harm. He listens to us attentively because He loves us, and He is concerned about us. But we must be obedient to the call and will of God, and be willing to yield the right-a-way to Him in every area of our lives. If we disobey, God may revoke the license, authority, and all privileges that have been given to us through Jesus Christ.

I believe that our Christian walk with God is like traveling on a narrow road. We must proceed with caution. We must have patience, and we should be fair to others even when they are unfair to us. We should give them the right-a-way even when it's not in their favor. And, God will reward you, and give you favor with others. Yield to God's will and to His ways. We must always watch and pray.

"Enter by the narrow gate; for wide is the gate and broad is the way that leads to destruction, and there are many who go in by it. Because narrow is the gate and difficult is the way which leads to life, and there are few who find it" (Matthew 7:13, 14).

Fall 1973

Russia sneaked up on the United States of America to attack and destroy. A few people and I were the only ones aware of this as we tried to lead peoples to safety. I said to God, "I'm not ready; I want it to be like you said in your Word. I want to be caught up to meet you in the air."

My Interpretation

Are you ready for the return of Jesus Christ? Jesus will come at a time when you're not expecting Him. He will come as a thief in the night. *Now* is preparation time for tomorrow may be too late. If today you hear God's voice, please do not ignore Him and harden your heart. Repent and acknowledge your sins and ask Jesus to forgive you.

Tell Him that you want to be ready to go back with Him upon His return to reign with Him forever. If you haven't made Jesus Lord of your life, please do it now. Tomorrow or even the next second may be too late. Please do not take risks with your eternal life.

If you have already accepted Jesus Christ as your Lord and Saviour, stay prayerful and be watchful. Do not compromise your faith and give no place to Satan. For, he is sneaky, conniving, deceiving, and only wants to steal, kill, and destroy you. Believe me, the devil hates you with a passion, and his only goal is to destroy your present and future life. Satan wants you to spend eternity with him (his demons, the anti-christ, and all the people who didn't believe in Jesus Christ) in torment in hell (that awful and dreadful place of torment that forever burns with fire).

Satan doesn't want you to be ready when Jesus returns. He doesn't want you to have eternal life with Jesus Christ, and he will do everything within his power to keep that from happening. You must be ready and warn others to be ready for Jesus' coming, and lead them to Him for safety.

"But the day of the Lord will come as a thief in the night, in which the heavens will pass away with a great noise, and the elements will melt with fervent heat; both the earth and the works that are in it will be burned up" (2 Peter 3:10).

"For you yourselves know perfectly that the day of the Lord so comes as a thief in the night. For when they say, "Peace and safety!" then sudden destruction comes upon them, as labor pains upon a pregnant woman. And they shall not escape" (1 Thessalonians 5:2, 3). "Watch therefore, for you do not know what hour your Lord is coming" (Matthew 24:42).

I also believe that someday the United States of America will be attack by her allies, and I believe that Russia will be one of them. The enemy wants to catch you by surprise. Stay awake, focus, faithful, prayerful, watchful, and be ready when Jesus comes.

Fall 1973

I was at my parent's house in North Carolina, when I heard a voice (the whole world, I thought, should have heard it because it was so loud and powerful) saying, "He cometh in a cloud and every eye shall see Him." "But I'm not ready yet!" I said to my mother.

My Interpretation

Ready or not Jesus is coming! God has given all of us plenty of time to prepare ourselves for the coming (return) of His Son Jesus Christ. The Gospel (Good News) of Jesus Christ is being preached today all around the world in nearly every nation. And even in those nations where the gospel of Jesus Christ isn't welcome, someway, and somehow God has provided a way for the harvest of souls. He loves us so much and wants no one to perish.

God have a select group of people who are risking their lives; and they're not ashamed, or afraid, to preach the Gospel of Jesus Christ. People are being told about Jesus, and are hearing and reading the Word of God. People are being saved, delivered, and set free from the snares and the clutches of Satan.

Therefore, when you and I stand before God one day, we can give Him no acceptable excuse as to why we didn't acknowledge and accept His Son, Jesus Christ as our Lord and Saviour. We cannot say that we didn't know, or that we have never heard the gospel of Jesus Christ. And you're reading this right now, so again, you'll have no excuse.

Jesus, "who desires all men to be saved and to come to the knowledge of the truth" (1 Timothy 2:4). "For the grace of God that brings salvation has appeared to all men, teaching us that, denying ungodliness and worldly lusts, we should live soberly, righteously, and godly in the present age, looking for the blessed hope and glorious appearing of our great God and Savior Jesus Christ, who gave Himself for us that He might redeem us from every lawless deed and purify for Himself His own special people, zealous for good works" (Titus 2:11-14).

"And this gospel of the kingdom will be preached in all the world as a witness to all the Nations, and then the end will come" (Matthew 24:14). "Therefore you are inexcusable" (Romans 2:1). "Then they will see the Son of Man coming in a cloud with great power and great glory" (Luke 21:27).

1973-1979

I had dreams but don't remember what I dreamt. I wrote down a few of my dreams but misplaced my notes. I shared many of my dreams with my mother in letters, but most of them I told her via telephone. I do remember dreaming about fire, and the world coming to an end. This is what frightened me the most. Oftentimes, I would call my mother in tears. She was the only one who could comfort me.

February 1980 [1]

I was looking through a game machine showing my daughters how to play the game. I hit the target and a bright shiny ball appeared, growing larger and larger, as it was coming out of the machine. It formed into the appearance of a man. He said, "I am a messenger, I was sent from heaven.

Let not your heart be troubled, you believe in God, believe in me also."
He then vanished.

My Interpretation

At the time when I had this dream I was going to a church where the pastor spoke well, sound good, and quoted Scriptures from the Bible. But one day he said some things that troubled my spirit very much. Things that I disagreed with as far as what I had read in the Bible. I was a baby in Christ, and I wanted to know the truth. Since God is omniscient and He knew that this was troubling me, He sent a messenger (an angel) to remove any doubt and negativity from my mind that had occurred through listening to this pastor. After this dream I looked for another church to attend.

What Jesus was telling me was simple for me to understand—"Sarah, do not be troubled by what you've heard (this pastor say) and what you believe. Listen, you already believe in God, My Father, now believe in Me, Jesus Christ (His Son) also."

So, if you're having a problem with the trinity, Jesus is saying the very same thing to you. A lot of people believe in God, Our Heavenly Father the Creator of the universe, but they don't believe in His only begotten Son, Jesus Christ (who gave His life on the cross for the sins of the world and God raised from the grave on the third day for our justification); and they have little or no knowledge of the Holy Spirit. And then there are some people that believes in Jesus Christ the Son, but do not believe in God the Father who gave His only Son (Jesus Christ).

Please know and understand that you can't have God, the Father, without His Son, Jesus Christ; nor can you believe in God unless you believe in His Son; or know God until you know His Son, and you can't get to God unless you come through His Son, Jesus Christ. You must believe in both. You can't believe in Jesus Christ, the Son of God, unless you believe in God, His Father, who gave His only begotten Son (Jesus) to die on the cross for our sins.

"For God so loved the world that He gave His only begotten Son, that whoever believes in Him should not perish but have everlasting life" (John 3:16).

Jesus said to him, "I am the way, the Truth, and the Life. No one comes to the Father except through Me" (John 14:6). ". . . Nor does anyone know the Father except the Son, and *the one* to whom the Son wills to reveal Him" (Matthew 11:27; Luke 10:22). Then they said to Him, "Where is your Father?" Jesus answered, "You know neither Me nor My Father. If

you had known Me, you would have known My Father also" (John 8:19).
". . . and from now on you know Him and have seen Him" (John 14:7).

"Whoever confesses that Jesus is the Son of God, God abides in him, and he in God" (1 John 4:15). "Whoever transgresses and does not abide in the doctrine of Christ does not have God. He who abides in the doctrine of Christ has both the Father and the Son" (2 John 1:9).

"He who believes in Him (Jesus Christ) is not condemned; but he who does not believe is condemned already, because he has not believed in the name of the only begotten Son of God" (John 3:18). "For the Father loves the Son . . ." (John 5:20). ". . . Has committed all judgment to the Son, that all should honor the Son just as they honor the Father. He who does not honor the Son does not honor the Father who sent Him" (John 5:22-23).

"For He (Jesus Christ) received from God the Father honor and glory when such a voice came to Him from the Excellent Glory: This is My beloved Son, in whom I am well pleased" (2 Peter 1:17). "The Father loves the Son, and has given all things into His hand. He who believes in the Son has everlasting life; and he who does not believe the Son shall not see life, but the wrath of God abides on him" (John 3:35-36). ". . . that you may know and believe that the Father is in Me, and I in Him" (John 10:38). "I and My Father are one" (John 10:30).

"Whoever denies the Son does not have the Father either; he who acknowledges the Son has the Father also" (1 John 1:23).

So it is without question that if one denies or does not believe in the Son, Jesus Christ; then that same one denies, or does not believe in Jehovah God, the Father. And, if one denies or doesn't believe in the Father, you also deny His Son Jesus, and do not believe in Him. You cannot believe in one without believing in the other one. And you can only get to God the Father, through His Son Jesus Christ.

February 1980 [2]

Dee (a lady I know) and I were returning from a walk, when I looked afar and saw a large crowd of people entering into a very large church. I said to her: "Noah must have died. Well, I am sure he is not sad because he's with God, and in our time he is 500 years old." (I was referring to Noah in the Bible.)

As we entered into a house, Dee went directly to the bathroom, and I looked into a room where a few people were gathered socially. Just as I was about to walk into the room to join them, I heard a voice coming from the next room. The door to the room was closed, and I thought I had seen an elderly man, whom I work with and respect very much, go into that room. In order to hear what the person was saying, I motioned for everyone to be quiet. Leaning over towards the room, I put my hand to my ear so that I could hear a little better.

Then I heard a voice like I've never heard before in my life. It sounded like waves of many waters and many claps of thunder, all at the same time. It was so powerful it shook and pierced my very soul, and I felt weak. I thought that surely the whole world must have heard His voice, and felt the earth shook. This voice was so authoritative, and so precise, that all doubt of whom this was faded immediately. I knew that this was the voice of Almighty God.

He said, "I am speaking to you in the name of the Lord thy God, this world is coming to an end soon!" (My mind then went back to this man I worked with, and I thought to myself, "I don't even think this man knows God)." I became very scared and woke up.

My Interpretation

This voice I will never forget, and immediately I knew that it was the voice of God. It was fearful, yet wonderful, it was powerful, and it pierced through my whole being. It was totally awesome in power and majesty.

Stop, look, and listen! God is trying to get our attention, and He can use whomever He chooses, even the very one you would least expect. God also wants us to know that this age is coming to an end soon. He always warns His people in order for them to get themselves ready for whatever occurs. God will use someone you may think isn't a Christian or a true believer in Christ. He sometimes uses people we admire and respect in order to get our attention. We should never judge people we don't really know personally. Only God knows and can see inside one's heart. We just may be surprised when you we see whom God chooses to use.

"The LORD thundered from heaven, And the Most High uttered His voice" (2 Samuel 22:14). "And I heard a voice from heaven, like the voice of many waters, and like the voice of loud thunder" (Revelation 14:2). "The voice of the LORD is powerful; The voice of the LORD is full of majesty" (Psalm 29:4). "And I heard, as it were, the voice of a great multitude, as the sound of many waters and as the sound of mighty thunderings" (Revelation 19:6).

This world, planet earth, is dying and is in utter chaos; and there is nothing that anyone can do about it. Not even the President, or any of the leaders in this world. Repent now and accept Jesus Christ into your life. For this world (as we know it) is coming to an end very soon. "Now I saw a new heaven and a new earth, for the first heaven and the first earth had passed away" (Revelation 21:1).

I'm not sure what Noah or the number 500 represents in my dream, if anything at all. However, in the book of Genesis 5:32, we read that Noah was 500 years old when he begot his sons Shem, Ham, and Japheth. After the flood, the whole earth was populated from these three sons. (Genesis 9:19) God told Noah that He was going to destroy man whom He had created because of the wickedness of man and his evil thoughts. Therefore, Noah was to build an ark according to God's instructions. Noah found grace in the eyes of God. He was a just man, perfect in his time, his generation, and he walked with God. He and his immediate family (8 people) were the only human beings saved from the flood. Noah was 600 years old at the time of the flood; and 950 years old when he died. (Genesis 6:18; 7:6; 9:29)

February 1980 [3]

I saw a very bright light shine from heaven upon the earth. In the light, I saw a very old man with a long white beard, and long white hair. A voice spoke from heaven and told me all about this man's life. The man was the biblical Saul. (I do not know which one, Saul of the Old Testament or Saul (better known as Paul) in the New Testament).

My Interpretation

What can be said about your life? The name Saul means "asked" or "being asked of God." Saul of the Old Testament was Israel's first king. (1 Samuel 15:1) It is said that Saul was tall and very handsome. He became king of Israel as a result of divine appointment by God and the Spirit of the Lord came upon him. He was a young man with great courage. Saul was also of the tribe of Benjamin. (1 Samuel 9:2, 17, 21; 10:1) However Saul wasn't perfect. You can read about his failures, jealousy (of David), disobedience, consulting a medium (witch, fortune teller), and his death. (1 Samuel 13:1-14; 18:5-16; 28:7; 31:4). The Lord regretted that He had made Saul king over Israel. Saul turned his back from following God, and he did not perform God's commandments. (1 Samuel 15:11, 35)

In the New Testament, Saul of Tarsus was a Jew of the tribe of Benjamin. He is a Hebrew and Pharisee. He was born in Rome but was raised in Jerusalem and was well-learned. Saul's Roman (or Gentile) name was Paul, which he used after his conversion on the road to Damascus. (Philippians 3:5; Acts 13:9; 16:37, 38; 21:39, 22:3; 23:6; 9:3-8). As he came near to Damascus, Jesus spoke to him (in a flashing light) in a verbal and real way. This changed the life of Saul (Paul) forever. He was called and ordained by God to preach the gospel of Jesus Christ to the Gentiles, proclaiming that He (Jesus) is the Son of God; He died for our sins and God raised Him on the third day for our justification. The Lord moved mightily in the life of Paul.

However before Paul's conversion he heartlessly persecuted the Church of God, so much as dragging Christians out of their homes and putting them into prisons; compelled them to blaspheme, and he executed them. (Acts 8:3; 9:1, 2; 22:4; 26:11) He was feared and hated by many people. He was an Apostle of Jesus Christ by the will of God (Ephesians 1:1), and wrote thirteen letters in the New Testament, and many believe that he may have written Hebrews (although the author is uncertain). Read more about Paul in the book of Acts.

"Therefore, if anyone is in Christ, he is a new creation; old things have passed away; behold, all things have become new" (2 Corinthians 5:17).

Do you know that our lives are as an open book to God? There's nothing hid that can be hidden from Him. Jesus knows all about you. He knows who you are, and what's in your heart. He knows what you're thinking, even before you think it. He knows what you're going to say, before you say it. He knows what you're doing, and why you're doing it. He knows where you've been, and where you are right now. He knows where you're going, and where you're destined to be. You can trust Him with your pass, present, and future. Our God is an awesome!

February 1980 [4]

I was sitting watching television when suddenly the program was interrupted and writing appeared on the screen. It read, "Don't be like Esau," referring to the biblical Esau. Then a voice came from the television, and it told me of all the times God was with me (while showing me pictures of my life on television)—and I didn't even know or realized it.

My Interpretation

Our God is all seeing, all knowing, and He's everywhere at the same time. God is always with us, guiding and protecting us from all harm. Even though we make mistakes and do things that we know we shouldn't do, God looks beyond our faults. He forgives us, and is always there for us— even when at times we may feel like He isn't. There's nothing we have done, or will do that God isn't aware of. Call on Him with your whole heart, and

He will answer you. He'll never leave you nor forsake you. (Provided you don't leave or forsake Him). He loves you but He will not make or force you to love Him. God will not violate our free will to choose who we want to serve, or where we choose to spend our eternal lives.

Esau was the son of Isaac and Rebekah. He was the older twin brother of Jacob. Esau sold his birthright to Jacob for a bowl of lentil stew. (Genesis 25:29-34) Birthright in the Hebrew family meant leadership and honor, and only the firstborn son had the right to receive such a privilege. Sadly, not only did Esau lose his birthright to his brother Jacob, but also his father's choice blessing through the deceit of Jacob and his mother Rebekah. (Genesis 27:1-29; 28:1-4) Isaac did give Esau a blessing but not one that he had hoped for. (Genesis 27:38-40) Thus began the sibling rivalry between the two brothers, and Esau vowed to kill Jacob his younger brother. (Genesis 27:41)

I believe that God is telling me (and you) not to throw away our birthright or spiritual inheritance from God. We're not to take it lightly. Sometimes we will do anything to satisfy the flesh. Be careful how you make trade and with whom, and do not be too anxious for anything. Don't be like Esau. Don't let Satan take your spiritual birthright and blessing.

"Be anxious for nothing" (Philippians 4:6). ". . . lest there be any fornicator or profane person like Esau, who for one morsel of food sold his birthright. For you know that afterward, when he wanted to inherit the blessing, he was rejected, for he found no place for repentance, though he sought it diligently with tears" (Hebrews 12:16, 17).

February 1980 [5]

I saw light shining on a wall, writing then appeared and the head title was **REVELATION NOTES** (in bold capital letters). I read all the notes but can remember only one: "He that believes in God, all things are possible."

My Interpretation

The word 'Revelation' means to reveal or make known something that was hidden; the manifestation of divine will or truth. God is simply telling me (and He's telling you): if I have faith, if I can conceive it, speak it, believe it, and trust Him; nothing in this life is unreachable, unobtainable, or impossible for me (or you).

"If you can believe, all things are possible to him who believes" (Mark 9:23). "With men this is impossible, but with God all things are possible" (Matthew 19:26). "But without faith it is impossible to please Him, for he who comes to God must believe that He is, and that He is a rewarder of those who diligently seek Him" (Hebrews 11:6).

Believe God to do the impossible in your life. Faith is the key that will open the door of impossibilities. It will make the impossible possible. Let faith arise in you.

February 1980 [6]

I was standing on a porch with one other person. A man and a woman were fighting inside the house. I thought about calling the police to break up the fight so that they wouldn't hurt each other. Pointing towards the house across the street from us I said, "Look! I belong over there, those people are Christians. Listen to them singing "Amazing Grace."

My Interpretation

This song is a beautiful hymn. Some of the words are: *Amazing grace, how sweet the sound that saved a wretch like me. I once was lost but now I'm found was blind but now I see.*

God is not the author of confusion, and we can call on Him in the midst of any trouble. There may be times when we'll have to separate ourselves from family and friends, especially if we're in harms' way. We can still love and pray for them from a distance. And, we can also be there for them to help them the best that we can.

But, if they are determined to keep fighting and hurting each other, then there's nothing that you or I can really do to stop them from doing it. However, there is something that Jesus can do, but they will have to call on Him for themselves. He's an expert in lost and found, and opening blinded eyes so that they can see. They will have to admit that they are a sinner, they are blind, wretched, and in need of a Saviour. They must ask Jesus Christ to forgive them of their sins, and they must repent of their sins. Jesus will help, save, and deliver whosoever will call upon Him in sincerity. His grace is truly amazing.

"Call upon Him while He is near. Let the wicked forsake his way, And the unrighteous man his thoughts; Let him return to the LORD, and He will have mercy on him; And to our God, For He will abundantly pardon" (Isaiah 55:6, 7).

But you know your place, you know where God has placed you, you know where you belong. So, "Come out from among them and be separate, says the Lord. Do not touch what is unclean, and I will receive you" (2

Corinthians 6:17). "For by grace you have been saved through faith, and that not of yourselves; it is the gift of God, not of works, lest anyone should boast" (Ephesians 2:8, 9).

If it weren't for the amazing grace of God we would all be lost. His grace is sufficient for us regardless of our circumstances. (2 Corinthians 12:9) You know that you belong in the family of God. Stay with God, and if you don't know Jesus Christ as your Lord and Saviour, invite Him into your life now!

February 1980 [7]

I was at my mother's house in North Carolina standing by a wood heater. I sensed that there was a spirit in the next room the door was closed. My mother, and my oldest brother knew this also but they did not seem frightened. My brother then asked me to come with him to the kitchen to get some fish so that we could cook it on the wood heater. Knowing I had to pass that room, I threw a chair at the door and it slightly opened.

Suddenly a tiny shiny ball appeared that grew larger and larger as it came towards me. It was a spirit that formed into a human. I was afraid, so I stooped down behind the wood heater hoping the spirit would not see me (I was holding my youngest daughter in my arms). The spirit reached his hand out to me and said, "Mandy (speaking to my mother), I come to take her for a little while." I was now no longer afraid because I knew that the spirit did not want to hurt me.

The spirit put something like a dab of white cream in the palm of my right hand and asked me if it hurt. I answered, "No." "Good, it's not supposed to," the spirit replied. Again, the spirit said to my mother while looking directly at me, "Mandy, I come to take her for a little while." I stood up and we walked outdoors. The spirit then asked me, "What is the most important thing to you right now in your life?" But before I could answer he disappeared. I felt that he knew what I was going to say (and it wasn't the right thing—but it was the truth).

My Interpretation

God knows us better than we know ourselves, and He should be number one in our lives. Sometimes God must get us alone or in a place where He can ask us questions that will bring about awareness in us to help us realize that we're putting someone or something else before Him. Loving God, and doing His will, should be the first and most important thing in our lives, and He should also be the most important person in our lives.

So I ask you: What is (or who is) the most important thing (or person) to you right now in your life? Be honest with yourself, because God already knows our thoughts before we even think them, and He knows us better than we know ourselves. (Psalm 139:1-4)

"You shall love the LORD your God with all your heart, with all your soul, and with all your strength" (Deuteronomy 6:5). "You shall have no other gods before Me" (Deuteronomy 5:7). Never put anyone or anything before Him. For our God is a jealous God. (Deuteronomy 6:15)

February 1980 [8]

I was on the subway, when I saw a crowd of people standing around a child that was demon possessed. I was afraid to go near the child thinking that the evil spirit might come out and possess me. When I looked again the child looked like my middle daughter, and I just could not walk away.

I went to the child and placed my two fingers (right hand from the thumb) on her forehead and said, "I rebuke you in the name of the Lord Jesus Christ." Instantly the child coughed up some nasty green substance (which was an evil spirit). It formed into a greasy looking bald-headed man, and he said to me, "All we need is you, and me, and we can overpower the earth." I replied in a powerful voice, "I do my Father's will. For this cause I came into this world." He immediately then disappeared.

My Interpretation

Satan will try to bring fear upon us to keep us from doing the work God called us to do. For fear and faith does not mix. The two can't walk together because they cannot agree. Fear says I can't do it, faith says it's already done. Fear causes things to stay in a dormant state. Faith speaks things into existence and causes things to move. Fear robs you of courage and of power. Faith increases your courage and gives you power, enabling you to speak to any mountain in your life, commanding it to be removed and cast into the sea.

Let the enemy know immediately where you stand with God. Do not be afraid of him. Once he knows your position with God and you give him no place in your life, and resist him, he will flee from you. (Ephesians 4:27; James 4:7) However he will come back, therefore you must always be ready for him with your sword, which is the Word of God.

"For I have come down from heaven, not to do My own will, but the will of Him who sent Me" (John 6:38). "But for this purpose I came to this hour" (John 12:27).

February 1980 [9]

Someone said that the President of the United States was very sick. I ran into an elevator and got off on the floor he was on. Sitting by his bedside was his wife and an African-American lady. The President's eyes were closed. I kneeled down and began to pray saying, "Oh Heavenly Father, heal your servant in Jesus name."

The President moved his hand slightly and his eyes opened slowly. I looked at his wife and then the African-American lady. The President seemed to have been reaching out to the African-American woman and me more so than his wife. At first, I thought this was very strange, but then I thought that perhaps it was because he was reaching out to God through us, and that he felt a sense of peace.

My Interpretation

Again, God is teaching me how to pray for people in high positions. The office that a person holds should have no bearing on how you pray. Some people when they're in the presence of high officials try to impress them by praying long prayers using big fancy words that God is not interested in, and others may need a dictionary to define your fancy words.

Regardless of whom the person is, even if it's the President of the United States of America, a short prayer of faith and sincerity will get God's attention. Pray what's in your heart believing that God hears and will honor your request. Sometimes a person may be reaching out to God through you. Allow the Holy Spirit to lead and speak through you.

"The effective, fervent prayer of righteous man avails much. And the prayer of faith will save the sick, and the Lord will rise him up. And if he has committed sins, he will be forgiven" (James 5:16, 15). ". . . and for a pretense make long prayers" (Mark 12:40). "And when you pray, do not use vain repetitions as the heathen do. For they think that they will be bear for their many words. Therefore do not be like them. For your Father knows the things you have need of before you ask Him" (Matthew 6:7, 8). "But the prayer of the upright is His delight" (Proverbs 15:8).

God is not interested in the big words or the length of your prayer, but He is interested in your heart. He's interested in your sincerity, love, faith, and your compassion for others. He is interested in your life-style and your relationship with Him. "But He hears the prayers of the righteous" (Proverbs 15:29).

February 1980 [10]

This is the second dream I had about the President of the United States. I was watching the President's special live speech from the White House on television. He was on the balcony speaking about the condition of the world. He spoke on how the people blame him for everything but it's not his fault. He said, "the people need to pray, what the world really needs now is prayer." He went on to say that a particular celebrity (can't remember the name) should stop talking about homosexuals and start praying. Then he started to preach, it seemed as though he became very excited. His wife warmly and softly put her hands on his shoulder as if it were to calm him.

The camera then came up closer, and I saw a strange look in his wife's eyes; a look of disapproval as if the President was not being sincere, and then the look faded. The First Lady smiled and began to sing the song, "*Wash Me in the Blood of the Lamb*." She sung it beautifully.

My Interpretation

Looks can be deceiving. Don't let Satan fool you—for he is a great deceiver. People are blaming God for the bad things that happens to them, and for the terrible condition that the world is in. It is not God's fault, its Satan's fault, and it is man's (our) fault. Honestly, what have you done to help make things better?

We all have a responsibility to do what is right, and to pray for our President, our children, one another, people in government, and for those in authority. If we would spend more time praying for each other and for our country (as well as foreign countries) instead of talking about idle things; I believe that our lives and the conditions of this world would be in better shape. We need to stop and take a close look at ourselves in the mirror at our lives, take inventory, and see what we need to put in and take out of our lives. We need to realize that we are not perfect. We need to call upon God, not man, for the healing of this world. Man has already done too much damage because of his love and greed for money, lust, and power.

We the people need to pray now as never before. We shouldn't point a finger at any one or any group of people. We are all at fault and need to ask God to wash us in the blood of the Lamb (Jesus Christ), and cleanse us from all unrighteousness.

"If My people who are called by My name will humble themselves, and pray and seek My face, and turn from their wicked ways, then I will hear from heaven, and will forgive their sin and heal their land" (2 Chronicles 7:14).

"Therefore I exhort first of all that supplications, prayers, intercessions, and giving of thanks be made for all men, For kings and all who are in authority, that we may lead a quiet and peaceable life in all godliness and reverence (honesty). "For this is good and acceptable in the sight of God our Saviour, Who desires all men to be saved and to come to the knowledge of the truth" (1Timothy 2:1-4).

What can wash away my sins? Nothing but the blood of Jesus! We must be washed in the Blood of the Lamb (Jesus Christ) who shed His precious Blood on the cross at Calvary for the sins of the world, and God raised Him from the grave on the third day for our justification. (John 1:29; 19:16-18; 20:1-18; Revelations 5:9, 12; Romans 4:25) We yearn to give up ourselves, and our lives, so as to press forward into the full power of that new life which Jesus Christ blood has provided for us. Oh, wash me in the blood of Jesus!

"Jesus Christ, the faithful witness, the firstborn from the dead, who loved us and washed us from our sins in His own blood" (Revelation 1:5).

February 1980 [11]

I was at my mother's house in North Carolina, when I heard a loud, strong, and powerful voice (I thought that the whole world heard it) saying, "He cometh in a cloud and every eye shall see Him." I cried to my mother saying, "Mother, I am not ready yet."

My Interpretation

Are you ready? It's time to get ready. Jesus is coming very soon. Please be ready when He comes. For He will come at a time when you least expect Him. It will be too late to change your way of living, or even ask God for forgiveness. You have already had plenty of time, and numerous chances.

"Blow the trumpet in Zion, And sound an alarm in My holy mountain! Let all the inhabitants of the land tremble; For the day of the LORD is coming, For it is at hand" (Joel 2:1). "Behold, He is coming with clouds, and everyone will see Him" (Revelation 1:7).

"Therefore you also be ready, for the Son of Man is coming at an hour you do not expect" (Matthew 24:44). "He who is unjust, let him be unjust still; he who is filthy, let him be filthy still; he who is righteous, let him be righteous still; he who is holy, let him be holy still." (Revelation 22:11) "For the day of the LORD is great and very terrible; Who can endure it?" (Joel

2:11). "And behold, I am coming quickly, and My reward is with Me, to give to everyone according to his work" (Revelation 22:12).

So, whether you believe it or not, or whether you're ready or not, Jesus Christ is coming again soon! If you do not know Him, I encourage you to please ask Him to come into your life, and forgive you of your sins. Be ready to go back with Jesus when He comes. Don't be left behind on this earth because you will go through the great tribulation. It will be a time like there has never been before, and there never will be a time like it again.

A word of encouragement for my sisters and brothers in the Lord: "Look up and lift up your heads, because our redemption draws near." (Luke 21:28)

February 1980 [12]

In another dream, I was at my mother's house in North Carolina, and it began to rain very heavily. The rain turned into hail, and the hail turned into fire. I began saying the prayer Jesus taught his disciples, Our Father, who art in heaven . . . (I woke up and I finished saying the prayer).

Our Father in heaven, Hallowed be Your name. Your kingdom come. Your will be done on earth as it is in heaven. Give us this day our daily bread. And forgive us our debts, as we forgive our debtors. And do not lead us into temptation, but deliver us from the evil one. For Yours is the kingdom and the power and the glory forever. Amen (Matthew 6:9)

I had this same dream again, on the same night, except this time I said the 23rd

Psalm: The Lord is my Shepherd (as I woke up again I finished saying the psalm).

The Lord is my Shepherd; I shall not want. He makes me to lie down in green pastures; He leads me beside the still waters. He restores my soul; He leads me in the paths of righteousness for His name's sake. Yea, though I walk through the valley of the shadow of death, I will fear no evil; for You are with me; Your rod and Your staff, they comfort me. You prepare a table before me in the presence of my enemies; You anoint my head with oil; my cup runs over. Surely goodness and mercy shall follow me all the days of my life; and I will dwell in the house of the Lord forever.

My Interpretation

The first prayer is often referred to as the Lord's Prayer. However, I refer to it as the prayer Jesus taught his disciples to pray. When we pray, we should not seek praise for the good deeds that we do for others, nor pray to be praise by men for excellence of words and long prayer. We must pray in faith and in the spirit. God wants to us pray and worship Him in spirit and in truth. He hears, delights in, and honors such prayers.

The second prayer reminds us that God is our Shepherd. He watches over us, protects us from seen and unseen dangers, leads, and guides us in our everyday lives. He's a very present help in times of trouble (Psalm 46:1), and that He will supply our every need according to His riches in glory by Christ Jesus. (Philippians 4:19) But we must believe, trust, and rely on Him to do just that.

I would like for you to read Matthew 6:9, and Psalm 23, for 7 days, expecting God to do something special in your life. And, ask Him to show Himself mighty and strong in your life. However, you must trust Him, have faith, and expect Him to move in your life.

February 28, 1980

A third time I dreamt about rain, hail, and fire in the same order as past dreams. My parents' house was burning, so I said to myself, "There's nowhere to run or hide, well at least I will die with my family." I looked outside by the front porch and it was raging with flames, but the flames would not spread, and we did not perish. I thought to myself, "We are the only ones saved, because surely this terrible fire destroyed everyone and everything in the whole world."

My Interpretation

Jesus can keep us in the midst of the rain, hail, and fire in our lives. No matter what Satan throws at us, Jesus promised that He would never leave nor forsake us. But we must have faith in Him and depend totally on Him. When Jesus appears in the sky upon His return, for some it will be a time of great joy, and for some it will be a time of great sorrow. For there will be no place to run nor to hide from His awesome presence.

The race is not given to the swift, nor is the battle given to the strong, but to him (or her) that endures to the end. (Ecclesiastes 9:11) For they that endure to the end will be saved. (Matthew 24:13) Pray that you, your family, and all who will accept Jesus as Saviour be found worthy to go back with Him upon His second return, and spend eternity with Him.

May 24, 1980

A small child stuck a needle into her finger and everyone standing around just knew that when pulling it out, it would be very painful (it was in quite deep). I went to the child, and asked her mother to stand on the child's side while I stood in front. I firmly held her finger, and said, "In the name of Jesus," while pulling the needle out quickly. The child did not even whimper.

My Interpretation

Children at one time or another, whether playing outside, inside, or just rambling for something may get a needle or splinter stuck in their finger, feet, or somewhere on their hand. And just at the thought of pulling whatever it is out they may start crying. The name of Jesus works in such matters when used with faith. This dream tells one what to do and say in such a case. This will also work for people of all ages.

You may feel like you are stuck in a painful situation right now and there is no way out. God is able and will help you. If you believe this, in faith, let us pray: "Father, in the name of Jesus, pull, and deliver me out of this situation. I trust you, and I thank you." Amen.

For the name of Jesus is a strong tower. In His name there is joy, peace, love, comfort, strength, encouragement, safety, healing, deliverance, wholeness, soundness, abundant life, a place of rest, eternal life, and everything that you need Him to be.

". . . and you shall call His name Jesus, for He will save His people from their sins' (Matthew 1:21). "Nor is there salvation in any other, for there is no other name under heaven given among men by which we must be saved" (Acts 4:12). "The name of the LORD is a strong tower; The righteous run to it and are safe" (Proverbs 18:10).

July 14, 1980

There were people walking in the street and something fell from the roof of a tall building. A lady quickly jumped to the side and the object missed her, but it struck a baby. The baby was pronounced dead. Someone said not to touch her, because when the police and doctor arrives, they will ask if the child was moved. The injured person should not be moved (although it depends on the situation) before medical help arrives.

I walked over and kneeled beside the baby placing my left hand on her forehead, and my right hand on her neck (it came to my mind that her neck was broken), and prayed saying, "Father, I know you can if you will. Not so much for my sake, for I believe, but for the ones who are standing around so that they will know that you are God." Instantly, the baby's eyes opened and I began praising God giving Him thanks. The baby who now looked to be around 2 years old was smiling. Her face and eyes were shining so bright. She was a beautiful child.

My Interpretation

God is able to do anything we can believe Him for. Without hesitation I walked over to the child believing that God would restore her life. This incident happened for a reason: to reveal the glory and power of God to the people standing around so that they would know and see the awesome power of God.

I believe God was also telling and showing me how to literally pray for a dead person (minutes after he or she is pronounced dead). For nothing is impossible with God.

"But Jesus looked at them and said to them, "With men this is impossible, but with God all things are possible" (Matthew 19:26). "Therefore I say to you, whatever things you ask when you pray, believe that you receive them and you will have them" (Mark 11:24). "If you can believe, all things are possible to him who believes" (Mark 9:23). But you *must* believe with *all* your heart and do not doubt. You must trust God.

July 24, 1980

I read the words on a wall, "God is merciful.

My Interpretation

Yes, God is merciful and His mercy endures forever (Psalm 103:8-12, 17; Luke 18:13; Jonah 4:2; 1 Chronicles 16:34; 2 Chronicles 30:9). Although we have no right to it and we certainly do not deserve it, God showers us with His mercy and His grace because He loves us, and because we are His creation. There's nothing you have done or said in this life that God will not forgive (except blasphemy against the Holy Spirit. (Matthew 12:31-32). God is ever so gracious, loving, caring, kind, sympathetic, and forgiving. All you have to do with a sincere heart is confess your faults and sins to Him, and He will forgive you.

"But God, who is rich in mercy, because of His great love with which He loved us, even when we were dead in trespasses, made us alive together with Christ (by grace you have been saved)" (Ephesians 2:4, 5).

Let us, therefore, come boldly to the throne of grace that we may obtain mercy, and find grace to help in time of need (Hebrew 4:16). Our God is love, and full of mercy and grace.

August 19, 1980

These words appeared before me, "For He is the Prince of the Living God."

My Interpretation

Jesus Christ is the Son of God. Therefore, He is the Prince of the Living God, Jehovah, Supreme Ruler and Governor. (Daniel 8:11) He is also called, the Prince of Life (Acts 3:15), the Prince of Peace (Isaiah 9:6), and the Prince of the kings of the earth (Revelation 1:5). "Him (Jesus Christ) God has exalted to His right hand to be Prince and Saviour" (Acts 5:31).

September 29, 1980

I was singing a song (God gave me) with these words, *"He's my lily of the valley. I know He's my bright morning star. What is His name? His name's Jesus! He's my lily of the valley. I know He's my bright morning star. I know His name. His name is Jesus!*

Then I heard a familiar voice say, "I heard His voice. Some people pray and don't listen. Listen for His voice when you pray." The voice speaking to me was that of a great gospel singer (Mahalia J), whom I admired and respected very much.

My Interpretation

I believe that this great gospel artist (Mahalia J) was truly an anointed woman of God. I believe that she loved God the Father, and Jesus Christ, His Son very dearly, and that she sung to, about, and for Him with all of her heart. I didn't know too much about her prior to this dream. However, after reading about her, listening to her CDs, and watching her DVDs, it was very easy for me to fall in love with her. There was a special glow on her face and a sparkle in her eyes.

Is Jesus your Lily of the Valley? Is He your Bright Morning Star? Do you really know Him? When you pray do you listen for His voice before you so quickly get off your knees? Wait a few minutes and listen attentively for His voice. Jesus wants you to know Him in a real and personal way. He wants to have a one on one relationship with you.

"I am the Rose of Sharon, and the Lily of the Valleys" (Song of Solomon 2:1). "I Jesus, I am . . . the bright and morning star" (Revelation

22:16). ". . . through His (Jesus) name, whoever believes in Him will receive remission of sins" (Acts 10:43). "Nor is there salvation in any other, for there is no other name under heaven given among men by which we must be saved" (Acts 4:12).

Call upon His name when you pray. And then wait, and listen for His voice to give you an answer. Don't be so quick to give on Him. He is the Lily of the Valley, and my Bright Shining Morning Star. What is His name? His name is "Jesus." Believe and trust in Him.

October 25, 1980

I was at a church and the pastor of this church was preaching on how people pretend to shout in the Spirit, and how some people quench the Spirit. While he was preaching my cousin was shouting. As the pastor was walked down the aisle preaching, I started to shake, I had been quenching the Spirit. I couldn't stand it any longer, nor could I sit still, for something inside of me just wouldn't let me, and I felt as if I would explore, if I didn't say something.

I jumped up and shouted, "I thank God for saving my soul, and I thank God for making me whole." I didn't want to say this, and I tried with all my might not to because I knew that by admitting that I was saved, I could no longer be involved in a relationship with someone I cared about very much. It would mean living a holy life before God, and I wasn't ready to do that.

My Interpretation

Shake Satan off you. Don't allow him to stop you from praising God. Satan will do everything within his power to stop you from believing in Jesus Christ, and accepting Him as Lord and Saviour. You see, Satan knows who Jesus is, and who God is. After all he once resided in heaven. He knows that God loves praise and worship. He knows that God inhabits the praises of His people. Be real with God, and He will be real to you. You may be able to fool some people sometimes, but you can never fool God at any time.

We should always give God thanks because He is so good to us; and it is also His will. Do not quench the spirit. (1 Thessalonians 5:19) Let go of anyone and anything that keeps, or hinders you from serving God. Let Jesus into your life, and let Him reign in over your life. Jesus is on His way back a second time to this earth, and it is time out for playing church games. He wants us to be ready and prepared to go back with Him. Praise and worship Him in spirit and in truth, and do not allow man, woman, child, Satan, demons, anything; or anyone between heaven and earth, on earth, or underneath the earth stop you. ". . . in everything give thanks for this is the will of God in Christ Jesus for you" (1 Thessalonians 5:18).

December 1, 1980 (Vision)

I was lying on my bed asking God what I should fast for. At the church I was visiting the congregation was asked to go on a fast for eight days for an upcoming revival. I wasn't really interested in fasting for obtaining material things, but I wanted to get better acquainted with God. I wanted to know more about Him and His way of doing things.

Suddenly I could sense that someone was in my room. Sitting up in the bed, I looked towards the window at my right, and saw the appearance of a man standing there. I could only see him from his waist down (from the waist up there was such brightness, I could not bear to look at him). I knew this was an angel. The angel said to me, "Ask for knowledge and understanding of the Scriptures."

Immediately I got on my knees, while still on the bed, and asked God for knowledge and understanding of the Scriptures as the angel was walking out of my bedroom. Just as I had finished asking God, the angel was entering back into my room, and touched me on my left shoulder. The touch was so powerful that it nearly knocked me flat on the bed, and I even heard the bone in my knee crack. I began to praise, and thank God for this visitation.

My Interpretation

God communicates with us through His Word (the Bible). Everything we need to know about Him is in the Bible (Scriptures, Word). There are many people who say they cannot understand the Bible, especially the original Kings James version. God will give you understanding and knowledge of the Scriptures if this is what you truly desire.

He will anoint your spiritual eyes to see, spiritual ears to hear, and your heart to receive what He's saying to you (and to the world) in His word. When going on a fast, why not ask God for (more) knowledge and understanding of His Holy Word (the Bible). Let His word lead and guide you. Let His word be your compass when you can't find your way, or if you're having trouble finding your way. The Holy Spirit will also help us. He's our teacher and will bring things to our remembrance, and He will give us revelations.

"Your word is a lamp to my feet and a light to my path" (Psalms

119:105). "Then you will understand the fear of the LORD, And find the knowledge of God. For the LORD gives wisdom; From His mouth come knowledge and understanding" (Proverbs 2:5, 6). "He stores up sound wisdom for the upright; . . . And knowledge is pleasant to your soul . . . Understanding will keep you." (Proverbs 2:7, 10, 11). "And in all your getting, get understanding" (Proverbs 4:7).

December 5, 1980

I heard a voice saying, "God will supply your every need."

My Interpretation

God assures us that if we trust and obey Him, He will take care of us and supply all of our needs. So, don't you worry about today or tomorrow; what you will eat, drink, where you will sleep, or how you will pay your bills. For, if God takes care of the lilies of the field, clothe the grass, and take care of the birds in the sky; surely my God will take care of you and me. Surely He will take care of our love ones. Surely He knows what we need. Trust Him to meet those needs in your life no matter how bad the situation looks.

Worrying will only steal your joy, your peace, and may affect your health, which will bring on more worries. I refuse to worry about anything else anymore because I trust God with my life, and He knows what is best for me. He is an on-time God, and He's faithful and true. However there is something that we must do also, and that is: Give Him first place in your lives. We must *seek first God's kingdom and His righteousness.*

"And my God shall supply all your need according to His riches in glory by Christ Jesus" (Philippians 4:19). "But seek first the kingdom of God and His righteousness, and all these things shall be added to you" (Matthew 6:33). "For your Father knows the things you have need of before you ask Him" (Matthew 6:8). "Therefore do not worry about tomorrow, for tomorrow will worry about its own things. Sufficient for the day is its own trouble" (Matthew 6:34).

But you must trust Him, love, obey, do things His way, and let Him be first in your life.

December 6, 1980

A preacher was saying that we should confess the Lord Jesus to people. (I was reminded of a note that I had posted on the bulletin board at work, regarding the goodness of the Lord. I mentioned how God had blessed my parents (they lost a lot of things in a fire) in great abundance, and I said that God is truly a rewarder of those who diligently seek him).

The preacher went on to say, "If you don't confess Jesus before man, neither will He confess you in heaven before His Father. When we gather around God's throne one day—and that day is sooner than some people think—oh, won't it be good to hear Jesus read in the book about how you confessed Him!" I smiled thinking how very much I would like that. He also spoke about having a mind like Jesus. Then the preacher said, "Make up your mind to serve the Lord, and don't turn back." I then woke up. (Read Hebrews 11:6, Matthew 10:32.)

In Real Life: With the dream still fresh in my mind, I knew that I would be unable to fall right back to sleep, so I turned on the radio as it was already set on a gospel station. I was shocked to hear a preacher saying, as he was about to go off the air, "Make up your mind once and for all to serve God, and don't turn back."

My Interpretation

It's time to serve the Lord in the beauty of holiness. It's time to tell a lost and dying world about the love of Jesus Christ, our Lord and Saviour. As Christians, it is time for us to let our light shine, so that people can see a difference in our lives, and will want what we have. Let love, faithfulness, joy, peace, longsuffering, goodness, gentleness, and self-control, which are the fruits of the Spirit radiate in your life. (Galatians 5:22) It's time to take a stand for whom you believe in; for the God of your salvation.

We are to have a mind like Jesus seeing things from His perspective— from His point of view. (1 Corinthians 2:1) The Holy Spirit enables us to comprehend the truth about Jesus thereby allowing us to see (through our spiritual eyes) things the way Jesus does. On the day I stand before the Almighty God of heaven and earth, I want to see Him open the Lambs' Book of Life to my name; and I want to hear Him say, "Well done Sarah, well done! Now enter into your rest with Me forever."

May I ask you a question, or better yet, ask yourself this question. Whom are you serving, God or Satan? Man or God? It's time for you and me to start running for Jesus with full speed. You may see what looks like a dead end just up ahead—but don't stop it's just a mirage to try and slow you down, to frighten you into turning back. It is a trick of the enemy. It is time for you and me to make up our mind, once and for all to serve God, and don't turn back. It's time for us to honor Him, obey Him, be devoted, and faithful to Him.

Make up your mind NOW to serve Him, and don't turn back for any reason. "Take heed to the ministry which you have received in the Lord, that you may fulfill it" (Colossians 4:17). "Therefore, since we are receiving a kingdom which cannot be shaken, let us have grace, by which we may serve God acceptably with reverence and godly fear" (Hebrews 12:28).

"If any man serves Me, let him follow Me; and where I am, there My servant will be also. If anyone serves Me, him My Father will honor" (John 12:26). "Therefore whoever confesses Me before men, him I will also confess before My Father who is in heaven. But whoever denies Me before men, him I will also deny before my Father who is in heaven" (Matthew 10:32).

January 4, 1981

I had three white envelopes in my hand ready for mailing. A voice spoke and said, "Mail only two, the last one is not to be mailed because the world will not be here." I said, "Lord, I don't have long. I've got to start working for you."

My Interpretation

The end of this age is near. God's time is not like time as we know it. One day is like a thousand years to Him. I'm not sure what the three white envelopes mean or represent, if anything. I do know that the work that God has for me to do (and you) must be done quickly. We have procrastinated and have been slothful concerning the things of God, and doing the work He's commissioned us to do. It's time to get busy while we have the chance. When Jesus comes I want Him to find me on the job—doing what pleases Him, and God the Father. Jesus told His disciples, "I must work the works of Him who sent Me while it is day; the night is coming when no one can work" (John 9:4). Night is approaching, and we must start working now!

February 1, 1981

I was on a subway train when a lady walked up to me and asked me what kind of Bible I read. I told her the King James Version because it's the original Greek text. She said for some people the King James Version was hard to understand. I told her that I could understand it (I was reminded of a vision I had 2 months ago in December). This lady named a book she read one time, and mentioned something about the letter L Volume 5.

However she told me to read the 6th chapter of Corinthians. I asked her which book the 1st or 2nd, but she never answered.

In Real Life: Then I woke up, thought about the dream for a while, and went back to sleep. Just before I woke up that morning, I heard a voice saying to me, "Don't forget to read the 6th chapter of Corinthians."

My Interpretation

I had been asking God some questions regarding some things dealing with my personal life. In this dream were the answers. Sometimes we expect God to be so puzzling and mysterious, and so when He speaks to us so clearly, we wonder whether or not it's really Him.

After reading the 6th chapter of 1st and 2nd Corinthians, I immediately understood why the lady in my dream did not specify which book (1st or 2nd). It was because both books contained the answers to my questions and much more. Please take a moment and read these chapters and have an ear to listen to what the Spirit of God says to you. Here He will speak to you about: lawsuits against another Christian, judging, overeating, immorality, and lifestyle. It tells us that we should not marry an unbeliever, or be unequally yoked together to an unbeliever, and much more.

Have a special ear to hear about sexual sin. When you engage in sexual activities outside of marriage, you are sinning against your own body. We were bought with a price, and that price was the blood that Jesus shed for us on the cross, our bodies therefore belong to Him. We should glorify God in our bodies. What we do with our bodies affects us physically and spiritually. It can affect our entire personality and leaves permanent scars. We must not corrupt our bodies through sexual immorality. For the sacredness of the believer's body is revealed in the Trinity: God will raise our body to life again, our body has been joined to Jesus, and our body is the temple where the Holy Spirit resides. Jesus purchased us with His own blood, and we're no longer our own. For, we now belong to God. (1 Corinthians 6:13-20)

"I beseech you therefore, brethren, by the mercies of God, that you present your bodies a living sacrifice, holy, acceptable to God, which is your reasonable service" (Romans 12:1). God isn't asking us to do something hard—it's reasonable!

"Do you not know that the unrighteous will not inherit the kingdom of God? Do not be deceived. Neither fornicators, nor idolaters, nor adulterers, nor homosexuals, nor sodomites, nor thieves, nor covetous, nor drunkards, nor revilers, nor extortionists will inherit the kingdom of God—and such were some of you. But you were washed, but you were sanctified, but you were justified in the name of the Lord Jesus and by the Spirit of our God" (1 Corinthians 6:9-11).

Therefore, "Come out from among them and be separate, says the Lord. Do not touch what is unclean, and I will receive you. I will be a Father to you, and you shall be My sons and daughters, says the Lord Almighty" (2 Corinthians 6:17-18).

There is so much more to digest and appropriate from the 6 chapters of first and second Corinthians, I just cannot tell it all on these pages. But don't just stop there, read the whole book of 1st and 2nd Corinthians, and be immensely blessed. Reading these chapters changed my whole life. And, I knew that I had to make some adjustments in my life, and let go of some things, and some people. It wasn't easy, but it was necessary.

February 12, 1981

JC, my brother, Tameeka, my youngest daughter, and I were at my mother's house. Something or someone was coming through the front door. My brother told me to run out the back door. I picked up my daughter and ran. When we got to the back door, my brother opened it and said with excitement, "Look, at God standing by the well!" I rushed to look, but he closed the door immediately as though he didn't want me to see. I said, "Let's pray." "Jesus, Jesus, Jesus" we both cried. I thought that my brother had disappeared and someone or something else was in the room, maybe the thing or person that was chasing us. I knew I had to pray harder. I was afraid and woke up.

My Interpretation

If we're in the place God has for us, and if we are being obedient to His will, then we as children of God, and joint heirs with Jesus Christ have no reason to run from Satan. Do not let the devil intimidate you. Satan will impersonate and he will use anyone available (family, friends, and strangers) to accomplish his task against you. But you must stand firm, look him eye-ball to eye-ball, and rebuke him in the name of Jesus. Remember, Jesus has given us power and authority over Satan and his demons. Stay prayed-up, so when you're faced with certain decisions, or get into tight situations, you won't have to pray so hard. But pray in faith with *no doubt* (that God won't do what His word says), and *no fear* (of failure in your own ability, of people, or of Satan). "For God has not given us a spirit of fear, but of power and of love and a sound mind" (2 Timothy 1:7).

April 28, 1981

I heard a voice saying, "Fast and pray often." Then I saw JC, my brother standing high in the sky, lovingly smiling at me shaking his head ('no') saying, "Don't you want to go to heaven?" (I was about to commit fornication, which is something that a born again Christian should not do).

My Interpretation

Fasting and praying combined can bring about miracles. I remember when I started my first 8 day fast God visited me in dreams nearly every night. He sent an angel to visit me to give me knowledge and understanding of the Scriptures. I could hardly wait to fall asleep at night so God could talk to me and show me more things. Or, I'd wait for a vision from Him while lying on my bed in my room. It was wonderful!

From the time I had this dream until now, Satan has been fighting me concerning fasting. At one point, it seemed impossible for me to fast because I'd get so hungry. My stomach would hurt, I'd feel nauseous, and my head felt like it would burst at any given moment. Many times I would start a fast but couldn't go through with it. I just had to eat even though I didn't feel hungry. One of my weaknesses was food. Satan knew this, and he used it against me to the fullest. Thank God for giving me victory over the flesh concerning my overeating habits. Foods no longer have me but I have it in control. Now I eat to live, and not live to eat.

People fast in various ways but you let God tell you how He wants you to fast. If He doesn't, then go with your heart and use common sense. (You should check with your doctor before going on any fast, if you take medication, if you have any illnesses, and especially if the fast is more than 1 day).

The way I generally fast is from 6:00 a.m. to 6:00 p.m., going without food and water, or just without food (however I'm led by God). I've also fasted from 6:00 a.m. to 3:00 p.m., going without food and water, or just without food. (This is a way that God showed me in a dream when I was having such a difficult time going without food). I have fasted with only 1 meal a day with water and juice. (This is when I fast for a week or more).

Please note: This is the way that I fast. I am not suggesting or advising anyone to follow. Use your own judgment, talk to God, and speak to your medical doctor before going on any fast, weight lost, or exercise program.

Don't you want to go to heaven? Having sex outside of marriage is wrong in the sight of God. (He sees and knows everything that we do). And if we want to go to heaven, we must stop committing fornication and other acts of sin. No one can force you to stop. It is your choice, and your decision. You get to choose where you will spend eternity: Heaven or hell?

"Nor let us commit sexual immorality" (1 Corinthians 10:8). "Do you not know that the unrighteous will not inherit the kingdom of God? Do not be deceived, neither fornicators, nor idolaters, nor adulterers, nor homosexuals, nor sodomites, nor thieves, nor covetous, nor drunkards, nor revilers, nor extortioners will inherit the kingdom of God" (1 Corinthians 6:9-10).

"Now the body is not for sexual immorality but for the Lord, and the Lord for the body" (1 Corinthians 6:13). "For this is the will of God, your sanctification: that you should abstain from sexual immorality; that each of you should know how to possess his own vessel in sanctification and honor, not in passion of lust, like Gentiles who do not know God" (1 Thessalonians 4:3-5). "For God did not call us to uncleanness, but in holiness" (1 Thessalonians 4:7). "Or do you not know that your body is the temple of the Holy Spirit who is in you, whom you have from God, and you are not your own? For you were bout at a price; therefore glorify God in your body and in your spirit, which are God's" (1 Corinthians 6:19, 20). "Therefore he who rejects this does not reject man, but God, who has also given us His Holy Spirit" (1 Thessalonians 4:8).

"For My eyes are on all their ways; they are not hidden from My face, nor is their iniquity hidden from My eyes. And first I will pay double for their iniquity and their sin" (Jeremiah 16:17, 18). God's eyes behold the good and the evil. Nothing is hidden from Him.

Stop sinning against your body. (Read 1 Corinthians 6:15-18) Say, 'No' to the devil, so you can go to heaven. Have respect for your body, because if you don't, neither will anyone else.

June 4, 1981

I was in a trance. I crawled out of bed, using every ounce of strength I had (words cannot explain how I felt), got down on my knees, and began to mourn and pray telling God that I accept Jesus Christ as my Lord and Saviour. As I was about to get up, I heard a voice say, "Pray for wisdom and knowledge to do the work God has given you to do." Quickly, I prayed saying, "Oh Lord, I pray for wisdom and knowledge to do the work that thou has given me to do." It was an awesome and wonderful feeling.

My Interpretation

The call of God was on my life but I wasn't ready for such a responsibility nor was I ready to give up the life I was living. Accepting Jesus Christ as my Lord and Saviour wasn't as yet on my agenda. Perhaps next year I'll find time for Jesus, I thought to myself. However, I found out that when the call of God is on your life, there's no place to run or hide, and your agenda doesn't really matter. It's all about God's agenda which is winning souls for Jesus.

When God commissions you to do His will, He equips you with everything you will need to accomplish the task. Satan will try to tell you differently, but don't believe him (you know he's a liar any way). If God is calling or has called you to do a work for Him, ask Him also for wisdom and knowledge to that work for His glory.

"I have taught you in the way of wisdom; I have led you in right paths. When you walk, your steps will not be hindered, And when you run, you will not stumble. Take firm hold of instruction, do not let go; Keep her (wisdom), for she is your life" (Proverbs 4:11-13).

"I am filled with the knowledge of the Lord's will in all wisdom and spiritual understanding" (Colossians 1:9). "For the LORD gives wisdom; From His mouth come knowledge and understanding" (Proverbs 2:6). "The LORD by wisdom founded the earth; By understanding He established the heavens; By His knowledge the depths were broken up, And clouds drop down the dew" (Proverbs 3:19). "Wisdom is the principal thing; Therefore get wisdom. "Get wisdom! Get understanding! (Proverbs 4:5).

June 17, 1981

I was going down in very clear water when I saw a great white whale. When I saw the whale, I thought of Jonah of Nineveh. The water was calm and crystal clear, and the whale seemed to be resting. I thought also about Stephen, how he was stoned to death for preaching the Good News of Jesus Christ. As the people were stoning him he looked towards heaven and saw Jesus. Then I saw myself standing upon the water listening to someone preaching the Gospel. Someone said to me, "Don't quench the spirit, and praise Him if you feel to." I then cried out in a loud voice, "Hallelujah!" Words cannot fully explain how good I felt inside.

My Interpretation

First, a little information about Jonah and Stephen: Jonah was a prophet who was born is Israel. He was called by God to preach repentance to the people of Nineveh in a town called Assyria. Jonah was afraid to go and neither did he want salvation offered to these people who professed no religion, and therefore he tried to run from God by a ship at the port of Joppa in route to Tarshish.

The men threw him overboard after realizing that it was Jonah, who had offended his God thereby causing such a terrible storm, which threatened their lives. A great whale swallowed him up. Jonah prayed to God while in the belly of the whale, and after 3 days he was disgorged on shore. Jonah obeyed God and went to Nineveh.

From the very first day Jonah preached the people received God's message and repented. God had mercy on them and abandoned his plan to destroy them. (Read the book of Jonah.) Our God is still full of mercy and grace, and He is a forgiving God.

Stephen was the first martyr of the apostolic church. He was one of seven chosen by God and the apostles to be a deacon, and he was described as a man being *full of faith*, the *Holy Spirit,* and *power,* and he performed great wonders and signs among the people. (Acts 6:5, 8) Because of envy and jealousy, his enemies set him up, and falsely accused him of speaking blasphemous words against Moses and God.

He was arrested by elders of the Scribes (Jewish leaders) and bought before the council. After Stephen addressed the council the Jewish leaders weren't too pleased to hear the truth, and they became furious. Their rage resulted in stoning Stephen. As the people stoned Stephen, he cried out with a loud voice to God and said, "Lord, do not charge them with this sin." And when he had said this, he fell asleep. (Acts 7:60; also read chapter 7 in its entirety) Wow! What a statement! I wonder if you, or I, were in such a position; what would we say, and how would we react?

Are you trying to run from the call of God? There's no place to run and no place to hide. Do you not want salvation for all people? Or, are you only concerned about yourself, your family, and your own certain group of people or race? Are you willing to preach the whole truth according to God's Holy Word (the Bible) with no compromise? Are you willing to die for the sake of the Gospel of Jesus Christ? Are you a Jonah, or are you a Stephen?

Pray for wisdom and knowledge to do the work that God has given you to do. Then do it willingly. Preach the Gospel of Jesus Christ to all people. Be humbled and honored that God has chosen you to minister to His people at such a time as this.

"Commit your way to the LORD, Trust also in Him" (Psalm 37:5). "Commit your works to the LORD, And your thoughts will be established" (Psalm 16:3).

June 23, 1981

I heard a calm voice saying, "First the lamb is shown, then the sheep. I have power to give life and power to take life; that was given to me of My Father (God)."

In Real Life: I woke up with chills and severe pain on my left side.

My Interpretation

John the Baptist referred to Jesus as the 'Lamb of God' who takes away the sins of the world. (John 1:29, 36) Jesus is called the Lamb of God because He was sacrificed for us (on the cross), as was the lamb (spotless) in the Jewish ritual. We (those who have been born again and do the will of God, those who have accepted His Son, Jesus Christ as Saviour) are His sheep. God shows Jesus, His Son, everything both spiritual and natural, and Jesus in turn reveals to us what He would have us to know. God the Father gave Jesus power to give life and to take life. At Calvary while Jesus hung on the cross, the Roman soldiers pierce Him in His side as water and blood ran out.

The nature of the sheep is to be gentle and submissive (Jeremiah 11:19; Isaiah 53:7), defenseless (Matthew 10:16; Micah 5:8), and always in need of guidance and care (Matthew 9:36; Numbers 27:17). The lamb and sheep depends totally on the Shepherd.

Jesus is the good Shepherd who gave His life for the sheep. (John 10:11; Matthew 18:12) The Shepherd has compassion, cares for, and protects the flock. (Matthew 9:36) The Shepherd looks for and restores those that have gone astray. (Matthew 18:12) God is the Shepherd of Israel. (Genesis 49:24) The LORD is my Shepherd. (Psalms 23) Shepherds and their flocks have a close relationship. (John 10:3, 4) Jesus told Peter to, "Feed my lambs and tend my sheep." (John 21:15-16)

June 30, 1981

I saw a church in my hometown on Main Street. I said, "Lord, could this be the church?" Three other people and I formed a circle, holding hands as we kneeled and prayed.

My Interpretation

God will show you were He wants you to go and minister to His people. You just stay in prayer and listen for His voice and instructions. You may be a little surprised at where and to whom He sends you. Never question God, just go and do what He tells you to do, even if it's in a place or area where you may not be welcome by some people (for whatever the reason).

"Proclaim the good news of His salvation from day to day. Declare His glory among all nations, His wonders among all peoples. For the LORD is great and greatly to be praised; He is to be feared above all gods. For He is coming, for He is coming to judge the earth. He shall judge the world with righteousness, And the peoples with His truth" (Psalm 96:2-4, 13).

"Go, therefore and make disciples of all the nations, baptizing them, in the name of the Father and of the Son and of the Holy Spirit, teaching them to observe all things that I have commanded you; and lo, I am with you always, even to the end of the age" Amen. (Matthew 28: 19, 20) Preach and teach the gospel of Jesus Christ to all people wherever God sends you.

July 4, 1981 (Vision)

I was lying on my bed. Suddenly, I was in a trance, and I sensed the presence of someone in my room. I turned my head toward the door. My eyes were closed, I tried to open them but I couldn't as an unusual brightness appeared. With every ounce of strength, with all my being it seemed, I said, "Jesus, I love you, because you first loved me." The voice coming from my bedroom door said, "Say, hallelujah! Go to the altar tomorrow."

In Real Life: I didn't go to church that Sunday because I didn't want to go to the altar. Knowing if I did go to the altar I would repent of my sins and give my life to Jesus. I just wasn't ready to do that. "I'll go next Sunday. My life is fine just the way it is," I thought to myself (not saying it out loud for fear that Jesus would hear me).

My Interpretation

What or whom are you holding on to that's preventing you from giving your life to Jesus? Regardless of what or who it is, you must let it or they go. Believe me nothing or no one is worth going to hell for. Satan doesn't want us to acknowledge Jesus as our Lord and Saviour. He knows that if we do this, he will no longer have dominion over our lives. We will then belong to Jesus because He has already paid the price for us (our sins) on the cross at Calvary over 2000 years ago. For we have been redeemed by the blood of Jesus Christ, and have been reconciled back to God. (Read Galatians 3:13; Ephesians 1:7; Romans 5:10, 11).

"But God demonstrates His own love toward us, in that while we were still sinners, Christ died for us" (Romans 5:8). "We love Him because He first loved us" (1 John 4:10). "In this the love of God was manifested toward us, that God sent His only begotten Son into the world, that we might live through Him. In this love, not that we loved God, but that He loved us and sent His Son to be the propitiation for our sins" (1 John 4:9, 10).

The word 'hallelujah' is the highest praise that we can give God. It expresses gratitude, love, and honor to Him. The *altar* reminds me of that most holy place as in the Tabernacle. It's a place where I can go and be one on one with God in His presence. It is a place of sacrifice, decision, and it is a place of change. It is a place of submission to God. It is a place where I am completely naked before God, as I pour out my heart and soul. I can hide nothing before Him.

It is a place where I deny myself, and humble myself before God. It is a place where I present my body as a living sacrifice, to do the will of God. It is a place where I can go and ask God to forgive me of my sins, and ask for salvation, mercy, grace, healing, and deliverance. It is a place where I go to praise and worship Him in the beauty of holiness as I kneel at His throne and sit at His (nail scared) feet. Jesus Christ is my Lord, Saviour, High Priest, Intercessor, Mediator, and Advocate. He is my Rock, Strength, Shepherd, Source, and my Healer. He is my Peace, Joy, Counselor, Protector, Guiding Light, and King. He is my Redeemer, Reconciler, Friend, Hope, and Comforter. He is everything to me, and He's all that I need.

You can come to His throne of grace and ask for forgiveness of your sins, mercy, and Jesus' help. There is no problem that is too big for Him to undertake and solve. He can relate to our situation, and understands us far better than anyone, and better than we understand ourselves. "For we do not have a High Priest who cannot sympathize with our weaknesses, but was in all points tempted as we are, yet without sin. Let us therefore come boldly to the throne of grace, that we may obtain mercy and find grace to help in time of need" (Hebrew 4:15, 16).

August 6, 1981

I saw a church and they were having service so I went in. An elderly lady walked directly to me singing, "Not to worry, God will supply your every need. Just have faith, trust in Him and believe."

In Real Life: My daughters were vacationing at my parents in North Carolina, and I wanted to pick them up. However I was a little short on money, knowing all my bills were due, and I had only one week vacation. The girls were not due to return home until Labor Day in September.

I telephoned mother and asked her what I should do. I knew that I could give her more money if I stayed at home, and I was hoping she would tell me to stay; not to worry about it, and wait and come home during the Labor Day weekend, but she told me that I had to make the decision. Finally I decided not to go. I went to bed but I couldn't sleep. I tossed and turned all night. I have never been so restless. It was at this time, that I had the dream I mentioned above regarding the lady singing that song to me. Suddenly no longer did I worry about not having enough money to make ends meet; I simply wanted to get to my parent's home. I felt an urgency that I must get there quickly.

After the dream I got up and called the bus terminal for travel information. I was told that the last bus to my hometown left at 4:00 a.m. I asked for a schedule of buses going to North Carolina that would get me closest to my hometown; by now I was desperate. I felt like I had to get there before Saturday night—it was now early Friday morning and it takes twelve to thirteen hours by bus to get home.

I decided to go to Wilson, North Carolina (approximately 30 miles from my parent's home) late Saturday evening. I cannot explain it, but I still had this strange feeling inside. As I walked into the house, I noticed the fan in my parents' bedroom and said to my mother, "I don't like that fan." "What do you mean you don't like the fan?" my mother replied. "I don't like that knocking sound that it's making," I said.

We all went to bed early as usual and everyone was at home except my niece Dianne who was at church. Dad was in his bedroom (with the noisy fan); my sister in her room; my niece Lisa in her room; my nephew Ken in his room; my mother and my daughters had made a place to sleep on the living room floor, and I was in a bedroom next to them near the kitchen.

I was sleeping when suddenly I heard a voice say, "Sarah, wake up!" I quickly sat upright in bed. I looked in the living room and it was filled with smoke and it was about to enter into my room. I then heard the same voice calmly and softly say, "Don't panic." Trying not to panic, I thought, "I must find the front door to open it before calling everyone, so that they can run outside, knowing how frightened they would be."

I ran past the living room (where mother and my daughters were sleeping) into my parent's bedroom, where dad was sleeping, and I saw the fan. That was it! The fan was on fire. I quickly opened the door, and yelled, "Fire!" Just as I said, "Fire," the fan burst into flames (until now it was just smoking and the fan was sitting on the floor which had carpet). I yelled to daddy, "It's the fan!" and he quickly jumped off of the bed, grabbed the fan and threw it out of the front door onto the dewy grass as I held the door open. "Don't tell me God isn't good!" I shouted as I got down on my knees and gave praise and thanks unto my God.

The dream I had and the urgency that I felt to get to my family became crystal clear. Now realizing that had I not obeyed God; and if I had not followed and obeyed the unction of the Holy Spirit, I truly believe that my three daughters, parents, sister, niece, and nephew could have perished in that fire. (The time was between 11:00-12:00 p.m.).

I was now relieved and no longer had that strange and heavy feeling. I felt as though my job was done, and I could have gotten on the next bus returning to New York City with a peace of mind.

My Interpretation

Trust God to supply every one of your needs. We must always listen with our heart. When the Holy Spirit is trying to lead and guide you, don't resist him. Jesus will get you where He wants you to go on time. Don't worry; just have faith, trust in Him, believe, and be obedient.

"And My God shall supply all your need according to His riches in glory by Christ Jesus" (Philippians 4:19). "God is our refuge and strength, a very present help in trouble" (Psalm 46:1). "Trust in Him at all times, you people" (Psalm 62:8). Listen to and be led by the Holy Spirit.

September 5, 1981

My parents and I were on our way home from shopping in my hometown. We had just passed Joiner's Cross Road, and I saw a great cloud of smoke about one mile away. Mother thought that our house was on fire, but as I looked more closely, I knew that the smoke wasn't that far away. As we were about to approach a curve, I said to daddy, "Turn around, we can't make it, there's too much smoke." Then suddenly there were great flames of fire. I wondered if anyone had called the fire department.

I looked to my left and saw a Caucasian man standing in his front yard watching the fire, with his hands on his hips, and I thought, surely he must have notified the fire department. As I turned around, I saw that another fire was about to start at a tobacco barn. The barn was silver or aluminum and box shaped. I had never seen a barn like this before. "Could this be happening to all of the tobacco barns?" I said to myself.

As I began to run, I noticed cows in a pasture. The cows started running. Knowing that I couldn't out run them, I quickly got off of the road, and stood to the side as they ran by. Then I heard a voice say, "Look how they (the cows) multiply." I looked and they were running with so much speed you could see their image, and they were multiplying as they passed by with such an unbelievable speed.

After all the cows had passed, I turned to start running when a lady suddenly appeared. I felt she wanted to stop me, and I didn't want her to, because I was ready to get away from there. The lady stopped me anyway, touching my elbow, she said, "Miss, you're a stranger here aren't you?" "Yes," I quickly replied. "Tell me," she went on, "What do you think this is?" Positioning myself to run, I said, "Miss, I don't know. All I know is that God is good, and Jesus is my Saviour." Then I took off running.

My Interpretation

We are just strangers here, our citizenship is in heaven, and this world is not our eternal home. It is for certain that strange things will happen all around the world as the end of this age draw closer and closer. Get on the run for Jesus, and run as if your life depends upon it—because it truly does.

And as you start doing the work He has given you, God is going to start multiplying your blessings. Hallelujah! So, position yourself and start running and watch Him move in your life and on your behalf as never before.

"For the Lord is good" (Psalm 100:5). "Good and upright is the Lord" (Psalm 25:8).

September 28, 1981

I was getting ready to go back with Jesus. Another lady, and I, was walking on our way to the place where Jesus was, and we saw other people. I spoke to two of them and said, "You still have a chance even in the tribulation. God is a good God. If you just call on Jesus and accept Him as your Lord and Saviour you will be saved." I continued walking (the lady was still with me) and saw Satan coming towards us, challenging me saying, "If you had power you could do this" (lifting himself up off of the ground). I told Satan that I did have power. Then I called on the name of Jesus, and lifted myself off of the ground higher than Satan.

The lady that was with me began to run, I ran also, and Satan started running after us. I saw a man standing outside a door. He had long hair (though it wasn't pure white) about shoulder length, his eyes sort of red (but not as red as fire). He opened the door just wide enough for the lady to go through. He had on a long robe (but it wasn't as white as snow). I started to go in, but he closed the door. I turned around and Satan was still standing there, but he didn't bother me (it was as though he couldn't move). Then I woke up very disturbed by this dream.

My Interpretation

Are you getting ready to go back with Jesus upon His return? Get ready, because He's coming soon! Stay in close fellowship with Him, be watchful, be careful, and be ready.

Remember that Satan can also appear as an angel of light. He will try to trick you into his trap. He's a counterfeiter. He'll try to set up house just like Jesus. He tries to make things look real when it's just an illusion. Watch that devil! He's cunning and he's conniving. Learn of his tactics. Do not be ignorant of the devices Satan uses and don't be intimidated by him. You don't have to prove anything to him.

He already knows that you have more power than he does. He just wants to occupy your time, and get your mind off Jesus so he can try and set you up in some way shape or form. He will try his very best to block and hinder your blessings from God—but he can't stop it, and he knows this. Never be afraid to face the enemy, because the Holy Spirit who is in you is greater, and more powerful, than anyone in this world (or underneath the earth for that matter).

"You are of God . . . and have overcome them, because He who is in you is greater than he who is in the world" (1 John 4:4). "But the Helper, the Holy Spirit, whom the Father will send in My name, . . . the Spirit of truth, whom the world cannot receive, because it neither sees Him nor knows Him; but you know Him, for He dwells with you and will be in you" (John 14:26, 17).

If you miss the rapture, I believe that those who call on Jesus Christ with pure hearts for salvation during the tribulation period will be saved. But you must be genuinely sincere.

"that if you confess with your mouth the Lord Jesus and believe in your heart that God has raised Him from the dead, you will be saved. For with the heart one believes unto righteousness, and with the mouth confession is made unto salvation" (Romans 10:9, 10). "For whoever calls on the name of the LORD shall be saved" (Romans 10:13).

"Then one of the elders answered, saying to me, who are these arrayed in white robes, and where did they come from?" And I said to him, "Sir, you know." So he said to me, "These are the ones who come out of the great tribulation, and washed their robes and made them white in the blood of the Lamb. Therefore they are before the throne of God, and serve Him day and night in His temple. And He who sits on the throne will dwell among them" (Revelation 7:13-17).

These people were saved through faith in the death of Jesus Christ, and they believed in Him for their salvation. They refused to take the mark of the beast (Satan), believing that if they did their soul would be lost forever. If you are left behind, please accept Jesus Christ into your life, and ask Him to forgive you of all your sins. Then tell others about Him, and win souls for Jesus during this time. Although you (Christians) will suffer persecutions, stay in prayer, be strong, encourage one another; reminding each other that you will soon reign with Jesus. Believe me it will be worth it all.

And whatever Satan says, or whatever he does (and you will greatly suffer) to you and your family, please *don't* worship the beast or his image, and *don't* receive his mark (666) or his name on your forehead or on your hand (or any place on your body). You will not be able to buy anything (food, clothes, milk or pampers for your) or sell anything. You may even be homeless, and you and your love ones may be tortured. But do not take the mark 666. Many will be killed because they refuse to worship the image of the beast. But DON'T you or your family receive Satan's mark (666 which is the number of a man and his name) any place on your body. For the moment that you do your souls will be lost forever, because the spirit of Satan, the devil will enter you. You (and your family except children newborn—12 years old) will spend eternity in torment in hell fire.

"If anyone worships the beast and his image, and receives his mark on his forehead or on his hand, he himself shall also drink of the wine of the wrath of God, which is poured out full strength into the cup of His indignation. He shall be tormented with fire and brimstone in the presence of the holy angels and in the presence of the Lamb. And the smoke of their torment ascends forever and ever; and they have no rest day or night" (Revelation 14:9-11).

It doesn't matter who you are, or how much money you have. You won't be able to buy or talk your way out of this one. "He (the beast, anti-christ) causes all, both small and great, rich or poor, free and slave, to receive a mark on their right hand or on their foreheads, and that no one may buy or sell except one who has the mark or the name of the beast, or the number of his name (666)" (Revelation 13:16, 17).

Satan will give great power and authority to the beast, this man who is the anti-christ. He will perform miracles and even make fire come down from heaven. He will deceive many and trick or talk them into receiving his mark (666) or name. (Revelation 13:2, 13, 14, 18)

"... it is the last hour; and the Antichrist is coming ..." (1 John 2:18). (I believe that he is already here, waiting for his hour, and will soon be revealed).

Please read Revelation chapters 12, 13, 14. Then read the entire book of Revelation so that you can be aware of what is about to happen on this earth. And even though during the tribulation period (7 years), you will have a chance to repent and accept Jesus Christ as your Lord and Saviour, why go through all the sufferings, why take the chance? Accept Jesus Christ now so you can go back with Him in the rapture when He comes. Ask Him to forgive you of your sins and come into your heart.

October 1981

I was in a trance-like state. I was lying on the sofa face down in the living room, when an evil spirit pressed hard on my back, trying to hold me down and said, "You know you got to let (calling the person by name) go; you know you got to let him go." It was as though the evil spirit was making fun of me, knowing how difficult it was for me to completely break off my relationship with this person. I then tried to get up off of the sofa, but the evil spirit said cunningly, "You can't." While lifting up with all the strength within me, I replied, "I can do all things through Christ Jesus who strengthens me." I then pushed the evil spirit off my back.

My Interpretation

You may love someone very much, and you feel like there's just no way that you can make it without him (or her). Well, I've got a shocker for you—yes *you can*, with the help of Jesus. I won't tell you that it will be easy because it won't. Satan will see to that. But just keep on reminding Satan, and yourself, that you can do all things through Christ Jesus who gives you the strength and power to overcome. God's strength is made perfect in our weakness.

"For the Lord is my strength" (Exodus 15:2). "I can do all things through Christ who strengthens me" (Philippians 4:13)

February 5, 1982

A Scripture was given to me with the interpretation but I can only remember the word, 'clean.' Then a lady said to me, "If you want to be in our group you have to give up Jesus, stop talking about Him, and stop believing in

Him. I quickly said, "No! I'll never stop preaching about Jesus; He is my all and all, He's my life."

My Interpretation

When the word *clean* is used in the Bible it refers to one being free from filth or dirt (and this is generally so); being ceremonially pure (Leviticus 10:10); and being metaphorically, innocent, and delivered from the power of sin. (Psalm 51:10; Acts 18:6; 1 John 1:9, Jeremiah 4:11) It refers to wholeness, healing and spiritual cleanliness. (Jeremiah 13:27; Matthew 8:2-3; 10:8; Luke 5:12-13; Psalm 51:7)

"Wash yourselves, make yourselves clean; Put away the evil of your doings from My eyes (Isaiah 1:16). ". . . and the blood of Jesus Christ His Son cleanses us from all sin" (1 John 1:7).

Don't let anyone talk you into not preaching about Jesus. You tell of His goodness, grace and mercy. Tell a dying world that Jesus saves. Tell the world that Jesus was born of a virgin name Mary, conceived by the Holy Spirit; Jesus died on the cross at Calvary over 2000 years ago for our sins, and that God raised Him on the third day for our justification. Tell the world that they must repent and be born again, and accept Jesus Christ as Lord and Saviour, if they want eternal life. Tell them that there is no other name given in earth or heaven whereby they can be saved—but the name of Jesus. Tell the world that Jesus is coming again soon to take His children home and the judgment of God will follow. Never ever stop talking about Jesus, loving Him, believing, and trusting in Him. He is our only Hope.

"But sanctify the Lord God in your hearts, and always be ready to give a defense to everyone who asks you a reason for the hope that is in you, with meekness and fear . . ." (1 Peter 3:15).

February 5, 1982

The same night in another dream, I was walking and saw a Catholic church. I wanted to stop and pray but hesitated because of all the candles and images inside the church. However, I found myself going inside going straight to the altar, and fell down on my knees crying out to God. I didn't notice the candles or images.

My Interpretation

There are people who will not set foot in a church unless it's of the same denomination as their church. If the church does anything a little different than they do they don't want to visit that church. I used to think the same way. But thank God for showing me that I can pray to Him anywhere I desire to. My heart and mind is focus on Him alone and not on the things that are around me. If God tells you to go and preach to a people who are of a different race, or denomination than you, do not hesitate to go. He does not care about the color of their skin, nor the inside walls of a church, or the denomination. He cares about winning souls for His kingdom.

"I was glad when they said to me, Let us go into the house of the LORD" (Psalm 122:1) "For My house shall be called a house of prayer for all nations" (Isaiah 56:7). "Do not judge according to appearance "(John 7:24).

March 10, 1982

I was looking up towards heaven and saw a spirit in the appearance of a man from head to waist, but I cannot remember what he looked like. He spoke not a word, but was using sign and hand language to give me a message. It took me a little while to understand, but I finally figured out the message. I then said (as I was stretching my right hand toward the spirit in heaven): "Reach out for love," using every ounce of strength I had to say it. (I have felt this same strange yet wonderful and powerful feeling several times before; I simply cannot find the right words to explain such a feeling). I knew I had the right message because the angel then disappeared, and I felt a sense of relief in my spirit.

My Interpretation

We seem to be reaching out to everyone—but the right one for love. God's love is unconditional. You have been looking in all the wrong places for love: your spouse, children, mother, father, sister, brother, relatives, boyfriend, girlfriend, fiancée, and friends. And the most you've gotten from the people you thought you could count on was headaches, pain, heartaches, and disappointments.

Let me tell you, according to the word of God, what true love does and does not do. "Love suffers long and is kind; does not envy; does not parade itself, is not puffed up; does not behave rudely, does not seek its own, is not provoked, thinks no evil, does not rejoice in iniquity, but rejoices in the truth; bears all things, believes all things, hopes all things, and endures all things. Love never fails." (1 Corinthians 13:4-8)

The greatest gift anyone can give is love. God desires for us to reach out to Him for love. He's reaching out to you and me with His arms wide open. He loves us so very much.

"For God so loved the world that He gave His only begotten Son

(Jesus), that whoever believes in Him should not perish but have everlasting life" (John 3:16). "In this love of God was manifested toward us, that God has sent His only begotten Son into the world, that we might live through Him. In this love, not that we loved God, but that He loved us and sent His Son to be the propitiation for our sins" (1 John 4:9, 10).

Why not reach out for love to the One who is *love*, and truly loves you: God our heavenly Father, and Jesus Christ His Son, who gave His life for you. He's waiting on you right now—just reach out!

March 11, 1982

I was reading Psalm 103 and 104.

My Interpretation

Psalm 103 is a Psalm of David. It's a psalm of praises for God's mercies, and reminds us not to forget all of His benefits. *"Bless the Lord, oh my soul, and all that is within me. Bless His holy name!* Psalm 104 tells us that we should praise God for His creation and providence. *"Oh Lord, how manifold are your works! Bless the Lord, oh my soul! Praise the Lord!"*

We should bless the Lord, worship and praise Him whether we feel like it or not (because it should be about Him and not us). With our whole heart we should bless His holy name, not only for all that He has done for us, doing for us, and will do for us, but because of who He is. What an awesome God we serve!

March 12, 1982

People were being held captive. The people were separated by race, and the poor were treated like animals. The overseer threw a banana, after half peeling it, on the ground for a poor man to eat. The poor man was in a field with live wire around it to prevent people from escaping. I did not like what the overseer had done to this poor old man, and I said so out loud.

The overseer heard me as he turned in my direction pointing a spear. I quickly hid behind my aunt Gold. Realizing that she may get hurt, I stepped from behind her, walking boldly toward the overseer (again feeling this powerful source of strength inside of me) saying in a loud, forceful and powerful voice, "The Lord is my light and my salvation; whom shall I fear? The Lord is the strength of my life; of whom shall I be afraid?" I then took the spear out of his hand and he ran into a corner scared and curled up like a frightened child. I set everyone free, preaching the gospel while doing so.

My Interpretation

Christians are to stand up for what is right, and there should be no compromise for the truth. We should not hold our peace because we are afraid of what man will do to us. A human being mistreating another human being because their skin is another color; or because they're of another ethnic background; or any form of discrimination against another human being is wrong. Start speaking out against these things. Do not be afraid, as long as you have God on your side, man can do nothing to you of spiritual damage. Take courage, declare the faith of the One you believe in, He will protect you from your enemies. The Gospel of Jesus Christ will make you free. And if the Son makes you free, you will be free indeed. (John 8:36)

David wrote in Psalm 27 verse 1: "The Lord is my light and my salvation; whom shall I fear? The Lord is the strength of my life; of whom shall I be afraid." "And do not fear those who can kill the body but cannot kill the soul. But rather fear Him who is able to destroy both soul and body in hell" (Matthew 10:28). My God is Almighty and awesome in power. There is none like Him in heaven, on earth, or in the depths of the earth.

May 30, 1982

I was in service at the church I attend, when a lady suddenly jumped up and said that she had to testify. She pointed to me and said that God gave her a message for me. I can't remember what she said, if anything, because I woke up.

My Interpretation

Be mindful of someone who tells you that they have a message or a word for you from God. Everything should be done decently and in order for God is not the author of confusion (1 Corinthians 14:33, 40). We should discern the spirits because all are not of God. (1 Corinthians 12:10; Hebrews 5:14) Some people just like to be in the spotlight.

Personally, I believe that God will converse with me about anything concerning me first; and then He will speak to the man or woman of God about those concerns merely as a confirmation for me. So if someone tells me that God gave them a message for me, or prophesies to me personally (or in general), and if God hasn't spoken to me about it; and if it's not in line with the Word of God it doesn't go any further than my outer ear. I will not accept it.

There are some people who like to use the term "God gave me a message for you," and then there are those who say they are prophets of God. Let's discuss false prophets for a little while (for if they are true prophets then they have nothing to worry about). The Word of God warns us against *false* prophets. (Read Matthew 7:15-16; 24:11, 24; 1 John 4:1; 2 Peter 2:1; Mark 13:22; Luke 6:26). And many times along with those false prophets are false witnesses. They work together to try and deceive the people. There are schools were a person can go and be taught how to be a prophet and or how to prophesy. Well, excuse me! But it is God who gives us the gift of prophecy (not man), and it is God and the Holy Spirit that teaches, and speak to and through us. Not man! (2 Peter 1:21) I do believe in prophecy and true prophets of God, and there many living today.

A prophet (of God) is a person who is led by God and speaks on His behalf. Prophecy is a spiritual gift given to one from God; and it's not to be taken lightly, misused, abused, or toyed with. Prophecy is for the church—for believers in Jesus Christ to: encourage, comfort, reveal, edify, and exhort the people of God. (1 Corinthians 14:3, 22) God may use prophecy to convict or convince unbelievers by revealing certain things about their lives (that only God and they would know) thus causing them to acknowledge God, repent and accept Jesus Christ as their Lord and Saviour; and they will tell others about their experience. (1 Corinthians 14:24, 25)

Those who prophesy must do so in order. For God is not the author of confusion. And since the spirits of the prophets are subject to the prophets, everything and every prophecy should be done in order, respectfully, and without confusion. The Holy Spirit is a true gentleman.

"Let two or three prophets speak, and let the others judge. For you can all prophesy one by one, that all may learn and all may be encouraged. And the spirits of the prophets are subject to the prophets. For God is not the author of confusion but of peace, as in all the churches of the saints" (1 Corinthians 14:29, 31-33). "Let all things be done decently and in order" (1 Corinthians 14:40).

Be assured that all false prophets will have their place in the lake of fire burning with brimstone (Revelation 19:20), and the false witnesses will not go unpunished. (Proverbs 19:5; 21:28) "Thus say the LORD GOD: woe to the foolish prophets, who follow their own spirit and have seen nothing!" (Ezekiel 13:3). They haven't seen or heard anything from

God. False prophets and teachers will surely be judged by God, and bring swift destruction upon themselves. (2 Peter 2:1; Matthew 7:22)

To know if God has truly spoken to someone who say that they are a prophet, or prophetess, and what will happen to that prophet (or false prophets) if they say something that God has not told them to say (speak lies): ". . . when a prophet speaks in the name of the Lord, if the thing does not happen or come to pass that is the thing which the Lord has not spoken; the prophet has spoken it presumptuously; you shall not be afraid of him. But the prophet who presumes to speak a word in My name, which I have not commanded him to speak, or who speaks in the name of other gods, that prophet shall die" (Deuteronomy 18:21, 22).

June 9, 1982

I was told in my dream to read 2 Timothy 3. Then I heard a voice saying, "Be not conformed to this world, but be ye transformed by the renewing of your mind." When I heard these words, I knew that I had either read them in the Bible (or heard someone say them) a long time ago.

My Interpretation

In 2 Timothy, the 3rd Chapter God was warning me (and He's warning you) that we're living in the last days (referring to the events that will take place at the end of human history and bring God's plan for the redemption of humanity to a climax, or the Christian era from Christ's death until His Second Coming). We're living in dangerous, difficult and evil times—not only for the Christians but for everyone. God tells us what the state of man will be like in the last days:

"But know this, that in the last days perilous times will come: For men will be lovers of themselves, lovers of money, boasters, proud, blasphemers, disobedient to parents, unthankful, unholy, unloving, unforgiving, slanderers, without self-control, brutal, despisers of good, traitors, headstrong, haughty, lovers of pleasure rather than lovers of God, having a form of godliness but denying its power. And from such people turn away!" (2 Timothy 3:1-5).

"And do not be conformed to this world, but be transformed by the renewing of your mind, that you may prove what is that good and acceptable will of God" (Romans 12:2). We must not follow after the world's way; but follow God's way. We must not think like the world thinks. But we must put on the mind of Jesus Christ, and think like He thinks. Pray and read the word of God. Ask Jesus Christ to come into your life. Repent and ask Him to forgive you of your sins. The Holy Spirit will transform your life. If you allow Him, He will change the way that you think, talk, walk, treat others, and the way that you live.

June 30, 1982

I was preaching in tongues (another language) in a foreign country in the language the people spoke and understood.

My Interpretation

I believe that someday God will use me to preach in a foreign country in their native language. It will not be done through an interpreter. I will literally and fluently speak in their tongue (language). God is showing me that He can use me (and you) anywhere He chooses, and we don't have to worry about a language barrier. Isn't our God awesome! (Read Acts 2:4-11)

"And they were all filled with the Holy Spirit and began to speak with other tongues, as the Spirit gave them utterance. And when this sound occurred, the multitude came together, and were confused, because everyone heard them speak in his own language. Then they were all amazed and marveled" (Acts 2:4, 6, 7).

July 7, 1982

Columbus, my oldest brother was trying to get a gun to fire but it jammed. "I need the gun," he said. "All I need is Jesus; the Word is my sword, more powerful and sharper than any two-headed sword," I replied. My brother then said, "Maybe I should come live by you." "You have to find Him (Jesus) for yourself," I responded.

My Interpretation

All you need is Jesus (the Word). You do not need guns, knives, or gangs. Those things will only lead you to death. But Jesus Christ will lead you to eternal life. For His word is the most powerful weapon one could ever possess and is all you or anyone needs. You must seek God for yourself. Love ones' spouse, friends, or gangs cannot do it for you. It's a *personal* thing and it's your choice. I pray that you will make Jesus Christ your choice.

"Seek the Lord while He may be found, Call upon Him while He is near" (Isaiah 55:6). "For the word of God is living and powerful, and sharper than any two-edged sword, piercing even to the division of soul and spirit, and of joints and marrow, and is a discerner of the thoughts and intents of the heart" (Hebrew 4:12). "Is not My word like a fire?" says the Lord, "And like a hammer that breaks the rock in pieces?" (Jeremiah 23:29).

August 5, 1982

A large number of people got off a bus with me. I thought we had traveled many miles. I got off the bus and walked into a church. The lights were on and I felt that someone was there. I thought to myself, "Daddy and uncle Rufus must have been praying all night." (My father is an elder and assistant pastor, and my uncle is a pastor). I then kneeled to pray. I looked at the altar and thought to myself: "I should go to the altar and pray." But I did not go.

My Interpretation

When we read about altars in the Old Testament in the Bible, it is a platform (usually made of large field stones, earth or unhewn field stones (Exodus 20:24-26), cedar and gold (1 Kings 6:20-22) upon which burnt and peace offerings were made to God, or to commemorate an event in which God had helped the person who's making the offering. It may have been a ritual sacrifice of animals or a burning of incense (Exodus 30:1-10).

There were two altars used in the Tabernacle. One was made of acacia wood and bronze, and was used for burnt offerings (Exodus 27:1-8; 38:1-7). The other one, the golden altar, was smaller and it was used to burn incense before the veil (Exodus 30:1-10; 40-5). The altars were a place used to offer prayers, praise and thanksgiving, and sacrifices to God. In the New Testament, in Christian worship, altars were not required for burnt offerings, since in the death of Jesus Christ, the final sacrifice for sin had been made.

For me, the altar is a very personal place where I offer myself and my life to God: a place where God sees and knows my innermost thoughts (for nothing is hidden from Him). Here, I am one on one with Him. It's a place of judgment, and I am standing in the most Holy Place, and on dangerous grounds before a Holy God; I must, therefore, be completely open and honest with first myself, and with God.

"Then I will go to the altar of God, to God My exceeding joy" (Psalm 43:4). ". . . bring your gift to the alter" (Matthew 5:23). "For My house shall be called a house of prayer for all nations" (Isaiah 56:7).

August 8, 1982

I was preaching to a group of people who were slaves (or they could have been field workers). I said in a loud authoritative voice, "This is what your father Abraham spoke about, 'and a virgin shall bring forth a child and He shall be called *Jesus*, for He shall save His people from their sins.'"

My Interpretation

We are to preach the gospel of Jesus Christ to all people; to those who are in bondage, darkness, and lost without hope. Let them know that there is salvation in the name "Jesus."

"And she will bring forth a Son, and you shall call His name *Jesus*, for He will save His people from their sins" (Matthew 1:21). "Therefore the Lord Himself will give you a sign: Behold, the virgin shall conceive and bear a Son, and shall call His name Immanuel (God-with-us)" (Isaiah 7:14). "For unto us a Child is born, Unto us a Son is given; And the government will be upon His shoulder. And His name will be called Wonderful, Counselor, Mighty God, Everlasting Father, Prince of Peace" (Isaiah 9:6). "Nor is there salvation in any other, for there is no other name under heaven given among men by which we must be saved" (Acts 4:12).

We are no longer slaves to sin or bound by Satan. Jesus came that we might be free. "Therefore if the Son makes you free, you shall be free indeed" (John 8:36).

August 13, 1982

I was in church singing gospel songs.

My Interpretation

God wants me (and you) to sing for Him. When one sings under the anointing of the Holy Spirit they can minister to the needs of the people. Broken hearts can be mended, and lives can be saved, delivered, healed, and changed forever.

"Like one who takes away a garment in cold weather, And like vinegar on soda, Is one who sings songs to a heavy heart" (Proverbs 25:20). "Make sweet melody, sing many songs" (Isaiah 23:16). "Sing us one of the songs of Zion!" (Psalm 137:3) "I will sing praises to my God while I have my being" (Psalms 146:2). "A merry heart does good, like medicine, But a broken spirit dries the bones" (Proverbs 17:22).

Therefore, "Let the word of Christ dwell in you richly in all wisdom, teaching and admonishing one another in Psalm and hymns and spiritual songs, singing with grace in your hearts to the Lord" (Colossians 3:16).

August 14, 1982

I was in church singing gospel songs.

My Interpretation

Singing gospel songs is a ministry, and when sung under the anointing of God: songs can minister comfort, healing, and deliverance to the listeners (as well as yourself). "Praise the Lord! Sing to the Lord a new song, and His praise in the assembly of saints." (Psalm 129:1) Gospel instrumental music can bring the same results when played under the anointing of God, and for His glory (and not for entertainment to seek the praise and glory of man).

"Praise Him with the sound of the trumpet; Praise Him with the lute and harp! Praise Him with the timbrel and dance; Praise Him with stringed instruments and flutes! Praise Him with loud cymbals; Praise Him with clashing cymbals!" (Psalm 150:3-5). The praises of God will always be in my spirit and in my mouth. I will sing unto Him.

August 16, 1982

I was in church singing gospel songs.

My Interpretation

I adore gospel music, and my favorite is praise and worship. Whenever I'm feeling discouraged or whenever my spirit needs uplifting, I begin to sing a gospel song or a hymn and make melody in my heart. It doesn't take long before I forget all about my problems because my focus is now on Jesus. The lyrics of the song become alive to me as I began to live in them; the music calms my soul, as I enter into the very presence of God through praise and worship. If I were gifted to sing and play gospel music I would truly use it for God's glory—and not mine own. Music (especially Gospel) is a wonderful gift that God has given to us to share with everyone in the world.

When God's written word, or His spoken word, does not seem to speak to some people; music (anointed) can minister to our hearts and our spirits, bringing us into the very presence of God. "Praise the Lord! For it is good to sing praises to our God; For it is pleasant, and praise is beautiful" (Psalm 147:1). "Sing to the Lord with thanksgiving" (Psalm 147:7). "Sing psalms to Him" (Psalm 105:2). "I will be glad and rejoice in You; I will sing praise to Your name, O Most High" (Psalm 9:2). "The LORD is my strength and song" (Psalm 118:14).

December 6, 1982

My sister had a lovely apartment which somewhat shocked or surprised me, because of her mental state (at that time). The rooms were very large. However, one bedroom needed some repairs. I thought to myself that no one could sleep in this room during the winter (or they would freeze to death) because of the cracks in the ceiling and walls.

The next day I visited my sister again but she wasn't home. The door wasn't locked so I went in. I was surprised to see that the entire apartment had been rearranged with new furniture. The room had been repaired, and had been divided into two bedrooms, and one bathroom. Everything was so pretty and clean. Then I heard a noise at the front door. I thought it was my sister, so I ran to the door and found it slightly opened.

I then saw this big thing (demon/evil spirit) with something in its hand knocking down the walls. It looked dreadful. I said to it loudly and without any fear, "Oh, no! I won't let you destroy her house again. She worked too hard to fix it," and the battle began. I jammed into it with my head while calling on the name of Jesus. The thing (demon/evil spirit) began backing out of the building into the street, where it turned into something like smoke and faded away.

My Interpretation

Don't give up praying for your loved ones. Walk by faith and not by sight. Stand on God's word. Once you clean your house (life) Satan will try to enter again. However he cannot get back in unless you let him in. Keep your house (life) clean and be careful to check all the places where Satan could gain entrance. Remind him that he has no more right over your life or your loved one, because you and they belong to God. You were bought with a price, the blood of Jesus, and you now belong to Him. Stand on the name of Jesus. Speak the word of God.

"When an unclean spirit goes out of a man (or person), he goes through dry places, seeking rest; and finding none, he says, I will return to my house from which I came. And when he comes, he finds it swept (cleaned) and put in order (a new life). Then he goes and takes with him seven other spirits more wicked than himself and they enter and dwell there; and the last state of that man (or person) is worse than the first" (Luke 11:24-26). He (Jesus) rebuked the unclean spirit saying to it: "I command you, come out of him and enter no more!" (Mark 9:25).

Fight Satan in the strength and power of the Holy Spirit. Resist him, give him no place to enter into your life, and rebuke him in the name of Jesus.

December 12, 1982

I was in an elevator that was going down quickly and was out of control holding several other people. As we were going down, I told the people to praise God and He would rescue us. They didn't want to, so I began praising Him myself. Suddenly we were on a bus, and there was a very bad storm with heavy winds and rain. Again, I asked the people to praise God, and if they would their lives would be spared. They still would not praise God nor would anyone answer me. I asked them one last time and one man said he would. I stretched out my hands toward his, took his hands and said, "We are saved." Then the storm was immediately over. I now found myself standing on a porch in front of a beautiful ocean. The waters were very calm.

My Interpretation

Some people just won't praise God even if their lives depended upon it. Praise God when no one else wants to. Praise Him when you're in difficult situations, in the midst of trouble—and He will bring you out victoriously. He will save you. "Save us, O LORD our God" (Psalm 106:47). "Look to Me, and be saved, For I am God, and there is no other" (Isaiah 45:22). "That whoever calls on the name of the LORD Shall be saved" (Acts 2:21).

December 1982

I saw something best described as a flame of fire on legs. My younger brother was running after it as he was yelling, "If I don't come back, you will know I turned pink." (I thought that the strange thing that was running was an evil spirit). As I turned to enter the house, I saw a tiny ball of brightness that became larger and larger. A spirit (angel) appeared and said, "Did you touch it?" "No," I answered. "Good, sometimes it's best to keep quiet," the angel said and then disappeared.

I opened the screen door and walked inside. I told mother that I had just seen an angel and what it had said to me. I turned around, sensing that someone else had walked in; there standing was a small man about three feet tall. I got chills knowing this was no ordinary man, but an evil spirit. He began talking as he started circling around me. I now realized that he was trying to make me angry and say something that would cause an argument. I was about to say, "Jesus" but my mother motioned for me not to, and I remembered what the angel had just told me. But I couldn't take this little fellow any longer.

I blurted out, "Jesus, Jesus, Jesus" I thought if I had just kept quiet a little longer, and the little evil spirit would have left me alone. The little man began backing out of the door into the front yard. The people inside the house began praising the Lord. There was a bright light shining in the yard (not all over the yard) from the house where the door was opened. Suddenly, I realized that I was leaving that light, for the rest of the yard was in total darkness.

Realizing I was going too far out into the yard, I began backing up, still calling on the name of Jesus. The little man quickly said, "No, don't back up, I can't go back to that house." I knew then that he was trying to lure me from the light into the darkness and fear began to invade me. I walked backwards to the screen door not taking my eyes off him. Feeling that I shouldn't turn my back to this evil thing, I kicked him with my feet, opened the screen door and rushed inside. I then woke myself up.

My Interpretation

Sometimes it is best to remain or keep silent and keep your mouth shut. Let Jesus fix it for you, because He knows just what to do. Satan's demons are standing around trying to provoke us into saying something negative, so they can act upon it, or gain access into some area in our life. They're waiting for us to do something negative that's not in line with the word of God. You see he can't do anything until you say something. Our negative words give him fuel or motorize him, just as our faith-filled words moves God.

Satan has a way of trying to lure us out of the light into darkness—out of the safety zone into his territory. And if you're not watchful, careful, and prayerful you will be in his territory before you know it; and by the time you realize it, it may be too late. Watch that devil.

Therefore submit to God. "Resist the devil and he will flee from you" (James 4:7), and give him no place in your life (Ephesians 4:27). Stay in the light. Jesus Christ is that light, and in Him there is no darkness. (John 1:9)

December 26, 1982

I heard someone saying, "Sometimes when people cry they feel guilty. Satan likes it when you feel guilty. Stop feeling guilty."

In Real Life: I woke up hearing a preacher on television; it was a Sunday morning, he was saying, "When you've accepted the grace of God you will stop feeling guilty." The preacher then quoted a scripture to read but I didn't quite hear it.

My Interpretation

To stop feeling guilty was a very hard thing for me to do even after I asked Jesus to come into my life. As a matter of fact, I couldn't open the door of my heart for Jesus to come in because I didn't think that I was worthy of His grace. Many times I had made promises to God that I didn't keep and vows that I didn't honor. I knew right from wrong. Satan thrives on your guilt because he knows this will keep you from accepting the grace of God. Once you have accepted the grace of God you will stop feeling guilty. Accept God's grace now and be free forever. God no longer remembers your sins, so why should you? For the Lord will give grace and glory. (Psalm 84:11)

Under the old covenant, God is merciful and forgives us of our sins: ". . . Says the Lord. For I will forgive their iniquity, and their sin I will remember no more" (Jeremiah 31:34). Under the new covenant God remains the same and says: "For I will be merciful to their unrighteousness, and their sins and their lawless deeds I will remember no more" (Hebrews 8:12; 10:17). "being justified freely by His grace through the redemption that is in Christ Jesus" (Romans 3:24). "To me, this grace was given" (Ephesians 3:8).

God's grace of forgiveness comes to us through Jesus, and because of His (God) love for us. For God so loved the world that He gave His only Son, and the Son (Jesus Christ) gave His life for us (and rose for our justification). We were bought with a price—the precious blood of Jesus. Don't you let anyone (no matter who the devil uses) make you feel guilty about your pass. Grow in the grace of our Saviour Jesus Christ, for His grace is sufficient. (2 Corinthians 12:9)

January 9, 1983

Pearlie and I were discussing my visit to North Carolina during the Christmas holidays.

She asked if I had seen her mother during my visit, and I told her yes. Then Pearlie said to me, "Sarah, you've been good to your brothers." We walked outside and saw that my two brothers were about to go the store. They asked us if we wanted anything and we said no. My sister (Jess) was sitting in the car with the door open with her feet resting on the ground. I asked my sister if she was going and she said no. So, I told her to come out of the car and shut the door. Gusty got a small twig from a tree; he was going to hit her because she wasn't moving. Columbus, my older brother, walked up to Gusty, warmly put his hand on his shoulder and said, "No man, you can't use that, and you can't hit her." As he was saying that I jumped off the porch saying, "No, don't tell him anything, because before I let him hit her with that switch, I'll take it and beat him with it!"

Then I suddenly felt this powerful feeling inside of me. I jumped on a tiny molehill of sand looking at Gusty directly in his face. I then looked towards heaven and saw two dark clouds that reminded me of (two dark clouds I saw in) a dream I had in 1980. Feeling this powerful source of energy within, I pointed at the clouds and said in a powerful loud voice,

"As sure as I'm standing here pointing my finger toward that dark cloud, before the end of 1983, she (now pointing my finger at my sister) will be healed, and she shall be delivered. These are not my words, but the words of Jesus Christ! Jesus said: if I could believe it, and receive it, it's mine. God had mercy on you Gusty, for it could have been you or me, and it's still not too late."

In Real Life: Before I went to bed, I had asked God what I could do to help regarding my sister's illness. In my dream I wanted to say that my sister would be healed in three months, but changed my mind thinking, what would people say if she wasn't healed, I would be embarrassed. I now realize that was the trick of Satan, he put fear in my mind; therefore, I could not use or stand on my faith. You cannot receive healing and deliverance from God if you have fear or doubt.

My Interpretation

Speak the word of God and believe the promises of God. Don't let Satan rob your love one (or you) of healing and deliverance. Speak in faith, and see in your spirit through the eye of faith, those things that you do not see in the natural; as though they already are. Do not let Satan rob you of God's blessings by bringing doubt, fear, and unbelief. Believe and trust God. Stand on His Word and promises no matter how bad or impossible things may be or look.

"For God has not given us a spirit of fear, but power and of love and of a sound" (2 Timothy 1:7) "For as many as are led by the Spirit of God, these are the sons of God. For you did not receive the spirit of bondage again to fear, but you received the Spirit of adoption by whom we cry out, Abba, Father" (Romans 8:14, 15). "Now faith is the substance of things hoped for, the evidence of things not seen." (Hebrews 11:1) "So Jesus said . . . Have faith in God. For assuredly, I say to you, whoever says to this mountain, 'Be removed and be cast into the sea,' and does not doubt in his heart, but believes that those things he says will be done, he will have whatever he says." (Mark 11:22-24) There is nothing too hard for God to do. Absolutely nothing! Just believe in your heart by faith what you say, when you say it; then receive them by faith in your spirit, and you will receive it (those things you say) in the natural from God.

January 12, 1983

I was preaching to a number of people saying, "Praise Him (Jesus) on the high sounding cymbals, praise Him with stringed instruments; Psalm 150, the last verse says: "Let everything that has breath praise the Lord. Praise the Lord!"

In Real Life: I went to church about one hour after this dream. The Holy Spirit spoke through the gift of tongues to the congregation, and the interpretation that came forth was: God said that He wants us to praise Him more. The minister read the scripture and it was the 100th Psalm; the pastor started his sermon with Psalm150, and the last verse was: "Let everything that has breath praise the Lord. Praise the Lord!"

My Interpretation

God desires a people that will praise Him with their whole heart. If you're alive you should give God praise for all of His mighty acts, and for all of the wonderful things that He has done for you personally, and for your loved ones. When we praise God we show Him love and adoration, and we honor Him. Praise and worship Him just because He is God, for He inhabits in the praises of His people. God is merciful, gracious, faithful, loving, giving, kind, and wonderful.

"Praise the Lord! Praise God in His sanctuary; Praise Him in His mighty firmament! Praise Him for His mighty acts; Praise Him according to His excellent greatness! Praise Him with the sound of the trumpet; Praise Him with the lute and harp! Praise Him with the timbrel and dance; Praise Him with stringed instruments and flutes! Praise Him with loud cymbals; Praise Him with clashing cymbals! Let everything that has breath praise the Lord. Praise the Lord!" (Psalm 150)

January 1983

I saw the word '***DIVINITY***' in large bold print as if it was branded on an extremely large piece of white paper or a white wall.

My Interpretation

The word *Divinity* as defined in the dictionary means the state or quality of being divine. The Godhead, God: a deity: such as a god or goddess, Godlike character, and theology. We as children of God, having been reborn of His Spirit, should have some of the essential nature, characteristics, and qualities of our heavenly Father.

Apostle Peter puts it this way: "As His divine power has given to us all things that pertain to life and godliness, through the knowledge of Him who called us by glory and virtue, by which have been given to us exceedingly great and previous promises, that through these you may be partakers of the divine nature, having escaped the corruption that is in the world through lust" (2 Peter 1:3, 4).

January 13, 1983

I had a dream about my favorite house. The last time I dreamt about this house was when it burned down. The house is now restored beautifully repaired and it almost looked brand new. I was in the front yard doing some work to the house, when I saw people coming from church. I felt a little embarrassed knowing that I should have been in church myself. The church was where a barn used to be.

My Interpretation

'House' is naturally interpreted as a dwelling place—a place in which to live, a house, or our home in heaven. It is also referred to as a place of worship—a church or temple (house of God), or even a person. Our body is the temple where the Holy Spirit dwells. (1 Corinthians 6:19, 20; 2 Corinthians 6:16)

Working on the house, reminds me that there are still areas in our lives that need to be worked on, which need repairing. It could be our heart, our character, renewing our mind with the word of God, our attitudes, our love and concern for others. Ask Jesus to help you work on renovating your house (interior and exterior). He is the best contractor for the job.

A barn is mainly used as a storehouse. However, this barn had been torn down and now in its place stood a house. God is tearing down some old stuff in our lives so that he can rebuild. Are you ready for a change in your life? God is ready to build, make repairs, fix, restore and renew some things in our lives. "For we know that if our earthly house, this tent, is destroyed, we have a building from God, a house not made with hands, eternal in the heavens" (2 Corinthians 5:1).

January 14, 1983

I was in church when I was filled with the Holy Spirit (Ghost). I felt the power of God in my feet, then all over me, and I couldn't keep still (although I tried). I did a praise dance. The feeling that I felt inside was wonderful and very powerful.

My Interpretation

Being filled with the precious Holy Spirit is a wonderful feeling, so much so that it's hard for me to explain. The Holy Spirit (also known as the Spirit of truth, Comforter and Helper) is given to us to lead and guide us into all truth (John 14:26); to comfort and help us, to teach us, to empower and strengthen us; to keep and protect us, to enable us to live a life that is pleasing to God, and to do the work He has assigned and called us to do.

". . . He will baptize you with the Holy Spirit" (Mark 1:8). "And I (Jesus) will pray the Father, and He will give you another Helper, that He may abide with you forever—the Spirit of truth, whom the world cannot receive, because it neither sees Him nor knows Him; but you know Him, for He dwells with you and will be in you" (John 14:16, 17).

"If you then, being evil, know how to give good gifts to your children, how much more will your heavenly Father give the Holy Spirit to those who ask Him!" ". . . but God, who has also given us His Holy Spirit" (1 Thessalonians 4:8) ". . . and do not take Your Holy Spirit from me" (Psalm 51:11).

January 25, 1983

I was talking to mother about a dream that I had telling me that it was time for me to change. I was reminded of a vision I had in 1968, wherein an angel appeared and said, *"In time you will change, I'll come back and let you know."*

My Interpretation

If God hasn't already spoken to you, don't be discouraged, and don't give up. Hold on and don't give up, for in His time, your change will come. God will surely let you know, but you must have an ear to hear, and a heart to believe so that you can receive what God says to you. Stay in prayer, and stay in His word, and believe His word.

". . . all the days of my appointed time will I wait, till my change come.

Thou shalt call, and I will answer thee: thou wilt have a desire to the work of thine hands. For now thou numberest my steps: dost thou not watch over my sin?" (Job 14:14-16 KJV).

January 25, 1983

I was going up towards heaven holding a small bottle of oil in my hand, asking God to anoint the oil so that I could use it to heal the sick, and I would give Him the glory.

My Interpretation

Olive oil (produced from the olive berry) is the oil that is most commonly used for anointing. To anoint one is to put oil onto the person's head, forehead, hands, or on any place of the body. The Holy Spirit anoints us to do the work God has assigned to us. The Holy Spirit is our Comforter, Helper, Counselor; he reveals things to us, lead us, and guides us into all truth. He enables us to understand our faith and to live the way God desires for us to live. (Read 1 John 2:20, 27; 2 Corinthians 1:21, 22).

Anointing the sick with oil should be accompanied with prayer (James 5:14-16). Anointing with oil was a large part of the Apostle's healing ministry (Mark 6:13). To anoint one with oil is also performed to consecrate the person to God, or to set he or she apart for an office. (Read Exodus 28:41; 29:7; 40:13, 15; Psalm 23:5; 2 Corinthians 1:21; Luke 4:18)

"Is anyone among you sick? Let him call for the elders of the church, and let them pray over him, anointing him with oil in the name of the Lord. And the prayer of faith will save the sick, and the Lord will raise him up. And if he has committed any sins, he will be forgiven" (James 5:14, 15). "The effective, fervent prayer of a righteous man avails much" (James 5:16).

February 5, 1983

I was at home in NC standing in the yard. I said to mother, "Let me go see my baby." I started walking toward the kitchen singing: *Amazing Grace will always be my song of praise, for it was grace that bought my liberty.* Entering the kitchen I saw my mother (whom I had just left outside in the yard), my sister, and two or three children.

My sister smiled at me as I said good morning, and that made me very happy (because most of the time she didn't talk or smile). I started to hug her but she got up as I went to touch her. My sister had a beautiful smile, and even her eyes looked different, they were so bright. I said to her, "I love you," as I sat at the table beside the child (three or four years old) whom I believed to be my baby daughter (who will be eight years old this month). I started hugging the child, and as I was embracing her, loving her, suddenly the child was my sister.

My mother was talking to someone about a church where they cast out demons, though she wasn't talking about taking my sister (who also needed deliverance), and this bothered me. My mother was telling this person that they took her brother to the church. I guess the person she was speaking to wanted to take someone there.

Suddenly, the power of the Holy Spirit came upon me, and it was very powerful. I got up, wrapped my arms around my waist, holding myself tight; I said to my sister (in a powerful voice), "Say with His (Jesus) stripes I am healed!" She couldn't say it. I started walking closer towards her as she backed up. I touched her and she fell to the floor. I held her by her feet, while still talking, but I do not remember what I was saying. Suddenly she stood up. I was standing in front of her, holding her hands. I said with a loud voice, "Say with His (Jesus') stripes, I am healed!"

This time she said it and was healed instantly. We began hugging each other, and jumping around while still embraced praising the Lord. I just couldn't praise Jesus Christ enough for the healing and deliverance of my sister. She was now free indeed from the stronghold of Satan.

My Interpretation

This dream tells me how to pray for a loved one (or anyone) that is demon possessed, or has a mental problem, and therefore does not have a mind or ability to pray for oneself. You can be an intercessor for a love one. Satan will tell you, and try to make you think that there's no hope for them, and that God doesn't hear your prayers—but Satan is a liar. You may not see light at the end of the tunnel; but just keep the faith, keep on believing, keep on praying, stay in God's word, and you'll reach the end of the tunnel where there's great light.

So, don't ever give up on healing and deliverance for a love one (or yourself) regardless of how bad the situation looks, or what anyone says. For Jesus will never give up on your love ones (or you). Let God's amazing grace be your song of praise. For His grace is sufficient.

". . . The effective fervent prayer of a righteous man (one who is in a right relationship with God) avails much" (James 5:16). "Surely He (Jesus) has borne our griefs And carried our sorrows . . . But He was wounded for our transgressions, He was bruised for our iniquities; The chastisement of our peace was upon Him, And by His stripes we are healed" (Isaiah 53:4, 5).

You don't have to go to a church or wait on someone else for healing or deliverance, or demons to be cast out of a love one, if you believe and have received Jesus Christ as your Lord and Saviour; if you have the baptism of the Holy Spirit; and if you are obedient to the word and will of God. You can call on the name of Jesus and trust Him for deliverance.

Jesus has given us the power and the authority to cast out demons. Jesus said, "And these signs will follow those who believe: In My name they will cast out demons; . . . they will lay hands on the sick, and they will recover" (Mark 16:17). He gave them power and authority over all demons, and to cure diseases. (Luke 9:1) "Lord, even the demons are subject to us in Your name" (Luke 10:17). When demons are spoken to in the power and authority in the name of *Jesus*, they must obey Jesus' name, and all that it represents.

February 22, 1983

My sister was trying to get in touch with me by telephone. My phone was ringing and mother picked it up. Just as I was coming for the phone she hung up. I knew she really wanted to speak to me; but my mother for some reason, seemingly didn't want her to. Then my father was telling me that my sister wasn't feeling well, and that her condition was getting worse, and she wanted me to come home. I told him to tell her that I would be coming home right away.

When I arrived in NC, my sister had gotten worse (they were in was my very special house). I began to pray to God and mourn in the spirit saying, "I can't stand seeing her like this anymore. You told me that all I had to do was come home." I kept mourning even harder for I did not know what else to say. My mother was praising God as she ran out of the house into the backyard where I was praying. "She's healed!" Mother shouted. I began praising the Lord dancing all over the yard. My sister is healed!

My Interpretation

Sometimes Satan will try to keep you from ministering to a loved one (and he'll use whoever he can, even those closest to you). Don't give up, for God always has a plan and it is sure to work. Just be obedient and go where He sends you, and say and do what He tells you. God will do the rest. We can't always understand everything as to why bad or unpleasant things happen to us or to a love one. But I know that God has a great plan for our life and He allows everything to work together for our good (so long as we love, trust, and obey Him). So, why not start praising Him right now for what He's about to do in your life and your love ones.

"Trust in the Lord with all your heart, And lean not to your own understanding;" (Proverbs 3:5). "Then you shall call, and the Lord will answer, you shall cry, and He will say, 'Here I am' (Isaiah 58:9). "Behold, I will bring health and healing; I will heal them and reveal to them the abundance of peace and truth" (Jeremiah 33:6).

March 3, 1983

I was looking at the beautiful skyline when I saw clouds rising. Then the clouds formed into something resembling a large arm (from the elbow down is all I saw), as it rose higher into the sky, forming into—what looked like a face. I cannot describe it or explain it exactly, but it seemed to have changed colors. I said to someone, "Come, and look at this!" Someone called me, but I shushed them motioning with my hand for them to come and see. Then this thing started coming towards the house, striking the earth with a laser, destroying everything that it struck. We ran out of the back door.

A man and I were standing on the corner side of the house when I realized that there was no place to run or hide. I saw a lady run into an old storage house. Noticing that the face did not see her, I thought maybe I would have a chance if I ran there also. Then the man standing with on my left said, "God said this little light of His, He's going to let it shine" (referring to me). I knew then that the face wasn't going to hurt us, and that we were saved. The man said, "Let's praise the Lord." I began to sing, "This little light of mine, I'm gonna let it shine."

My Interpretation

Troubles are coming but God will keep us safe in the midst of it. As Christians we are to let our light shine forth, so that people will see a difference in us, and in the way that we live. Then hopefully they will desire to have what we have in Jesus Christ.

"You are the light of the world. A city that is set on a hill cannot be hidden, nor do they light a lamp and put it under a basket, but on a lamp stand, and it gives light to all who are in the house. Let your light so shine before men, that they see your good works and glorify your Father in heaven" (Matthew 5:14-16).

Regardless of your age, race, religion, or gender we are to tell the world about the love of

God. We are to demonstrate that love by helping them and by introducing them to Jesus Christ. "For God so loved the world that He gave His only begotten Son, that whoever believes in Him should not perish but have everlasting life" (John 3:16).

"But even if our gospel is veiled, it is veiled to those who are perishing, whose minds the god of this age has blinded, who do not believe, lest the light of the gospel of the glory of Christ, who is the image of God, should shine on them. For we do not preach ourselves, but Christ Jesus the Lord . . ." (2 Corinthians 4:3-5). "For it is the God who commanded light to shine out of darkness who has shone in our hearts to give the light of the knowledge of the glory of God in the face of Jesus Christ" (2 Corinthians 4:6). Jesus Christ is the light of the world. (John 8:12. 9:5; 1 John 1:5) I thank God for considering me as one of His little lights, and for letting me shine for His glory.

March 21, 1983

I was sitting in the house with my mother, brothers, daughters, nephew, two relatives, and two dear friends when I heard the sound of an airplane in the sky. The sound came closer and closer. I looked out of the window and heard and saw blasts of explosions. The airplane was discharging bombs. I yelled and told everyone to get out of the house. Everyone started hollering, and I started praying. Once outside the house, I could feel the heat, it was muggy and extremely hot. It was difficult to breathe. I prayed even harder. Suddenly I was lifted up off of the ground about four feet. A loud and powerful voice said, "They have believed, but have not received."

Then it was over, and everyone returned inside the house to the same rooms that they were in before. I began writing down what had happened. My mother said, "Writing it down on paper is no good, you have to do it." Then she told me what the voice had said, the part that I couldn't, but I still can't remember what she said. Mom got a paper and pen as though she was going to write it down for me. My brothers then said that they were going gambling, and I thought to myself, "How could they think of doing such a thing after what had just happened!"

Suddenly I was in a church talking to the pastor and told him what had just happened. He was writing on a piece of paper, and said: "What does an apprenticeship mean (or do)?" I quickly said, "But I don't want to do an apprenticeship." As I was looking on the paper that this pastor was writing, I read: Mount (?) Choir Singers (I don't remember the complete name of the church), and apprenticeship.

After seeing this I realized that he knew I wanted to sing. As though he was reading my mind, he said, "I know, but think about it." I turned to go for a walk on the church grounds to think about what the pastor said. I saw a big burial ground which frightened me, and I noticed right beside me a tree with hymn books on it; and right away I thought this was a Baptist Church. The name of the church was on the hymn book, but again I can't remember the name.

Then I saw a flyer (or program) with the name of a funeral home on it. I left the church ground and found myself hopping and skipping on the most beautiful pavement of smooth stones. Skipping on each stone, like a little girl playing hopscotch, I said with each skip, "*What—must-I-do-to-be-a-Christian?*"

My Interpretation

When I had this dream, I wasn't a born again Christian. However, I was going to church more than usual, and I knew God was calling me into the ministry. According to the dictionary, an apprentice is one who is bound by a legal agreement to work in return for instructions (as in a trade); one who is learning a trade or occupation; a beginner; a learner. One in such a case would be considered as doing an apprenticeship with the proprietor, the one with whom he entered into the legal agreement.

2 Timothy 2:15 tells us that we should study to show ourselves approved unto God, a worker who does not need to be ashamed, rightly dividing the word of truth. We must learn all about Jesus and His way of doing things. He wants you and me to enter into a legal agreement to study His word, to learn as much as we can about Him.

"For all Scripture is given by inspiration of God, and is profitable for doctrine, for reproof, for correction, for instruction in righteousness, that the man (or woman) of God may be complete, thoroughly equipped for every good work" (2 Timothy 3:16-17).

A burial ground or cemetery is a place where the dead body is buried (some people say laid to rest). It is time to die to oneself and lay to rest our old way of doing things. It is time to bury the old man and be resurrected into a newness of life. The tree with hymn books represents songs, covering, and shelter. A funeral home represents death, sadness, mournful, sorrow, and a profound lost. Hopping and skipping represents being playful, happy, joyful, and care free.

What must I do to be a Christian? In order to answer that question, one must first know the definition of the word 'Christian.' According to the dictionary a 'Christian' is one who professes, and affirms his or her belief in Jesus as Christ, and lives according to His teachings; following the religion based on His life and teachings. Christians should show love and compassion for one another, and for all people, manifesting the qualities or Spirit of Jesus Christ.

What must I do to be a Christian? I must ask Jesus to forgive of my sins and repent. I must profess, affirm, and declare to the world that I believe in Jesus Christ, the Son of God, that He died on the cross for my sins (and yours), and that God raised Him from the grave on the third day for my justification. "For I am not ashamed of the gospel of Christ, for it is the power of God to salvation for everyone who believes" (Romans 1:16).

I must follow His life and teachings. I must have the Spirit of Christ in me. I must live and walk in the Spirit (and I will not fulfill the lust of the flesh). I must display the fruits of the Spirit (love, joy, peace, longsuffering, kindness, goodness, faithfulness, gentleness, self-control). I must show love and compassion for others, and be concerned about their well-being and their salvation (regardless of race, religion, or gender). I must love my neighbor as I love myself. I must read God's word to transform and renew my mind, for truth, and guidance: and allow God to speak to my heart through the Holy Spirit and His word (the Bible). I must be born again (in my spirit with God's Spirit). Read John 3:3-8; Romans 10:9-10;12:2; 1 John 1:9; 2 Timothy 2:15; Galatians 5:14,16-26; 1 Peter 1:23.

April 12, 1983

I was singing a song entitled, *"Hold on Your Change Will Come."*

My Interpretation

When you feel like giving up, don't! Hold on your change will come. Jesus knows all about your hurt, pain, afflictions, disappointments, financial problems, domestic problems, and the struggles you're going through here on earth. He's going to do the impossible for you and show Himself mighty and strong in your life. Just hold on to your faith in Him, and trust Him.

"According to Your mercy remember me; For Your goodness' sake, O LORD. The troubles of my heart have enlarged; Bring me out of my distresses! Look on my affliction and my pain, And forgive all my sins. Consider my enemies, for they are many; And they hate me with cruel hatred. Keep my soul, and deliver me; Let me not be ashamed, for I put my trust in You. Let integrity and uprightness preserve me, For I wait for

You" (Psalm 25:7, 17-21). I will hold on because I know that my change is surely coming soon. I will wait!

April 14, 1983

I was thinking about the above dream and the song "H*old On, Your Change Will Come.*"

My Interpretation

Our citizenship is in heaven, and our physical bodies will be changed when we go to our eternal home. We eagerly await for the return of our Saviour, the Lord Jesus Christ, who will transform our lowly body that it may be conformed to His glorious body. (Philippians 3:20, 21) Therefore, no matter what you're going through right now, no matter how painful it is, just hold on because Jesus is coming to take us home. Your change is about to come. For we shall all be changed.

"If a man dies, shall he live again? All the days of my hard service I will wait, Till my change comes" (Job 14:14). ". . . but we shall all be changed— in a moment, in the twinkling of an eye, at the last trumpet . . . For this corruptible must put on incorruption, and this mortal *must* put on immortality." (1 Corinthians 15:51-53) We must be changed before we can go to our new eternal home.

April 21, 1983

I read these words in the sky: *Repentance from Worldliness.*

My Interpretation

God was telling me (and He's telling you) to turn away from the way that we're going, desiring and lusting for the things of the world; doing things and living the way the world does. As Bible believing Christians we are in this world, but we are not to be a part of it by doing ungodly things, or doing anything contrary to God's word. He tells us how to live.

Once you ask Jesus Christ to forgive you, and you repent of your sins, and invite Him into your life, there must be an inward change of the heart; and then a total transformation begins to take place (inward and outward). The old you die and you become a new creation in Christ Jesus. You will think, speak, and live a different life style from your old one. You will want to live a life that's pleasing to God and do things His way, not your own way, and not the world's way.

"If you were raised with Christ, seek those things which are above, where Christ is, sitting at the right hand of God. Set your mind on things above, not on things on the earth" (Colossians 3:1, 2) "And do not be conformed to this world, but be transformed by the renewing of your mind, that you may prove what is that good and acceptable and perfect will of God" (Romans 12:2). "For, there is a way that seems right to man, but the end thereof is death" (Proverbs 14:12; 16:25).

So let us stop following the world, but turn to Jesus and start following Him and do things His way. Jesus' way leads to eternal life because He is the Way, the Truth, and the Life. (John 14:6) The world's way lead to eternal torture in the lake of fire and total separation from God. (Revelation 20:15; 21:8, 27). Do not love the world or the things (worldly possessions) in the world because they are all temporary. I do not associate myself with world as it relates to the world's system way of doing things. I try to set my mind and stay focus on heavenly things, and doing things God's way so to please Him; for my citizenship and permanent residency is in heaven.

"For what will it profit a man if he gains the whole world, and loses his own soul? Or what will a man give in exchange for his soul?" (Mark 8:36, 37). "For the wages of sin is death, but the gift of God is eternal life in Christ Jesus our Lord" (Roman 6:23).

May 1983

I picked up the phone to make a call. I heard voices and one of them seemed to have been the operator trying to clear the line. She seemed to have hung up and I continued to listen. Then I heard a voice say, "Sarah, Sarah Jones!" He went on talking to me, but I couldn't hear clearly what the person was saying because someone turned on my television. I tipped over to the doorway of the room, trying to signal my daughters with my hand that I was going to turn off the television, and for them to be quiet.

As soon as I turned the television down, the person immediately stopped talking. But in my mind I felt like the person was telling me that they knew that I wanted to live for the Lord and wanted to do right. The person said something about a hindrance, or maybe I wasn't trying hard enough to get rid of that hindrance.

My Interpretation

God knows who you are and He knows where to find you. Are you really trying hard enough to change your old life style? Are you really doing your very best to live right according to God's word? God knows your heart, and He knows what's standing in the way of you giving your heart completely to Him. "You ran well. Who hindered you from obeying the truth? This persuasion does not come from Him who calls you" (Galatians 5:7, 8).

Don't allow Satan to trick you. Get rid of anyone or anything that tries to hinder you from doing the work and will of God. Man does not have a heaven or hell to put you in, but God does. And when you stand before Him on judgment day, you will have to stand all by yourself.

May 1983

I was pregnant and went to get an abortion. Then suddenly I had given birth to a beautiful son. I thought to myself—how could I have had this child when I had an abortion? The baby had somehow grown in my fallopian tubes. And even though I had given birth to the baby, he belonged to my sister. As I was holding the baby boy in my arms adoring him, I thought to myself; if I had a son he would look just like this child. As my sister was leaning on the porch, not too far from me, I realized that she was herself again (mentally) and she was very beautiful. Realizing this, I got down on my knees and prayed, saying, "Lord, I thank you for making her born again and healing her gradually."

My Interpretation

Are you pregnant with a word from God? I'm pregnant with a message from God, and Satan is doing everything he can to make me abort. He's trying to abort my mission but God will perform a miracle, and I will give birth and bring forth this message from God in a way that will seem impossible to me. Just when Satan thinks he's won, Jesus steps in and does a new thing that blows Satan's mind. We should intercede for loved ones (especially those who are mentally and physically ill). We may have to be a spiritual surrogate mother for them. Also we must be born again of the Spirit. For, that which is born of the flesh is flesh, and that which is born of the Spirit is spirit. (Read John 3:3-8)

"Cry aloud, spare not; Lift up your voice like a trumpet" (Isaiah 58:1). "Pangs as of a woman in childbirth" (Jeremiah 50:43). "Heal me, O LORD, and I shall be healed" (Jeremiah 17:14).

May 1983

I sensed the presence of someone standing by me telling me something, and I quickly wrote down what was said before I forgot. "I will do whatever God commands me to do. Whatever He asks me, I will do." (I was saying it aloud as I wrote it down on paper.)

My Interpretation

Many times we tell God that we'll do whatever He asks and tells us to do, but we don't keep our word for one reason or the other. We really do not mean to be disobedient, and thank God that He knows our heart. However, it is now time for us to focus fully on the call God has upon our life. He wants to hear you say with your whole heart, "I will do whatever You command me to do, and whatever You ask me, I will do it." Submit to God and let His will be your will, and let His will be done in your life. If you need to be reminded of the promise you made to God, write it down on a piece of paper and post it up somewhere so you can read it often.

John 15:14 reads: "You are my friends if you do whatever I command you." It is time that we surrender all—our very will to God. God has called and ordained you to do a work for Him. Do it—stop wasting precious time (that you will never have again). God is with you.

"Before I formed you in the womb I knew you; Before you were born I sanctified you; For you shall go to all to whom I send you, And whatever I command you, you shall speak. Behold, I have put My words in your mouth" (Jeremiah 1:5, 7, 9).

February 24, 1984

I was in a church. A man whom I did not know said to me, "Sister Sarah, I pray your strength in the Lord."

My Interpretation

I'm reminded of Jesus when He prayed for Peter. And the Lord said, "Simon, Simon (Peter)! Indeed, Satan has asked for you, that he may sift you as wheat. But I have prayed for you, that your faith should not fail; and when you have returned to Me, strengthen your brethren" (Luke 22:31-32).

We as Christians should always pray for our sisters and brothers strength in the Lord, because we do not know what fiery darts Satan is throwing at them. But we do know that if we're having trouble with the devil, then so are they. We know that Satan comes (and his desire is) to steal, kill, and to destroy. (John 10:10) That alone should be reason enough for us to pray for one another. Jesus said in that same chapter and verse

(John 10:10): "I have come that they may have life, and that they may have it more abundantly."

"Seek the Lord and His strength" (Psalm 105:4). "The Lord will give strength to His people; The Lord will bless His people with peace" (Psalm 29:11) "God is our refuge and strength, a very present help in trouble" (Psalm 46:1). "And He shall strengthen your heart" (Psalm 27:14). ". . . and pray for one another" (James 5:16).

My sisters and brothers, in the name of Jesus, I pray your strength in the Lord always. Will you also pray the same for me? God bless you and thank you so very much.

March 1, 1984

A man was holding people hostage. I spoke the Word of God to him, and he gave his life to Jesus and released the hostages.

My Interpretation

The word of God will change your mind, change your heart, set you free, give you a new outlook on life, and it will give you a chance to choose eternal life. Don't allow Satan to hold you hostage and keep you in bondage. Read the word of God—for His word is powerful and there is life in His word. Accept Jesus Christ as your Lord and Saviour. Then witness to others and tell them about the love of God.

"For the word of God is living and powerful, and sharper than any two-edged sword, piercing even to the division of soul and spirit, and of joints and marrow, and is a discerner of the thoughts and intents of the heart" (Hebrews 4:12).

March 23, 1984

A woman and a child were in a crusade and there were thousands of people. She got up to testify about the healing of her child. As she was talking, I looked at the child and thought, "This child looks perfect, nothing is wrong with her." I began to praise God.

My Interpretation

You'd be amazed as you hear testimonies concerning healing and many other wonderful and miraculous things God is doing for people. Yes, God is still working miracles in the lives of people all over the world, and He can work a miracle for you. His only requirement is faith.

But He (Jesus) said to them "where is your faith? (Luke 8:25) "Now faith is the substance of things hoped for, the evidence of things not seen. But without faith it is impossible to please Him, for he who comes to God must believe that He is, and that He is a rewarder of those who diligently seek Him" (Hebrews 11:1, 6)." . . . your faith has made you well. Go in peace, and be healed of your affliction" (Mark 5:34, 36).

April 29, 1984

My pastor was shaking hands with some people, as they remained sitting in their seats. When he got to me he sat down beside me and said, "Haven't I seen you here before?" "I have been coming here for over two years, and have only missed two or three Sundays," I replied. "Evening service?" the pastor asked. "No, morning service," I responded. He then said (smiling), "You see, and this is my first time calling you out. I'm going to be keeping my eyes on you, get ready; I'm going to be keeping my eyes on you!"

My Interpretation

Be faithful in your service for Jesus. In case you're not aware of it God has His eyes on you. So be ready for you do not know when God will call upon you to do a work for Him concerning His people. Your pastor is also watching you to see how faithful you are in the things of God, church affairs, and how much you have grown in your ministry. He may call you at God's given time to bring forth a message from God. Get ready, so you can—be ready.

"Behold, the eye of the LORD is on those who fear Him, On those who hope in His mercy," (Psalm 33:18). "The eyes of the LORD are in every place, Keeping watch on the evil and the good" (Proverbs 15:3). "The eyes of the LORD are on the righteous, And His ears are open to their cry" (Psalm 34:15). God is watching us and He hears us.

May 16, 1984

I was giving my testimony as to how I came to the Lord. I told the people that Rhonda, my oldest daughter, was a great inspiration to me. She was saved (accepted Jesus Christ as her Lord and Saviour) at the age of thirteen, and was more faithful to God than I was.

My Interpretation

I honestly do not testify as often as I should. However, this dream reminds me that I should mention my oldest daughter, Rhonda, who was and still is a great inspiration to me. She was saved at the age of thirteen. My daughter read her Bible, prayed, listened to gospel music, and had bible class in our home on Wednesday night for the young people living in our building and community. She also started a ministry of mailing tracts from our home to people.

I remember that night on New Year's Eve. We were at home and she told me that she wanted to go to church. We all got dressed and went to the church that we'd been attending. That night she was baptized and received Jesus Christ as her Lord and Saviour. She has never been the same, and God have blessed and given her favor with people she comes in contact with, and in all that she does.

Frankly, at the time, she was more faithful to God than I was, and I felt a little embarrassed. She read her Bible, believed God's Word, had enough faith for the two of us, and started a home bible study (which was a blessing to many young people). I was (and still am) very proud of her. And even today her love for Jesus Christ and her faith encourages me, and her two younger sisters. To God I give the glory! ". . . And a little child shall lead them" (Isaiah 11:6).

May 18, 1984

I went forward to sing a song in church. I said to the congregation, "I will sing unto the Lord a new song." The song was in the tune of *Precious Lord*. The title was: We *Lord*. ("We" in French means, "Yes") It was a beautiful song.

My Interpretation

Jesus Christ wants us to say yes to Him (in any language) and allow Him to reign in and over our lives. He loves us and wants us to surrender our lives to Him. Say "yes" to His will, His way, and to His plan and purpose for your life. For He know what is best for us. Perhaps someday I will write a song and title it 'Yes Lord,' and sing it in the tune of *Precious Lord*. This will be my new song that I will sing unto my Lord. Why don't you sing unto Him a new song, and say 'yes' to Him, right now?

"Praise the LORD! Sing to the LORD a new song, And His praise in the assembly of saints" (Psalm 149:1). "He has put a new song in my mouth—Praise to our God" (Psalm 40:3).

July 3, 1984

A man was trying to attack me telling me something about meat. I said to him, "The word of God is my meat." I began quoting scriptures and preaching. I felt the power of the Holy Spirit. The man (evil spirit) immediately departed.

My Interpretation

The word of God is my meat, my food, and my strength. The weapon that will defeat Satan is the word of God. Memorize scriptures, and mediate on God's word day and night. Stand on His word, have faith in His word, and trust His word for there is life and power in the word of God. In fact, everything we need is in His Word. "It is written, 'Man shall not live by bread alone, but by every word of God'" (Luke 4:4).

July 4, 1984

I said, "Though He (God) slay me a hundred times, yet will I trust Him."

My Interpretation

Regardless of trials, tests, bad news, misfortune, sickness, bills due, rent due, and unemployed. But I am determined that no matter what the case may be: "I will trust God, my Father; I will trust Jesus Christ my Saviour at all times. I love Him and nothing, nor no one, can separate me from Him.

Job 13:15 "Thou He slay me, yet will I trust Him." Job was saying "no matter what illness is upon me; or how my body feels; no matter what others may think or feel about me; no matter what I lose (family or material things); no matter what God does to chastise me, I will trust Him; for I know my Redeemer lives.

(Although God didn't put the sickness on Job; He allowed Satan to afflict Job to prove that Job was an upright man. In other words—Job was being tested). So don't you worry, because what you're going through right now is only a test. Trust Jesus Christ and believe His word and promises. Our Redeemer lives and He reigns forever!

"To You, O LORD, I lift up my soul. O My God, I trust in You" (Psalm 25:1, 2). "I trust in the mercy of God forever and ever" (Psalm 52:8).

July 4, 1984

I was singing in the choir at the church I attend.

My Interpretation

In the Old Testament, singers held a very important place in temple worship (1 Chronicles 9:33). ". . . and appointed two large thanksgiving choirs . . ." (Nehemiah 12:31). "The singers sang loudly with Jeremiah as their director" (Nehemiah 12:42). There are many Scriptures that you may read regarding singing, worship and praise songs unto God, and musical instruments. Singing praise and worship songs under the anointing, is a ministry that God has placed you in. You have a great responsibility to God and to the souls that have been assigned to you for harvest.

"... admonishing one another in psalms and hymns and spiritual songs, singing with grace in your hearts to the Lord" (Colossians 3:16). "I will praise You with my whole heart; Before the gods I will sing praises to you. I will worship . . . And praise Your name" (Psalm 138:1, 2).

July 18, 1984

I saw myself give up my spirit. As people were gathered around me, I looked down on them smiling. As the Spirit of God heavily came upon me, my eyes became very heavy, and I felt as though I was about to hear from the Lord. This feeling that I had is very hard for me explain. All I can say is—it was a glorious feeling! There are no words that can explain how wonderful and powerful I felt.

My Interpretation

I believe when the spirit leaves the body one can actually view their body (if only for a moment) before crossing over or going on to their next life. They can also see everyone who's surrounding them. "Then the dust will return to the earth as it was, And the spirit will return to God who gave it" (Ecclesiastes 12:7).

July 23, 1984

My employer spoke to me regarding a raise. (In real life, I did get a raise on 7/22). He told me that I should use the money wisely and to put aside a penny for bread. Then he said, "Be meek and humble." I looked at him and thought that this was a little strange coming from him (he's Jewish but conservative as far as religion is concerned).

My Interpretation

Don't be so quick to judge others. God has no respect of person. He can and will use anyone He so chooses. Have an ear to listen for the voice of God from the least one you'd expect. Be a good steward over the things He has given you. Be meek and humble. We must be gentle, kind and patient with others. We should not allow ourselves to be easily provoked by others. We should be submissive to God and to His will.

"Blessed are the meek, For they shall inherit the earth" (Matthew 5:5)."But the meek shall inherit the earth, And shall delight themselves in the abundance of peace" (Psalm 37:11).

We must humble ourselves. We must be lowly in spirit, not displaying arrogance, not thinking more highly of ourselves than we ought to; and that you're better than everyone else. We must be careful how we stand otherwise we might fall. We must not be too proud or assertive.

Isaiah 57:15 reads: ". . . I dwell in the high and holy place, with him who has a contrite and humble spirit, to revive the heart of the contrite ones." Jesus said in Luke 14:11: "For whoever exalts himself will be abased, and he who humbles himself will be exalted." ". . . God resists the proud, but gives grace to the humble" (James 4:6). Be meek and humble in your behavior, attitude, and spirit.

September 30, 1984

A man said: "When I say 'thank you Jesus, praise the Lord' I mean it, and I always feel something good inside." I began to mourn very hard crying to Jesus, thinking that just this morning I said: "thank you Jesus," but felt nothing. Then I was looking up into the sky and saw many animated cartoon figures. I asked someone standing beside me if they saw it too, and they said, "Yes." We all wondered what did this mean. "But this is animated," I said. "These are things to come (or things that come and go or fade away)."

Then I saw another figure and truly it was amazing. As I walked down the steps into a yard, I looked up into the sky and saw an awesome sight. I could not take my eyes off this sight, and I began speaking in tongues. Then I saw a round ball like a symbol of the earth spinning around and around. There was writing on it and I tried to look closer to see what it read. Finally I saw it clearly, and it read: *Know God Saves. I Am the Lord thy God.*

Then I literally saw myself, in my dream, waking up, rushing out of bed getting dress for church. I had only a few minutes to get there before service start.

In Real Life: I woke up and looked at the clock; it was 11:48 a.m. I hurriedly got out of bed and dressed for church. During the service God spoke (through someone using the gifts of tongues and interpretation of tongues) and said that many of us seek to know His will. God also told us not to throw away the Word, and for us to read the Bible. (He said more, but I don't remember what it was). An Elder (whom I greatly respect) of the church was speaking that morning and his subject was: *That I Might Know Him.* As I watched television that morning as I was getting dressed, the preacher's subject was: *That I Might Know Him.*

My Interpretation

Our salvation is not based on our feelings but our faith in Jesus Christ, and what He did for us at Calvary. We should always give God thanks and praise Him whether we feel like it or not. For He is worthy of all praise, glory, and honor. We should never forget what He has done (and is doing) for us. He is so good to us. He constantly endows us with His love, mercy, and grace.

God wants to reveal Himself to us. He wants to become more real to us. He wants a personal relationship with us. He is telling us to study and read the Bible. For God speaks to us through His word. In His word we can discover His will for us. In His word we learn about Him in a more personal way, and His way of doing things, and handling certain situations. In His word we have His mind and thoughts.

In His word He tells us how He wants us to live, and how we should live as children of God. God wants you to know that He can save you no matter what you have done in your pass. After you have given your heart to God, your pass has passed (whether it was years or months ago; yesterday, today, or even 1 second ago. It has passed and no longer exists). God loves you. Oh, my friend, I pray that you will give your heart to Him, so that you might know Him. For, there is life in His Word.

"that I may know Him and the power of His resurrection, and the fellowship of His sufferings, being conformed to His death" (Philippians 3:10). "For I am God, and there is no other; I am God, and there is none like Me" (Isaiah 46:9).

Accept Jesus Christ as your Saviour and Lord today. 'Therefore He is able to save to the uttermost those who come to God through Him, since He always lives to make intercession for them" (Hebrews 7:25).

October 28, 1984

I walked into a church and started to sit in the back but decided to go up front to sit in the second row. As I sat down, the pastor of the church came to me and said, "No time for playing with your finger (I was biting a tiny bump that was on my pinkie), I want you to testify." He quickly stepped back (as I was shaking my head, 'no') and he said to the congregation, "I have someone here who is going to testify." I felt the urge to testify about the blessing God gave me during revival under the tent in July and August, but I didn't. It's time to talk about all that God has done for you, and about His wondrous works.

My Interpretation

Time is out for playing back-row sitters. Keep your focus on Jesus Christ rather than on little things that can wait or doesn't really matter. It is time to come to the frontline and stand up for truth. It's time for us, as Christians, to move forth in the church of God and tell others about the love of Jesus Christ. We must testify to others and tell of God's goodness. Be bold and courageous, and have no fear; then move when God tells you to. Don't allow Satan to steal your testimony. Don't keep silent any longer. "And they overcame him by the blood of the Lamb and by the word of their testimony" (Revelation 12:11).

October 31, 1984

I saw some barns. I had a dream about these very same barns a few months ago. But this time, they sat closer in my dream (in my prior dream they were far away) and there were five additional barns. The colors of the barns were silver and they were shaped like a box. I was at my favorite house. I went outside and looked across the road to my left and saw the barns; feeling a little frightened, I said sorrowfully, "Oh, no!" Then I began to mourn very hard.

My Interpretation

The stage is being set. The time is approaching and is very near; there will be great sorrow and mourning upon the earth as never before, nor will there ever be again. Hold firm your faith, and trust in God in spite of what you will see. If you don't know Jesus as your Lord and Saviour, I implore you to invite Him into your life today. And if you abide in Him, He promises to abide in you, and never forsake you. Whatever comes and whatever happens, do not fear because—Jesus will be right there with you.

"For you yourselves know perfectly the day of the Lord comes as a thief in the night. But you, brethren, are not in darkness, so that this Day should overtake you as a thief" (1 Thessalonians 5:3, 4). "Therefore let us not sleep, as others do, but let us watch and be sober" (1 Thessalonians 5:7). Jesus is coming soon! Are you ready?

October 1984

I was teaching on love and stealing.

My Interpretation

The word of God tells us that we should pursue love. (1 Corinthians 14:1) If we do not have love (in our heart) we have become as sounding brass or clanging cymbal, and we are nothing. (1 Corinthians 13:1, 2) "You shall love your neighbor as yourself. Love does no harm to a neighbor" (Romans 13:9-10).

"By this all will know that you are my disciples, if you have love for one another (John 13:35). And now abide faith, hope, love, these three; but the greatest of these three is love (1 Corinthians 13:13). For God so loved the world (you and I) so much, He gave His only begotten Son, Jesus Christ.(John 3:16) Love is so powerful and will never fail. Love wants what is good and best for us. Love shelters and protects us. You can trust and rely on true love.

Concerning stealing: One of the Ten Commandments is thou shall not steal (Exodus 20:15). In the book of Romans 13:9 "You shall not steal." Let him who stole, steal no longer, (Ephesians 4:28). All thieves will have a place in the lake of fire.

Therefore, let us cast off the works of darkness, and let us put on armor of light (Romans 13:12). Love does not steal, but gives. Let us walk in the love of Jesus Christ our Lord.

October 1984

I was in a car with two other people. They were speaking about attending church on Sunday's only, and that they did not go during the week. The lady said that it was in the Bible, and at that point, I said to her, "Where? Show me! God said that we should always pray without ceasing. That means we should always pray!" Then I began to preach (the driver, who was male, and the lady were in the front seat; I was in the back seat).

My Interpretation

For some reason I associated attending church regularly with praying regularly. In the book of Hebrews 10:25 it reads: "Not forsaking the assembling of ourselves together, as the manner of some is; but exhorting one another, and so much the more, as you see the day approaching."

As children of God we should encourage one another. As we gather together in love and on one accord with the same purpose: to worship and praise the One and Only Almighty God, we draw strength from each other, we up lift one another, we get energized, and we encourage one another to continue to be faithful to God. Other Scriptures you can read are: Psalm 107:32, and Psalm 111:1.

It is good and pleasant for us to dwell together in unity (Psalm 133:1) because there's strength; and it's pleasant because there's joy. For the joy of the Lord is our strength. So I feel that it is very important for us to attend church and fellowship with our brothers and sisters in Christ as often as we can—and not just on Sunday.

Prayer is much like our natural food. We cannot survive very long without it. In Luke 18:1 Jesus tells us that, men ought to always pray and not to lose heart. "Praying always with all prayer and supplication in the Spirit, being watchful to this end with all perseverance and supplication for all saints" (Ephesians 6:18). And Jesus tells us to "watch and pray lest you enter into temptation: the spirit indeed is willing, but the flesh is weak" (Matthew 26:41; Mark 14:38).

Although we may not feel like praying or going to church some time, that still isn't an excuse to give in to those feelings. As a matter of fact that's when we should really press our way out to church and spend extra time with God in prayer; giving Him a sacrificial praise. Satan will do everything he can to keep us from worshiping and praising God. He knows that we will be strengthened and blessed by God. There is strength in unity, and power in prayer.

December 10, 1984

I saw writing in the sky, it read: *Only good things come from above.* I looked again and it read: *350,000 will be put to death.*

My Interpretation

God wants us to have the very best of everything right here and right now on earth. He gives us the very best. Every good and perfect gift comes from above (James 1:17). I have no idea what the 350,000 (put to death) means. It may have or have not already happened.

December 22, 1984

I was standing above a very large city, seemingly on a mountain with an angelic spirit being. As the angel stretched out his arm and pointed toward this city; lights suddenly came on one by one, very fast, until the whole city was flooded with light. It was a beautiful sight to behold. I began speaking in tongues, praising God as I thought about His goodness.

My Interpretation

As Christians, "We are the light of the world. A city that sets on a hill cannot be hidden" (Matthew 5:14). "For so the Lord has commanded us: I have set you to be a light to the Gentiles that you should be for salvation to the ends of the earth" (Acts 13:47).

"To open their eyes and to turn them from darkness to light, and from the power of Satan to God, that they may receive forgiveness of sins and an inheritance among those who are sanctified by faith in Me" (Acts 26:18).

God doesn't want us to hide what He has given us, but share it with all. "Let your light shine before men, that they may see your good works and glorify your Father in heaven" (Matthew 5:16). Jesus is the light of the world. Turn on the Light, and tell others about Him.

God has called me to do a great work for Him, but until now I have been disobedient to this great call of God on my life. I have given Him so many excuses such as: I wasn't qualified, I don't speak well enough, I wouldn't know what to say to His people, I don't know what to do, to wait until my children were old enough to take care of themselves; and I was too busy with work and other everyday things. I truly thank God for His forgiveness, mercy, kindness, grace, and for His patience. I thank Him for not leaving me or forsaking me, and for looking beyond my faults and seeing my needs.

Work while it is still day. Stop procrastinating and do what God has called and ordained you to do. Tell the world that God loved us so much that He gave His only begotten Son that whosoever believe in Him will not perish, but have eternal life. Tell the world that Jesus Christ is the Son of God; He was born of a virgin name Mary by the Holy Spirit; He died on the cross for the sins of the world; and He rose on the third day from the dead (grave) for our justification. Tell them that Jesus is now seated in heaven at the right of God, the Father. Tell them that He is Lord and Saviour; He is the Way, Truth, Life; He is the Light of the world; and He is coming a second time to judge the world, and to take His children to their eternal home which He prepared over 2000 years ago.

Tell them that Jesus Christ is the Saviour of the world. He forgives us of our sins, saves, heals, delivers, and set free. But we must believe and have faith in Him.

(Read John 3:16; Matthew 1:18-25; John 19:16-18, 30, 33-35, 40-42; John 20:1-29; Romans 4:25; 5:1; 10:9; Hebrews 8:1; 1 John 1:5; 5:12; John 1:4, 9; Revelations 22:12).

December 26, 1984

I was preaching about God's grace.

My Interpretation

When we speak of God's grace we talk about the free mercy of God, or His unmerited favor, His love, and His graciousness. No matter what hardships or sicknesses we encounter, we should remember that God said that His grace is always enough, ready, and is available to us.

"My grace is sufficient for you, for My strength is made perfect in weakness" (2 Corinthian 12:9). "For the grace of God that brings salvation has appeared to all men" (Titus 2:11). "And of His fullness we have all received, grace for grace. For the law was given by Moses, but grace and truth came through Jesus Christ" (John 1:16, 17) ". . . the only begotten of the Father, full of grace and truth" (John 1:17).

"But where sin abounded, grace abounded the more, so that as sin reigned in death, even so grace might reign through righteousness to eternal life through Jesus Christ our Lord" (Romans 20, 21). ". . . through whom also we have access by faith into this grace in which we stand, and rejoice in the hope of the glory of God" (Romans 5:2) We have been justified by Jesus' grace. (Titus 3:7)

January 16, 1985

I was preaching and praising God in tongues.

My Interpretation

Tell others about the good news of Jesus Christ and praise Him in your heavenly language. Give Him the highest praise—praise that He alone is worthy of. For in Him we live and move and have our being. (Acts 17:28) He is the air that we breathe, and we can do nothing without Him.

"I will extol You, my God, O King; And I will bless Your name forever and ever. Great is the Lord, and greatly to be praised; And His greatness is unsearchable" (Psalm 145:1, 3). Great is our Lord, and mighty in power" (Psalm 147:5).

February 4, 1985

I was at a church that I use to visit very often, when this lady got up and asked if anyone wanted or needed healing or prayer; and if so she would pray for them. I felt that she was out of order and so did the bishop of this church. A man walked up to her to stop her from *laying hands* on people and was trying to avoid a big scene. Then the bishop walked over to her and she began to pray thinking that the bishop was in agreement with her. But I saw from the look on his face that he did not approve nor was he in agreement with her.

After this woman had prayed for this one lady (and she was healed), she softly and sweetly left. As she was approaching the door, a man in the pulpit began to speak (supposedly) in prophecy against the lady. I noticed that the pastor had indicated to this man to do this. That is another reason why I knew this prophecy was not of God. Realizing this, I couldn't stand it any longer; I stood up and said, "Now I know what the Lord called me for, to exploit this kind of falseness in the church." And then I woke up.

In Real Life: I woke up, and then I went back to sleep and had a dream about this same church, and the same bishop, concerning the doctrine he teaches. This is what I dreamt:

A woman was sitting across from me telling me how she heard that this bishop didn't believe in the text (or only studied the text when he needed to). She said that her teacher, nor she, believes in what the bishop teaches. I told her that as long as he preached the full Bible and its truth, but she should certainly read the Word for herself.

My Interpretation

I believe that there is a time and there is a place for everything. Things concerning the church should be done decently and orderly. (1 Corinthians 14:40) There will come a time when false prophets and teachers will try to stop the work and plan of God. They will try and deceive the people of God. I am against false prophets pretending to be led by God (but actually being led by Satan and their own fleshly thoughts). And it is time for this sort of thing to be exposed. Beware of false prophets, who come to you in sheep's clothing, but inwardly they are ravenous wolves. You will know them by their fruits" (Matthew 7:15-16).

Read the Bible for yourself so that you will not be children, tossed to and fro and carried about with every wind of doctrine, by the trickery of men, in the cunning craftiness of deceitful plotting (Ephesians 4:14). Read and allow God to speak to you and teach you.

February 15, 1985

I was at church and was about to go into the pulpit. I began speaking in tongues so powerfully (that when I awoke from the dream I had a headache for a second). Satan tried to enter my mind trying to make me believe that my speaking in tongues was not of God. I then said with much authority, "Satan can only do to me what God allows him, and furthermore, he (Satan) cannot do any more than I want him to do."

My Interpretation

Satan never gives up and he's always trying to place doubt, fear, and unbelief in our minds and in our hearts. He knows that he is limited as to what he can do in our lives; but he doesn't want you to know it. Always resist him and give him no place in your mind, heart, or in your life. Satan is nothing but a liar, thief, robber, deceiver, imitator, an accuser, and he's conniving. He can even appear as an angel of light. So be careful and watch that devil. Also remember that he can only do what God allows him and no more than you want or let him do.

"And they were all filled with the Holy Spirit and began to speak with other tongues, as the Spirit gave them utterance" (Acts 2:4).

February 19, 1985

An elderly man (with lovely white hair) was telling me to start fasting. He proceeded to tell me how he fasted. At first he couldn't fast from 6 a.m. to 6 p.m. because he got too hungry. He fast from 6 a.m. to 3 p.m., then gradually from 6 a.m. to 6 p.m. The elderly man went on and told me to start fasting now because there would be trouble ahead in the choir that I was in.

My Interpretation

During the time I had this dream I was having problems with fasting. I tried fasting from 6:00 a.m. to 6:00 p.m. but would get hungry and eat. In this dream God was telling me of another way of fasting, and this way would work for me. Please note: This is my dream and the way that God communicated with concerning fasting. I am not advising anyone else to do this. Use common sense and consult with God and your medical doctor. ". . . that you may give yourselves to fasting and prayer." (1 Corinthians 7:5) "So we fasted and entreated our God for this, and He answered our prayer." (Ezra 8:23)

March 4, 1985

I was standing in front of this person and she laid her hands on my forehead and prayed for me. She said, "When I'm like this, I let Jesus take full control." As she touched me, I felt the power of God run through my body (it was so powerful that I literally jerked from a bent knee position on my bed). I woke up and the unbearable migraine headache which I had all day and most of that night was completely gone.

My Interpretation

This lady was operating in the gift of healing. When operating in this gift, the individual must allow Jesus to take absolute and total control. The individual must decrease so that Jesus can increase allowing the Holy Spirit to work in the office of healing. ". . . to another gifts of healing by the same Spirit" (1 Corinthians 12:9).

God gives us spiritual gifts (empowered by the Holy Spirit) to use for His glory, to minister to the needs of His body, the church; for edification and exhortation to His people; as well as for our spiritual growth. (Please read Romans 12:6-8; 1 Corinthians 12:1-11, 28).

March 27, 1985

I heard someone say (referring to me): "Where is the preacher?"

My Interpretation

I was surprise of bishop's voice I heard asking this question because I didn't think that he believed in women preachers. Although I never understood why, since God is God and He can choose and use anyone He wants to carry out His will; His plan; and His purpose. A preacher is one who proclaims the Gospel of Jesus Christ and or delivers a sermon; and this can be male or female. This can be me (or you).

"The Spirit of the Lord is upon Me, because He hath anointed me to preach the gospel to the poor; He hath sent Me to heal the brokenhearted, to proclaim liberty to the captives, and recovery of sight to the blind, To set at liberty those who are oppressed; To proclaim the acceptable year of the Lord" (Luke 4:18, 19). "Preach the word! Be ready in season and out of season. Convince, rebuke, exhort, with all longsuffering and teaching" (2 Timothy 4:2).

"For if I preach the gospel, I have nothing to boast of, for necessity is laid upon me; yes, woe is me, if I do not preach the gospel" (1 Corinthians 9:16). Where are the preachers?

March 27, 1985

I was reading a bereavement card. I thought that the card was from me, telling people not to mourn for me when I die.

My Interpretation

I died to sin (to the old life that I was living). I have been crucified with Christ; it is no longer I, who live, but Christ lives in me; and the life, which I now live in the flesh I live by faith in the Son of God, who loved me and gave Himself for me. (Galatians 2:20) And when I leave this life to enter into my eternal life with my Heavenly Father, and Jesus Christ my Saviour; please do not mourn for me. Please know that I am happier than I have ever been or could ever be. My absence from this body signifies my presence with God. (2 Corinthians 5:8)

"For to me, to live is Christ, and to die is gain. . . . having a desire to depart and be with Christ, which is far better" (Philippians 1:21, 22).

March 27, 1985

I was in a hospital looking for the ladies room, when I saw a little girl five or six years old. The nurse asked me if I was her mother (I was just standing there looking at the child. There was something very special about the little girl). "She caught my eye. No, I am not her mother," I responded. That part of the hospital was the children ward. The part that I was in prior to that was the maternity area, because everyone I saw looked as though they were about to go into labor, and ready to deliver at any time.

My Interpretation

We are now in labor, the pain is just about over, and we're about to give birth to a new life. We're about to give birth to: our ministry, new ideas, new jobs, new relationships, new leadership, writing books, writing screen plays, producing movies, and to spiritual gifts (for the ministry) as we began to walk in the calling wherein God has called us; planned and purposed for our lives. Get ready for a great explosion of the Gospel of Jesus Christ. We're about to have the greatest revival ever on earth. God is calling us to heal and deliver His children because Jesus is on His way back a second time. Great miracles are about to happen. I believe that Jesus is going to use the not so popular one; the one no one has ever heard of before; the one who has only a high school education; the one who didn't complete high school; the one you and others thought would not succeed; and the one you thought God couldn't or wouldn't use.

Let us also pray for the health, safety, and wholeness of all the little children around the world. Pray that no weapon Satan forms against them prosper. Pray that their parents will love and cherish them. Pray that goodness and mercy follow them all the days of their lives, and that they will dwell in the house of God forever. Amen.

March 29, 1985

I dreamt about *love*. I asked God to show me how to love, and to put more love in me.

God was showing me how to demonstrate "love for one another." You simply *put others before yourself.* I told God that I understood the dream.

Now, before this I had a dream while still in a dream. I had asked God to give me more love for people. There was this lady who needed help with her luggage. She had gotten tired, so she stopped and sat on her luggage. She was asking for help, and although there were many people passing her, not a single one stopped to help her. I was ahead of this lady, but I had turned around and went back looking for someone, after realizing that they were not with me. As I walk over to help this lady, I cried out to God asking Him to show me how to love, and put more love in my heart for others.

My Interpretation

So many people profess that they serve a God of love, yet they themselves fail to demonstrate compassion and love for all people (regardless of color, religion, or gender). As people of the Most High God, we need to show more love and compassion for our fellow man. We need to be concerned about one another. If you want to know how to love—simply put others before yourself. Love your neighbor as you love yourself. (Romans 13:9)

"Though I speak with the tongues of men, and of angels, but have not love, I have become sounding brass or a clanging cymbal. And though I have the gift of prophecy, and understand all mysteries and all knowledge, and though I have all faith, so that I could remove mountains, but have not love, I am nothing. And though I bestow all my good to feed the poor, and though I give my body to be burned, but have not love, it profits me nothing" (1 Corinthians 13:1-3)

Love suffers long and is kind; love does not envy; love does not parade itself, is not puffed up; does not behave rudely, does not seek its own, is not provoked, thinks no evil; does not rejoice in iniquity, but rejoices in truth; bears all things, believes all things, hopes all things, endures all things. Love never fails' (1 Corinthians 13:4-8). "And now abide faith, hope, love, these three; but the greatest of these is love" (1 Corinthians 13:13).

April 1, 1985

I looked at my father and said, "Satan I rebuke you in the name of Jesus, take your hands off him. He belongs to God."

My Interpretation

In real life, I found out later the same week that my father had not been feeling well. I prayed with him over the phone, and repeated the same words (above) that I had told Satan in my dream. My father got better. I especially thank God for this dream because from that point on I began to pray often for my father (a great man of God).

In Reality: My beloved father went to his eternal home to live with Jesus six months after this dream. And yes, I do know for certain that daddy is with Jesus Christ and God my heavenly Father, because God told me so.

I'd like to share this with you because someone may need to hear it. In a dream during the home going service for my father, I began speaking in the gift of tongues and the interpretation came through me. God said to the people "Do not weep for my servant (referring to my dad): for he is well, for he is with Me. But weep for yourselves and for your children." What an awesome word from God! I knew for certain that my earthly father was now with my Heavenly Father. (This message I was to share with my family and the people at the home going service.)

April 2, 1985

As I was leaving a large place where people were assembled, I noticed a group of people reading a paper that a woman was passing out. I saw some kind of an inscription, and the name of someone was written on the paper. After seeing this, I began to speak out loud saying, "There is no other name in heaven or in the earth whereby you can be saved except the name of Jesus. For Jesus said, "You can't get to the Father, but by me. The only way that you can get to God is through Jesus Christ."

The people slowly returned the paper to the lady. As the woman was about to pass by me I told her that I would pray for her. "Ask God to reveal to you to who you should be praying to. If you sincerely ask Him, He will surely show you," I said to her.

My Interpretation

There is no other name in heaven or on earth where in a person can be saved except the name of Jesus. If you sincerely want to find out the truth as to whether or not you're serving the right God; why not ask God to show you. I guarantee you that He will—if you're sincere. Don't just take man's word for it—don't even take my word. For neither man nor I have a heaven or a hell to put you in. But God does. Read the Bible and let God speak to your heart through His living word. "Nor is there salvation in any other, for there is no other name under heaven given among men by which we must be saved" (Acts 4:12).

May 26, 1985

I was witnessing to many people telling them about the Good News. When I said, "Every knee shall bow and every tongue must confess that Jesus is Lord," a man then said something and I demonstrated to him how he (and everyone else) would have no other choice but to bow. I called a small child of about four years old, but the child would not come to me. I then asked the man to stoop down to about the height of a four year old child. I placed my hand on his shoulders holding him down preventing him from getting up.

(At this time, the child wanted to come to me, but I said no because he didn't want to come when I first asked, and I had now began the demonstration). Move when God tells you to because by the time you decide to; He may would have already chosen to use someone else who's willing to obey His voice.

I said, "If I were to hold a small child down like as such, he would not be strong enough to get up on his own, for my strength overpowers a child's strength and he would have no other choice but to stay here. When Jesus comes, every knee shall bow and every tongue shall confess that Jesus is Lord. They will have no other choice. They may not want to, but they will have no other choice." It then began to rain hard and hail started falling. This man got very frightened. I began to praise God saying, "Glory, glory to God, hallelujah!"

My Interpretation

This dream illustrates that whether one wants to or not—one day they will bow down before Jesus Christ and confess that He is Lord of Lord. "For it is written, as I live, says the Lord, every knee shall bow to Me, and every tongue shall confess to God" (Romans 14; 11).

"That at the name of Jesus every knee should bow, of those in heaven, and of those on earth, and of those under the earth, and that every tongue should confess that Jesus Christ is Lord, to the glory of God the Father" (Philippians 2:10,11). You will have no other choice.

June 4, 1985

I heard the voice of a man trying to say something but seemed to be having a problem saying it. I knew what he was trying to say, so I yelled with a loud voice for him to hear me: "Seek ye first the kingdom of God and His righteousness and all these things will be added unto you. I know it is in Matthew, but I don't know which chapter!"

Suddenly, there was a great explosion with lots of water and fire. It was an awful sight to see and it was very frightening. People began to run for their lives. I ran to a ditch thinking to myself that there is no place to run or hide so I may as well just lie down in this ditch and die. I thought there was no need of trying to out run or hide from what was happening.

I laid down in the ditch and as I closed my eyes to die, I could literally feel my spirit leaving my body. Immediately I opened my eyes and said, "No, I'm not ready to die!" I got up out of the ditch and started running for my life in hope that this great disaster would stop eventually; and that the smoke, fire, or flood wouldn't catch up with me.

My Interpretation

We must not allow the cares of this world grip our lives. People are so stressed out over yesterday, today, and tomorrow. We're so materialistic and wrapped up in self. We're putting everything and everyone first when we should put God first in all that we do. God assures us that He will take care of our every need, because He loves us. But if you want Him to do this for you, you must do this for Him: "But seek first the kingdom of God and His righteousness, and all these things shall be added to you" (Matthew 6:33).

So do not worry about what you will eat, what you will wear, how you're going to pay your bills and the cares of this world. Why worry about something you cannot change. And if you can change it, then there is no need to worry. Satan wants you (and I) to give up and lie down and die. But don't you give up, don't give in; keep on running in the race, be encouraged and keep the faith. Do not fear when disaster strikes. God is with you, and wants you to live.

"I shall not die, but live, And declare the works of the Lord" (Psalm 118:17).

June 10, 1985

I was in this large place with many seats. I was high upon the steps when this lady appeared before me asking me if I knew the song, "Holy, Righteous." I told her that I did not know all the words to the song, and asked her if she knew the lyrics. She said yes. I then asked her if she would sing it before the choir arrived (thinking that if anyone heard her sing they would take it from me and sing the song themselves). She sang the song and it was beautiful. She got to one part and told me to use my own words. She said to me, "The Lord wants to give you those songs to sing" (it was another song also, but I can't remember it).

My Interpretation

I heard a choir in a church I attended sing this song, but I do not know the song or the artist. However I do know that Our God is Holy and Righteous, and He is calling us to live a holy and righteous life. ". . . but as He who called you is holy, you also be holy in all your conduct" (1 Peter 1:15).

June 13, 1985

Satan confronted me as he tried to bring fear upon me. I began speaking in tongues and he fled.

My Interpretation

Satan is a fallen angel and he is real (Isaiah 14:12). He is also known as: Lucifer (Isaiah 14:12); devil (Matthew 4:1); dragon (Revelation 12:7-9); serpent (Revelation 20:2); Beelzebub chief ruler of the evil spirits or demons (Matthew 12:24); ruler of darkness (Ephesians 6:12); and angel of the bottomless pit (Revelation 9:11).

In the Old Testament, Satan is called Abaddon in Hebrew and Apollyon in Greek, that is, *destroyer* (Revelation 9:11). Know for a fact that Satan does not care for you nor does he even like you. He only wants to steal, kill, destroy and take you to hell (John 10:10). That's who and what he is, that's his nature. He doesn't want us to receive anything from God (Mark 4:15). He's our adversary, accuser, and he is a liar. (1 Peter 5:8; Job 2:6; Revelation 12:10; John 8:44)

Satan is a transformer (2 Corinthians 11:14), and he tries to hinder our prayers to God and our mission for God (1 Thessalonians 2:18), but he cannot stop us unless we allow him. The Son of God was manifested for this purpose—that He might destroy the works of the devil (1 John 3:8). Therefore, we have the victory through Christ Jesus.

Don't be intimidated by Satan. The Bible tells us that Satan walks about *like* a roaring lion, seeking whom he may devour (1 Peter 5:8). He wants us to fear him, he wants us to believe that he's so strong and powerful he wants to deceive us. Fight him with the sword (word) of God and give him no place (Ephesians 4:27). Resist him and he will flee from you (James 4:7). For greater is He (Jesus Christ) who is in you (and me), than he that is in the world (1 John 4:4). Glory to God!

June 19, 1985

The Rapture had come.

My Interpretation

The word *rapture* to me means being caught up or transported to meet God in the sky, as He takes us His children, His church, His body of believers, to our eternal place of residency.

Will you be ready to go back with the Lord when He comes? Will you be 'caught up' or 'rapture' when He returns? Will the Lord find faith here on earth when He returns? Oh, how I want to be ready. For in a moment, just one moment, we will be changed and caught up to meet Him in the sky.

"For the Lord Himself will descend from heaven with a shout, with the voice of an archangel, and with the trumpet of God. And the dead in

Christ will rise first. Then we who are alive and remain shall be caught up together with them in the clouds to meet the Lord in the air. And thus we shall always be with the Lord" (1 Thessalonians 4:16, 17).

You don't want to miss it! For this world will be in the worse state ever after the rapture. Once God takes His people off this earth there will be there no open churches, no Bible to read, and no gospel to hear. The antichrist will be in control of the world for seven years. The first three and a half years he will be okay so that he can gain everybody's trust (especially the Jews), but you will be under his dictatorship.

Then at the ending of the first three and a half years, or the beginning of the next three and a half years he will show his true colors, you will see him for whom he really is. Life on this earth will be unbelievable, unbearable, and you will wish for death but death will flee from you.

Don't let the rapture come and go without you. Watch and be ready when Jesus comes.

June 20, 1985

I was singing a song God gave me entitled: The Lord Understands.

My Interpretation

Sometimes we feel like God doesn't know or isn't paying any attention as to what is going on in our lives. We just feel like He doesn't really understand us as well as we'd like for Him too. But we're so wrong when we feel this way. God understands and is concerned about everything that goes on in our lives regardless of how big or how small we may think that it is. Jesus Christ, the Son of God, is our High Priest who understands, who is compassionate, and can sympathize with our weaknesses; because He too was in all points tempted as we are—but He *did not* sin. (Hebrew 4:15). God has a great plan and purpose for our lives. He loves us.

Great is our Lord, and mighty in power; His understanding is infinite" (Psalm 147:5). ". . . You understand my thought afar off. You comprehend my path and my lying down, and are acquainted with all my ways (Psalm 139:2, 3). ". . . for the Lord searches all hearts and understands all the intent of the thoughts" (1 Chronicles 28:9).

So don't be afraid in keeping anything from God, or to come to Him regarding your problems. God has perfect knowledge of us, and He knows us better than we know ourselves. Pray that their parents will love and cherish them. Yet even though God knows our every thought and everything about us, He still wants us to talk to Him about it and to make our request known to Him and to fellowship with Him. He is our Heavenly Father and we are His children, and He is very much concerned about what goes on in our lives.

June 24, 1985

I was speaking in tongues. All I had to do was praise the Lord out of my heart, aloud, not with my mouth closed. (And I began speaking in my heavenly language.)

My Interpretation

This dream shows how one can speak in tongues. One must praise the Lord aloud out of their whole heart; and let the Holy Spirit take full control of your mind, spirit and body.

"And they were all filled with the Holy Spirit and began to speak with other tongues, as the Spirit gave them utterance" (Acts 2:4). "And these signs will follow those who believe: In My name they will speak with new tongues . . ." (Mark 16:17).

July 1, 1985

A woman was blaming God for a fire that destroyed her home. I started preaching and my subject was: "Why Do You Blame God; Why Don't You Blame Satan?"

My Interpretation

People have a tendency to blame God when things go wrong in their lives or when tragedy strikes. Yet God loved the world so much that He gave His only Son, Jesus Christ, that whoever believes in Him will not perish, but will have eternal life (John 3:16). Jesus came that we might enjoy life to the fullest here on earth, and that we might have eternal with Him. It amazes me that Satan (evil) is hardly ever blamed for anything that happens or goes wrong in this world.

People accuse and convict God without a trial or jury; and Satan is never even brought in for questioning. Now that you know, you had better stay on guard. Because your adversary is walking about like a roaring lion; looking for someone to devour their hopes, dreams, and life. Satan's plan is to steal, kill, deceive, and destroy you and your loved ones. His only desire and plan is to take whomever he can to live in eternal torment and flames with him and his demons (fallen angels). His plan for you is eternal torment and separation from God. This is his way of revenge (getting back at Jesus) because he was kicked out of heaven, and he knows that he is doomed for eternity. He is a deceiver, destroyer, thief, disguiser, imitator, conniver, and a liar. See him for what and who he truly is. Don't let him deceive you any longer. And, please pray for our children daily because Satan is after them more than anyone else.

Jesus said in His Word, "The thief does not come except to steal, and to kill, and to destroy (John 10:10). . . . He (Satan) was a murderer from the beginning, and does not stand in the truth, because there is no truth in him, for he is a liar and the father of it" (John 8:44). But, "I have come that they may have life, and that they may have it more abundantly" (John 10:10). Satan the devil knows how his story will end, and he wants you to join him in the conclusion.

"The devil, who deceived them (the people), was cast into the lake of fire and brimstone where the beast and the false prophet are. And they will be tormented day and night forever and ever" (Revelation 20:10).

July 14, 1985

Pastor Ken another person, and I, were standing in front of a river. A white boat was sitting in the center of the water. Pastor asked us if we wanted to go out into the deep where the boat was to do a little fishing. While pointing to the area, he said, "I caught two on this side and one on that side yesterday." As he was speaking, I found myself with a fishing pole in my hand, and I suddenly had a bite. Pastor Ken said in excitement, "Pull it baby, pull it!" (He calls many of the church members 'baby'). But as I looked around and saw the waters surrounding me, knowing that I could not swim, I was afraid to pull on the pole for fear of falling into the waters.

Pastor Ken kept telling me to pull, so finally I did, gently and caught a small fish. As he was taking the fish off of the hook for me, I had another bite on the other side (I had a fishing pole on my left and right). Again, pastor told me to pull it, and again I was afraid, even more so because I was now further out into the deep waters. Finally, I pulled but the small fish jumped off the hook back into the water. I lost that fish.

My Interpretation

It's time for us to launch out and step into the deep and win souls for Jesus. Because of fear we have been safely standing on shore, waiting for someone else to do what God has commission you to do. People all over this world are hungry for the word of God. People in parts of this world are losing their lives for the sake of the gospel. And here we are afraid and too comfortable to move out from our safe haven. There are some people who have gone back into the world for lack of love and encouragement. We lost that soul because we were too comfortable at where we're at; afraid of where we may have to go; and too careless with what God has placed in our hands.

Step out into the deep and fish for souls for Jesus Christ before it's too late. Stop being afraid and take a step of faith. It's time to launch out into the deep, and do what you have never done before; go where you've never gone before; and see where God takes you. Trust Him to lead, guide, and direct you in all that you do. Have faith in God and rely on Him. You will never discover what God's plan and purpose is for your life until you step out in faith on His word, and do what He tells you to do. Don't be afraid of change, and let "change," change you.

"Launch out into the deep and let down your nets for a catch" (Luke 5:4). 'Follow Me, and I will make you become fishers of men" (Mark 1:17).

July 14, 1985

I heard someone singing a song entitled: *God's Tomorrow*. Al told me that was the song pastor wanted someone to learn and sing for him and that he (Al) had the lyrics. I wanted so much to give him my phone number to call me with the lyrics so that I could learn the song and sing it for the pastor—but I didn't.

In Real Life: About two weeks after this dream, my pastor stated one Sunday morning that there was a song that had been on his heart, and he wondered if anyone knew it. The name of the song was, "God's Tomorrow." Well no one responded with a yes. So, pastor said that he would be grateful if someone would learn the song and sing it. A couple of weeks later, a lady in our choir sang the song. It was a very beautiful song.

My Interpretation

This was an opportunity for me to learn that song and sing for the pastor; but because of my fear—I missed it. Our fear of being incapable of doing something will cause us to miss our blessings. Be confident because God always prepares you, and equips you to do all that He tells you to do.

In God's tomorrow there's no sickness, pain, tears, or sorrow. There is love, peace, joy, happiness, and wholeness. His tomorrow is so much brighter and better than today. "For I consider that the sufferings of this present time are not worthy to be compared with the glory which shall be revealed in us" (Romans 8:18).

July 15, 1985

My sister was healed. Her skin began to get clear right before my eyes. Satan began to tell her that she wasn't healed, and he also tried to tell me the same thing. I began to rebuke him in the name of Jesus, as I began speaking in tongues as the Spirit of God gave utterance.

My Interpretation

Satan is a liar. He tries to put doubt, fear, and unbelief in your mind and heart. Satan knows that as long as he can keep us bound by these things, we cannot receive anything from God. As Christians we are to walk by faith, and not by what we see with our eyes. (1 Corinthians 5:7) Trust in Jesus Christ for your healing.

"Surely He (Jesus) has borne our griefs (sicknesses) And carried our sorrows (pains) . . . But He was wounded for our transgressions, He was bruised for our iniquities; The chastisement for our peace was upon Him, And by His stripes we are healed" (Isaiah 53:4, 5). "Who Himself bore our sins in His own body on the tree, that we, having died to sins might live for righteousness—by whose stripes you were healed" (1 Peter 2:24).

August 5, 1985

A group of Caucasians didn't want Blacks to move into a particular building. One Caucasian man started walking from the top of the stairs (like he owned the world) talking. I started walking towards him (I didn't want to live in this building, I was just passing by when I saw what was going on), saying in a great powerful voice, "I come in the name of Jesus. I can do all things through Christ Jesus who strengthens me. I do not fear what man can do to me." As I was saying this, Satan tried to bring fear upon me, but I resisted and blocked out all fear.

My Interpretation

Stand up and fight for what is right. Do not fear what man can do to you. You have God as your shield and buckler. He will fight your battles. Man can only deal with your flesh he cannot touch your soul. Isn't that good news? Aren't you glad about that?

"I can do all things through Christ who strengthens me" (Philippians 4:13). "And do not fear those who kill the body but cannot kill the soul. But rather, fear Him who is able to destroy both soul and body in hell" (Matthew 10:28).

September 9, 1985

I was in church speaking in tongues.

My Interpretation

I was speaking in a heavenly language to God that is known by Him, Jesus Christ, and the Holy Spirit. "And they were all filled with the Holy Spirit and began to speak with other tongues, as the Spirit gave them utterance" (Acts 2:4). "For he who speaks in a tongue does not speak to men but to God, for no one understands him; however, in the spirit he speaks mysteries" (1 Corinthians 14:2).

September 9, 1985

A childhood friend (Suey) whom I haven't seen for many years telephoned me, and she sounded wonderful. She asked me to hold on for a moment because she had to do something. The moment turned into minutes. Finally, a woman picked up the phone and I told her that I was holding for Suey. "She's about to leave for the hospital right now," the woman said. I was surprised to hear that because Suey didn't sound (nor had she mentioned that she was) ill. I hung up the phone and began to pray for her and I spoke in tongues. The thought that quickly entered my mind was: This is what God wants me to do—*pray for the sick*.

My Interpretation

Sickness or mishaps can happen without warning and at any given moment. God tells us to pray for one another. (James 5:16) Some people have a special gift for praying for the healing of others. It is called the gift of healing (1 Corinthians 12:9, 28). When we pray for the healing of others we can pray in our own native language, or pray in the spirit. And when we're not sure how to pray for certain conditions or situations, allow the Holy Spirit to converse with God through us.

"For if I pray in a tongue, my understanding is unfruitful" (1 Corinthians 14:14) "Likewise the Spirit also helps in our weaknesses. For we do not know what we should pray for as we ought, but the Spirit Himself makes intercession for us . . ." (Romans 8:26). "Now He who searches the hearts knows what the mind of the Spirit is, because He makes intercession for the saints according to *the will* of God" (Romans 8:27). Pray in faith with love and compassion. And keep your heart and mind on Jesus.

September 12, 1985

Mother, another person, and I were returning to mom's house, when we saw a large tree lying across the road. This huge tree had stood in our front yard close to the house. I looked at the tree, then looked at our house, and began thanking and praising God that it didn't fall on the house; knowing that my daughters and other members of my family were in the house.

My Interpretation

The Spirit of God reminded me that: though tall and big trees may fall in our lives, and burdens seem unbearable; God will and still protects His children. And even when our children are not with us, He's watching over and protecting them from all danger and harm. There is no need for us to worry. Our heavenly Father and Jesus our Saviour will protect us and our family.

"No evil shall befall you, Nor shall any plague come near your dwelling. For He shall give His angels charge over you To keep you in all your ways" (Psalm 91:10, 11).

September 27, 1985

I saw writing in the sky. I was moving fast so it was difficult for me to read; so I said, "No, Lord, No Lord, I want to read it!" for I could only read part of it. Then I heard someone reading, and I turned around and saw that it was Ursula, my middle daughter. She read: "God will take care of His children and He will be with them." "Where are you reading that from?" I asked her. She pointed to her Bible. I then said, "Thank you Lord, you knew that I wanted to know what the writing read."

My Interpretation

God wants you and me to know that He will take care of us. No matter what we may be going through He will never leave nor will He forsake us. (Hebrew 13:5) He promised to be with us always, even until the end of this age. (Matthew 28:20) So do not be discouraged, but be encouraged because God will take care of you. Just believe, rely on Him, and trust Him.

"casting all your care upon Him, for He cares for you" (1 Peter 5:7). "Cast your burden on the LORD, And He shall sustain you; He shall never permit the righteous to be removed" (Psalm 55:22).

November 22, 1985

I was at a church; a woman was singing the song, "Oh, What a Beautiful City."

My Interpretation

I can only imagine that the city the woman was referring to is the New Jerusalem. The Bible describes it as a city paved with pure gold, crystal clear waters, walls made of jasper, walls adorned with all kinds of precious stones, gates made of pearl, and so much more. There is no night, nor light of the sun there, for our Lord God gives light in the New Jerusalem. Oh, what a beautiful city! (Read Revelation chapters 21 and 22 for more about your new eternal home)

"Then I, John, saw the holy city, New Jerusalem, coming down out of heaven from God, prepared as a bride adorned for her husband" (Revelation 21:2).

December 1985

In Real Life: One evening I was on my knees praying about a situation, which I did not quite know how to pray for. After acknowledging this to God, I suddenly started speaking in tongues, and God said to me: "No weapon formed against you will prosper." (This was my first experience speaking in tongues, and I heard the interpretation in the spirit). The Holy Spirit then led me to Isaiah 54:17:

"No weapon formed against you shall prosper, and every tongue which rises against you in judgment, you shall condemn. This is the heritage of the servants of the Lord, and their righteousness is from Me, Says the Lord." Isn't this a great and awesome promise of God?

February 1, 1986

I was singing in a choir on the train. The song was: This Little Light of Mine, I'm Going to Let It Shine.

My Interpretation

We as Christians and children of the Most High God must be an example to those who have not yet invited Jesus Christ into their lives; and have not accepted Him as their Lord and Saviour. God has commanded us to be a light to those who live in darkness, and to those who do not believe in Him, or in His Son, Jesus Christ. (Acts 13:47)

In the book of Matthew 5:14-16, Jesus said: "You are the light of the world. A city that is set on a hill cannot be hidden. Nor do they light a lamp and put it under a basket, but on a lamp stand, and it gives light to all who are in the house. Let your light so shine before men, that they may see your good works and glorify your Father in heaven."

However in order for our light to shine, we must walk in the light. Jesus is the light of the world. (John 8:12) Therefore let us put on the armor of light. (Romans 13:12). This little light of mines, I will do my very best to let it shine everywhere I go, and in everything that I do; so that people may see Christ in me, and glorify the Father.

February 15, 1986 (Vision)

I saw a bright light in my room.

My Interpretation

I believe that this was an illumination of God's presence in my room. The joy and peace that I felt was indescribable. The light was overwhelmingly beautiful. "In Your presence there is fullness of joy (Psalm 16:11). "Cast me not away from thy presence" (Psalm 51:11). "For with You is the fountain of life; In Your light we see light" (Psalm 36:9).

February 15, 1986

There was a lot smoke and very dark clouds in the sky. The people began screaming and there were very strong winds (like one has never heard before). I began praising the Lord.

My Interpretation

I'm reminded of how it will be on the day that Jesus returns to earth. Some people will be screaming in fear of Him, and some will be ushering Him in with praises. What will you be doing? Are you ready to meet Him? If not, get ready now, because Jesus is coming soon!

"And behold, I am coming quickly, and My reward is with Me, to give to every one according to his work" (Revelation 22:12).

February 18, 1986

I was singing a beautiful gospel song.

My Interpretation

I love to sing and listen to gospel music—songs of worship and praise, and songs that glorifies God Our Father, and our Lord and Saviour Jesus Christ. "Sing us one of the songs of Zion" (Psalm 137:3). "I will sing praises to my God while I have my being" (Psalm 146:2). "You shall surround me with songs of deliverance" Selah (Psalm 32:7).

February 24, 1986

I was speaking in tongues (language).

My Interpretation

"Though I speak with tongues of men and of angels, but have not love, I have become as sounding brass or a clanging cymbal" (1 Corinthians 13:1).

March 10, 1986

I was speaking in tongue (a heavenly language given by God; that only God, Jesus, and the Holy Spirit understand).

My Interpretation

"For he who speaks in a tongue does not speak to men but to God, for no one understands him; however, in the spirit he speaks mysteries" (1 Corinthian 14:2).

However, there is also the gift of tongue that God bestows upon certain individuals. It is a gift from God. This tongue is given to chosen ones by God to bring forth His word to the church for edification. There is also the gift of interpretation of tongue, which must be operational along with the gift of tongues, either by the person who speak in tongue or by someone else who has the gift of interpretation. (1 Corinthian 12:10, 30; 14:13, 22)

March 19, 1986

I was at my late father's wake and I was speaking in tongues. God also spoke through me with the interpretation and said, "Don't weep for my servant (speaking about my father) for he is well, for he is with Me. But weep for yourselves and for your children." (This is the second time that I had this dream).

My Interpretation

When our loved ones die in this world, if they are saved, immediately their spirit is in the presence of God. It is okay to mourn because we love them and their presence in this world will be missed. But if they are saved, you can also be happy for, and with them, because they are in that place Jesus has prepared for them long ago.

We should weep for ourselves and for our children because we have not finished the race, we have not finished our course. We have yet to reach the finish line. So we must continue to pray, live according to the word of God, abide in Christ, and be obedient to His will; stay in the race, and work out our own salvation with fear and trembling. (Philippians 2:12) If you don't know Jesus Christ, invite Him into your life today.

"We are confident, yes, well pleased rather to be absent from the body and to be present with the Lord" (2 Corinthians 5:8). But Jesus, turning to them, said, ". . . do not weep for Me, but weep for yourselves and for your children" (Luke 23:28).

March 22-24, 1986

I was speaking in tongues (language).

My Interpretation

"He who speaks in a tongue edifies himself. . ." (1 Corinthians 14:4). This is not the gift of tongues (that requires interpretation), but rather praying in the spirit. When we don't know what or how to pray for a situation; the Holy Spirit intercedes, takes over and prays through us to God, the Father, in another language unknown to us.

"Likewise the Spirit also helps in our weaknesses. For we do not know what we should pray for as we ought, but the Spirit Himself makes intercession for with groanings which cannot be uttered" (Romans 8:26).

April 17, 1986

A few people and I were camping in the backyard of a house. It was very dark and there were no stars in the sky. Suddenly, one other person and I sensed that someone or something was coming behind us, and we began to run. We ran towards the front of the house. When I got to the front, I felt some kind of force pulling me into what looked like a big dark hole or tunnel. I was trying with all my might not to be pulled in by this force. I thought to myself that the person who out ran me must have gotten pulled into this darkness. I felt a strange coldness and sensed that it was death.

I heard a voice and turned around and saw someone standing at the corner of the house. At first I thought it was the person that I was running from, but it was an angel. He said, "You're strong, you are very strong, but He (God) can take you right now if He wanted to. He's going to let you stay, because there is work here for you to do. Do you want to stay?" "Yes," I replied quickly. Immediately, I was released from this mighty, forceful, and tremendous pull.

Then we began walking and the angel said, "He wants you to learn." The angel was telling me all the things that God wanted me to learn. I noticed the number six (the 6th chapter of the Book of Revelation came to my mind) on a board, or post with a little blood right behind the number, and it seemed as though I was sitting on a horse as I was reading this. I woke up very puzzled about this dream.

My Interpretation

God is Almighty and all-powerful; and we are nothing, and can't do nothing without Him. 2 Timothy 2:15 tells us to study the Word of God to show ourselves approved to God, a worker who does not need to be ashamed, rightly dividing the word of truth. We as believers, as God's ambassadors, and as God's children; should be able to handle the word of God skillfully. God's word should be handled respectfully, tactfully, correctly and accurately.

Reviewing the Book of Revelation chapter 6, it speaks about the Seven Seals and the opening of those Seals by Jesus Christ the Lamb of God). With the opening of the first seal a white horse appeared; second seal—a fiery red horse; third seal—a black horse; and the fourth seal—a pale horse. Great power was given to each rider on the horses to cause the most horrible things to happen; and bring judgment on the earth (this is not the final judgment).

The devastation will be very great, unbelievable, and unbearable. There will more wars, tremendous floods, deadly earthquakes, no peace, more people killing one another, price increases (food, clothing, housing); and countless will be homeless and hungry. A great number of people will be put to death, die from hunger and diseases, and by the beasts of the earth.

The fifth seal speaks about the saints, the children of God who have been faithful, stood firm for the name of Jesus, and died for their testimony. They are ready to see the wicked people on the earth punished for their sins. When the sixth seal was opened, there was a great earthquake, the sun turned black, and the moon became as blood. People will run to find a hiding place to hid from the face Jesus; but will find none.

The seventh seal is opened in Revelation chapter 8. There was silence in heaven for about half an hour. Seven angels (who stood before God) were given seven trumpets. As each angel sound the trumpet great punishment will befall upon the earth and the people upon the earth. The seas, oceans, rivers, springs of water, fire, fishes, trees, grass, ships, and much more will be destroyed. You can read about all seven seals in Revelations chapters 6, 7, 8, and what they represent, what has happened; is now happening; and what is going to happen on this earth all around the world.

I believe that some of these events has already happened, are happening now, and will happen in the 21st Century. I believe these are events that will take place on the planet earth during the Great Tribulation; a time (seven year period) in which judgment is poured out on a world that has rejected Jesus Christ. This is a time when the wrath and judgment of God is displayed.

"For the great day of His wrath has come, and who is able to stand?" (Revelation 6:17).

This will be a time on earth like never before and will never be again. Please open your heart and accept Jesus now as your Lord and Saviour, and you won't have to go through this great tribulation. My friends, Jesus is real; the Great Tribulation is real; hell is real; heaven is real; just as death is real. All are just as real as you and I. Please, read Revelation chapter 6. Then read the entire book of Revelation, you will be blessed (for God has promised to bless those who read it), informed, encouraged, and hopefully be ready when Jesus Christ returns.

April 18, 1986

My sister, mother, and I were sitting in the house when I saw a beautiful newborn baby. My sister picked up the baby. I thought she just wanted to hold the baby, but to my surprise she threw the infant onto the floor. I sat there frozen with shock, I couldn't move although I tried to with all of my might.

This happened a third time and I pointed to her repeating three times in a stern voice, "Don't you touch that baby again!" My mother was eating and she said, "Oh, why don't you leave her (my sister) alone now." "Okay Sarah, I won't touch her if you don't want me too, but I don't think you should say that to me and you're supposed to be a child of God," my sister said.

Well, that did it! I quickly stood up (now with no difficulty), with my left hand outstretched walking directly towards her and my hand rested upon her forehead. I felt an electrifying heat or a current flow through my arm and hand. I opened my mouth to say "Jesus," but nothing came out—I couldn't talk. I then looked in her eyes and saw an evil spirit. My hand stayed upon her forehead, knowing now that I was battling with Satan. Although I still could not speak; in my mind I kept saying, "Jesus, Jesus." I felt within my heart that I could have cast the evil spirit out had I not feared, but used my faith, and believed God's word.

My Interpretation

You must have faith and confidence in yourself (as a child of God), in God and His Word, and you cannot have any doubt or fear; especially when you're dealing with Satan and his demons. Fear and doubt is like a fuel needed for Satan to operate in our lives. He feeds on fear, doubt, and unbelief. Just as faith and trust is like a fuel needed for God to operate in our lives.

Satan will use anyone he can, and often times the very one closest to us to deter your faith, and he wants to keep you from obtaining what God has for you. Your weapon against Satan is the word of God, and your faith is your shield. Do not listen to him, and do not fear him. He may have a bad bark but he has no bite. He may be a good imitator, but Jesus is the Originator. Remember, faith is always active, it (you) must do something in order for it to work (for you).

Our perfect love in God, our heavenly Father, and in Jesus Christ, our Lord and Saviour, casts out any fear that Satan would try to bring upon us. (1 John 4:18) And, He (the Holy Spirit) who is in us is greater than Satan, his demons, and those who are in the world. Remember even our faith is based on the ability to choose. We must believe what we say.

"If you have faith and do not doubt . . ." (Matthew 21:21). "For our God has not given us a spirit of fear, but of power; and of love, and of a sound mind." (2 Timothy 1:7)

Do not allow the enemy to rob your sick love one, or anyone (that's unable physically or mentally to call on Jesus for themselves) of their healing and deliverance. Pray for them in faith, trusting, and believing God for their healing

April 19, 1986

My mother and I were sitting in a room waiting for my father to come home (although we knew that he was dead), and I saw a bright light. I began speaking in tongues. My father appeared and smiled as he hugged me and softly walked over to my mother and hugged her lovingly. He spoke not a word. He looked very happy and much younger.

My Interpretation

Our loved ones and friends are waiting patiently for us to arrive to our eternal home. As believers in Jesus Christ when we close our eyes in this life, our spirit (which still lives on) is immediately in the presence of God where our loved ones and friends (if they were saved, believed and accepted Jesus as Saviour and Lord) will greet us with lots of hugs and kisses. They are anxiously and happily awaiting our arrival.

"For we know that if our earthly house (body), this tent (body) is destroyed, we have a building from God, a house not made with hands, eternal in the heavens". (2 Corinthians 5:1) "We are confident, yes, well pleased rather to be absent from the body and to be present with the Lord" (2 Corinthians 5:8).

April 22, 1986

I was at church having a good time with the Lord. The pastor and other ministers were sitting on the pulpit. A young woman was either speaking or singing under the anointing of God. She began to minister to individuals. Using the gift of knowledge as the Holy Spirit led her she prayed for some, and laid hands on others. The young woman was looking for another lady that had a special testimony. Unexpectedly, I realized that someone was in back of me. It was the young woman pouring oil on the center of my head. I began to tremble (the power of God's anointing) as I felt the oil being poured on my head. It was a lot of oil.

My Interpretation

Oil is symbolic of the Holy Spirit. It was used (especially olive oil) in the Old Testament and the New Testament for anointing someone for God's service and for healing the sick.

And the Lord said, "Arise, anoint him; for this is the one!" Then Samuel took the horn of oil and anointed him (David, the youngest son of Jesse), and the Spirit of the Lord came upon David from that day forward. (1 Samuel 16:12, 13).

"But you have an anointing from the Holy One" (1 John 2:20). "Now He who establishes us . . . in Christ and has anointed us is God . . ." (2 Corinthians 2:21). "Is any one among you sick? Let him call for the elders of the church, and let them pray over him, anointing him with oil in the name of the Lord" (James 5:14). God, having anointed us, also placed a seal upon us and given us the witness of the Holy Spirit in our hearts as a guarantee. (2 Corinthians 1:21, 22)

April 25, 1986

I was praising the Lord, praying, and speaking in tongues.

My Interpretation

I was praying in the spirit. Sometimes when we pray about certain situations concerning ourselves or someone else, we may not know quite how to petition God regarding the problem, and we do not always know what we should pray for. There may be even times when our bodies are just plain tired, and yet we still pray. That is when the Holy Spirit steps in and prays to the Father through us, in a language that only God and the Holy Spirit understand. It's a wonderful feeling.

"Likewise the Spirit also helps in our weakness. For we do not know what we should pray for as we ought, but the Spirit Himself makes intercession for us with groanings which cannot be uttered. Now He who searches the hearts knows what the mind of the Spirit is, because He makes intercession for the saints according to *the will of God*" (Romans 8:26, 27).

May 5, 1986

Suddenly, people began leaving church. I saw my father (though he didn't look or acted like himself) also leaving. I followed them towards the door wondering why they were leaving the church, and where they were going. There was a great noise that sounded like a herd of cattle coming from the outside. Quickly, I looked out the door and saw thousands of people running for their lives. Someone yelled, "The world is on fire!" I looked to my left and saw flames of fire a short distance away. I said, "I'm waiting here in the church." "We'll be safe in the church," the pastor replied.

I walked back towards my seat speaking in tongues, and praising God. Then I noticed that the people were no longer screaming, so, I went back to the door to look outside. I looked to my right, and saw that the fire had passed over the church. The few people that stayed in the church were saved. The fire had destroyed everyone and everything.

My Interpretation

Do not follow anyone, especially if you're not sure who they are or where they're going. They may be leading you in the wrong direction. They may be leading you into danger, away from safety, and away from Jesus Christ. Stay in church no matter what's going on in the world. You'll be safe *with* and *in* Jesus Christ our Lord and Saviour. Continue to pray, praise, and worship God. For the fire and storm in your life is passing over. And regardless of what happens in the world it will not affect us. God promise to take care of us—and He will.

"Your way, O God, is in the sanctuary" (Psalm 77:13). "For in the time of trouble He shall hide me in His pavilion; In the secret place of His tabernacle He shall hide me" (Psalm 27:5) "The name of the LORD is a strong tower; The righteousness run to it and are safe" (Proverbs 18:10). "But whoever trusts in the LORD shall be safe" (Proverbs 29:25). "He is a shield to those who put their trust in Him" (Proverbs 30:5).

June 6, 1986

I spoke in the gift of tongues at a funeral service, and God also spoke through me with the interpretation. I said, "No fornicator, whoremonger, liar, adulterer, cheater, murderer, stealer, etc . . . will enter into the kingdom of God."

My Interpretation

Although some may think a funeral service is not the place or time to tell people such things—but I beg to differ. I think that it is the right place and the right time. Some people may never set foot in a church other than to attend a funeral service. It is a time they realize that one day they too will die. It is a time where death is more real to them, because they are staring death right in the face. Now we have their attention. It is a time for us to speak to the dead (spiritually) that's living, and speak to the living so that they will never die (spiritually).

Remind them that this (first) death is of the body (flesh) only, but for their spirit (which never dies) it is the beginning of eternal life either in the place that Jesus has prepared for those who love and accepted Him as God's Son; Lord and Saviour; a place called heaven or paradise. It is a place of awesome beauty and we will be with our Father God, and Jesus Christ His Son, our Saviour forever.

Remind them of a place that has been prepared for Satan, demons, wicked people, and all those who detest and reject Jesus Christ. It is a place called hell that burns eternally with fire and brimstones. It is a place of total darkness and indescribable eternal torment. Tell them what the Word of God says. As God's ambassador it is your (and my) responsibility to tell them the truth.

"Do you not know that the unrighteous will not inherit the kingdom of God? Do not be deceived. Neither fornicators, nor idolaters, nor adulterers, nor homosexuals, nor sodomites, nor thieves, nor covetous, nor drunkards, nor revilers, nor extortionists, will inherit the kingdom of God" (1 Corinthians 6:9, 10). "Now the works of the flesh are evident, which are: adultery, fornication, uncleanness, lewdness, idolatry, sorcery, hatred, contentions, jealousies, outbursts of wrath, selfish ambitions, dissensions, heresies, envy, murders, drunkenness, revelries, and the like; of which I tell you beforehand, just as I also told you in time past, that those who practice such things will not inherit the kingdom of God" (Galatians 5:19-21). "But there shall by no means enter it anything that defiles, or causes abomination or a lie, but only those who are written in the Lamb's Book of Life' (Revelation 21:27).

"But the cowardly, unbelieving, abominable, murderers, sexually immoral, sorcerers, idolaters, and liars shall have their part in the lake which burns with fire and brimstone, which is the second death" (Revelation 21:8). "The devil, who deceived them, was cast into the lake of fire and brimstone where the beast and the false prophet are. And they shall be tormented day and night forever and ever" (Revelation 20:10).

"Then Death and Hades were cast into the lake of fire. This is the second death" (Revelation 20:14). "And anyone not found written in the Book of Life was cast into the lake of fire' (Revelation 20:15). ". . . to be cast into hell, into the fire that shall never be quenched—where 'Their worm does not die And the fire is not quenched'" (Mark 9:43, 44).

Eternal death and torment will be the final destiny for those who choose to reject Jesus Christ as Lord and Saviour. If you do not want this to be your final destiny, please ask Jesus Christ to forgive you of your sins, and make you a new creation in Him. Now, repent, turn from your old lifestyle and turn to Jesus' lifestyle. Read the Bible (God's word) to learn of His ways, and His will and purpose for your life.

For, "Eye has not seen, nor ear heard, Nor have entered into the heart of man The things which God has prepared for those who love Him" (1 Corinthians 2:9). You can read Revelation chapters 21, and 22, for a brief description of where our eternal place of residency with the family of God will be; the awesome, and indescribable beauty of it.

June 20, 1986—Vision

I was in a trance. I heard my father's voice coming from another room. I was in my bedroom. It was so wonderful to hear father's voice once again.

In Real Life: *My* dad went home to live with God in 1985. He was a humble man, a good provider for his family and a wonderful person. All of my life I remember him being in church. He was a deacon, minister, elder, assistant pastor, and he loved God. The subject of the last sermon he preached was "love." Although I was home on vacation that Sunday, I didn't go to church. Several people told me that daddy really preached, and that there was something different about him, and his preaching. My mother told me the very same thing.

Daddy had asked me if I was coming to church. I told him no because my nephew-in-law was coming to finish painting the house. I'm sorry that I missed seeing and hearing daddy preached his last sermon here on earth. I remember us sitting on the porch one warm evening in September 1985. I read a few scriptures, we talked, we laugh, and we prayed. When we were at the bus station for my return to New York, daddy was sitting in a chair inside the station (which he never did. He always stood on the outside). I went inside and asked him if he was okay as I touched his cheeks. He said yes, as he looked at me with his loving smile. Daddy just kept looking and smiling so lovingly at me as if it would be his last time seeing me (here on earth). And it was. (I truly miss my daddy).

All that week I had been cleaning my parent's house: painting, putting down new rugs, and throwing out things that weren't needed. I didn't understand why I suddenly decided to do all this work, but God knew. God knew that within three weeks He would call daddy home to be with Him. He knew that I would be in no mental or emotional state to prepare the house at such a time. God will always prepare us for whatever situation we have to face, and for whatever we have to do.

"Precious in the sight of the Lord is the death of His saints" (Psalm 116:15). "So teach us to number our days" (Psalm 90:12). "For it is soon cut off, and we fly away" (Psalm 90:10).

October 2, 1986

There was a river of blood in a wide area. My father was driving, mother was in the front seat, and I was in the back. Daddy drove around the blood (he was an excellent driver) in a very small path. I told him to drive slowly in case we came to another river of blood, because the path had a lot of blind spots. In a short while we saw a river of clear water, and I began praising God, thinking of His marvelous works. I then looked out the car window to see if it was raining blood, but it wasn't. Suddenly, I was in my house, and a woman (Kob) from the church I attend was there also. I looked out my window and it was raining blood.

My Interpretation

Blood is the symbol for life. The outpouring of blood symbolizes total dedication to God. Jesus Christ shed His precious blood for us on the cross for the remission of our sins. Water symbolizes purification, cleansing and or refreshment. As we travel in life, the path we take may have blind spots, and it may be hard to see our way out of certain situations. Don't be afraid. Began to praise God while thinking of His marvelous works, and trust Him to lead you, guide you, and bring you out victoriously.

What can wash away our sins, and what can give us a new life, make us a new person, and make us whole again? The answer is: "Nothing but the blood of Jesus!" There is power in the blood of Jesus. Power to: heal, forgive, redeem, reconcile, change, save, and set souls free.

". . . My blood which is shed for you" (Luke 22:20). "In Him (Jesus Christ) we have redemption through His blood, the forgiveness of sins" (Ephesians 1:7).

October 11, 1986

I looked towards heaven and saw the image of the face of Jesus. (This is what came to my mind. But, my memory of His face seemed to have instantly faded. It's hard to explain).

My Interpretation

According to the dictionary the word *image* means to make or produce a likeness of a person (or object). A reproduction of a person that closely or precisely looks like another. I think a good example would be twins. The word of God tells us that Jesus is the image of the invisible God, and the first born over all creation. (Colossians 1:15) We are also made in God's image.

God said, "Let us make man in our image, according to our likeness" (Genesis1:26). ". . . since he is the image and glory of God . . ." (1 Corinthians 11:7) "Who being the brightness of His glory and the express image of His person . . ." (Hebrew 1:3).

October 21, 1986

I was on the subway train when it stopped between stations. A woman was having difficulty breathing. I lifted my hands towards heaven, praying and speaking in tongues concerning this woman. And I thank God for Jesus; and for being in my life.

My Interpretation

We must not hesitate to pray for and help one in need. We should always be about our Father's business regardless of where we are or who is around us. We must be confident that anything we ask the Father in the name of Jesus in faith, He will grant our request. We should give thanks to God our Father, in the name of Jesus Christ our Lord, for all things, and at all time. (Ephesians 5:20)

So Jesus answered and said to them, "Assuredly, I say to you, if you have faith and do not doubt, you will not only do what was done to the fig tree, but also if you say to this mountain, 'Be removed and be cast into the sea,' it will be done. And whatever things you ask in prayer, believing, you will receive" (Matthew 21:21, 22). Allow the Holy Spirit to take control when you do not know how to pray concerning certain situations. For, the Spirit Himself makes intercession for us with groanings which cannot be uttered. He searches the hearts and knows what the mind of the Spirit is, because He makes intercession for the saints according to the will of God. (Romans 8:26, 27)

October 27, 1986

I was singing a song God gave me: "Jesus, Why Do I Think of You All the Time?"

My Interpretation

I think of Him (Jesus) all the time because I love Him, He saved my soul, and because I have been redeemed by His Blood. Because of Him I have been reconciled to God and restored to a right relationship with Him, and He has forgiven me of my sins. I think of Jesus all the time because He gave His life (died on the cross suffering the shame and separation from the Father) for me; and because He rose on the third day (out of the grave) for my justification, and with all power in His hands; because He has given me and all who will believe in Him eternal life.

I think of Jesus because He is now seated at the right hand of the Father in heaven making intercession for me, and for my family; because He watches continuously over us, keeping and protecting us; because He is God and besides Him there is no other; because He is the best thing that has ever happened to me, and the best thing that will ever happen to me.

I think of Him because He is the Bishop and lover of my soul, and He's sweet as a honeycomb; because He lights my way when I cannot see clearly; because He makes my crooked ways straight and my rough ways smooth; because He is my strength, when I'm weak; because He supplies my needs and my wants. He fulfills the desires of my heart, and He is my best Friend. When I'm sad, just the thought of Him makes me happy. I forget about everything and everyone that cause me hurt and pain. Jesus is my song, my joy, my strength, and my life.

Jesus is my all and all, He is everything I want and need. He is the first one that I think about when I awake in the morning, or in the middle of the night, and the first and last one I think of before I fall asleep at night. I cannot help but think of Him all the time. How often do you think of your Lord and Saviour? Is it only when you need something from Him?

"My heart is steadfast, O God, my heart is steadfast; I will sing and give praise" (Psalm 57:7). ". . . I trust in the mercy of God forever and ever. I will praise You forever, Because You have done it" (Psalm 52:8, 9). Let nothing or no one separate you from the love of God.

October 29, 1986

I was in church. I had an unction to go up front to tell the people to praise God and thank God, for truly He's worthy to be praised. Someone went up before me because I hesitated. I felt very sad about this.

My Interpretation

Whenever the Spirit of God tells you to say or do something you should not hesitate. Just get up and do it. God is not going to tell you to do something that you can't do. He's going to be the one speaking through you anyway. He just requires your vocal cords.

If God can't use you because of your stubbornness, fearfulness or disobedience, He will use the one that will obey and willing to be used by Him. Do not hesitate when God tells you to do something. He has a plan and purpose, and He knows what He is doing. Are you willing to yield yourself fully to God so He can use you? Are you now ready to fully surrender your total self to Him and to His will? Rebuke the spirit of fear and shame in Jesus name.

..."Whoever believes on Him will not be put to shame" (Roman 10:11). "I can do all things through Christ who strengthens me" (Philippians 4:13).

November–December, 1986

All spiritual dreams were about preaching and speaking in tongues praising God.

My Interpretation

God wants to use us to preach the Gospel of Jesus Christ. He wants to use us to bring the message of salvation and deliverance to His people. He desires for us to walk by faith and not by sight. "So then faith comes by hearing, and hearing by the word of God" (Romans 10:17)

"How then shall they call on Him in whom they have not believed? And how shall they believe in Him of whom they have not heard? And how shall they hear without a preacher? And how shall they preach unless they are sent? (Romans 10:14, 15).

"The Spirit of the Lord is upon Me, Because the Lord has anointed Me To preach good tidings to the poor; He has sent Me to heal the brokenhearted, To proclaim liberty to the captives, And the opening of the prison to those who are bound; To proclaim the acceptable year of the Lord, And the day of vengeance of our God; To comfort all who mourn, . . . To give them beauty for ashes, The oil of joy for mourning, The garment of praise for the spirit of heaviness; The planting of the Lord, that He may be glorified" (Isaiah 61:1-3).

I implore you to read and hear the God's word as often as you can. The time will come when in this country; yes, the United States of America that the word of God which we are blessed to read and hear so freely will be no more.

"Behold, the days are coming," says the LORD GOD, "That I will send a famine on the land. Not a famine of bread, Nor a thirst for water; But of hearing the words of the LORD. They shall wander from sea to sea, and from north to east; They shall run to and fro, seeking the word of the LORD, but shall not find it" (Amos 8:11-12). I believe that this day is coming soon, and it will be worldwide.

October 6, 1987

I was in church with a group of people. A woman said that if we memorized one or two Scriptures we would be rewarded. She gave one or two scripture cards to each person and she gave me several. I wondered, "Why is she giving me all these scripture cards? I can't remember all of these Scriptures." Tameeka, my daughter, was with me and encouraged me to remember at least one. I'm not sure of the Scripture, but I think it was in 2 Peter.

Then I suddenly saw people standing in a line in front of the building where I work. I was about to get on the line when a man approached me and led me to the front. I then noticed that the pastor of the church I attend was praying for the people on the line, one by one. Someone laid hands on me and began praying, and I began to feel the power of God all over my body.

In Real Life: I woke up and stayed awake for about 20 minutes. Again I fell asleep and had the same dream regarding the scripture cards. The same scripture was quoted, but I still cannot remember the scripture. I do remember reading the words: "*The Most High God.*"

My Interpretation

We should study and memorize scriptures so when Satan attacks us in our mind and body, we can use the word of God as a weapon against him. Jesus did this when Satan confronted him after He had fasted 40 days and nights. (Matthew 4:1-10). Satan cannot stand against the word of God. It might be surprising to see the number of people in your work place who desire prayer. God wants to use us to minister to the needs of every people. No matter who or where they are. When God gives you the opportunity to bless others; use it.

2 Timothy 2:15 tells us to study the word of God to show ourselves approved unto God, a worker who does not need to be ashamed, rightly dividing the word of truth. The word of God is our sword. It is the only weapon that can stand against the fiery darts that the enemy attacks us with. It is the only weapon that can and will ultimately destroy Satan. He (Satan) cannot stand against The Most High God, who is our Heavenly Father, Ruler, and Creator of heaven and earth. (Genesis 1:1; 14:20) Nor can he stand against the Son of The Most High God: Jesus Christ our Lord and Saviour. (Mark 5:7, Luke 8:28) And, we are the servants of The Most High God; therefore, he cannot stand against us. (Daniel 3:26) Glory to God! We are His children.

November 8, 1987

I saw lightning and dark clouds. Looking from my kitchen window I saw that the clouds were moving to the right towards my house. They were going to pass over the house. As the clouds grew closer the sky became clear. I looked to my left and saw a moving cloud of red lightning and it looked very frightening. It moved over a two-story house and stood; the lightning struck the house and it burst into flames. It was a horrible sight and I felt so sad knowing that all who were in the house, if anyone, had perished. Returning to my senses, I quickly picked up a little child. I was about to run out of the house thinking it would be next, but the lightning stopped. I heard my mother say, "Yes, the end of the world is soon."

My Interpretation

God knows where we are, and He knows where we're going. He is Almighty and He is an awesome God. The end of this age is rapidly approaching. Jesus is soon to return to earth. Can't you see the signs? Read Matthew chapter 24 regarding some of the signs and things that will happen prior to the second return of Jesus Christ.

November 8, 1987

I was singing a beautiful gospel song along with a man and woman.

My Interpretation

I love to sing and listen to gospel music. When one sings under the anointing of God it can minister to the needs of the people just as teaching or preaching the gospel. Healing and deliverance can take place; and the lives of many can be encouraged, revived, restored, renewed, and changed. That's the kind of gospel music I'm in tune with.

December 8, 1987

As I was passing by a large church, I looked through the window and saw a man who goes to the same church as I do. Suddenly I was in this church, and asked two young girls for directions to get out of the church, but they wouldn't direct me. They walked away, so I followed them. They went to the area where the preacher was speaking. I saw a lady sitting and I told her about the behavior of the young girls. We held hands while praying for the girls, and I began speaking in tongues. The one thing that bothered me was that I had food in my mouth, and therefore, couldn't speak in tongues effectively until I took it out. The young girls were set free.

My Interpretation

Pray for a child who has a disobedient or rude spirit. Never have food, gum or anything in your mouth while in the sanctuary in church; you are disrespecting the house of God, and you never know when God will call upon you to minister to someone. You cannot be used by God effectively until you have been cleansed. If there's anything in your life displeasing to God you must get rid of it. You cannot see clearly enough to remove the speck out of anyone eye, until you first remove it from yours. (Luke 6:41-42)

February 1, 1988

A man was standing very high up on what appeared to be a train. He was telling someone that his partner died overnight and that he was in prayer all night—and he prayed all the time. "We are living in perilous times and prayer is the only way," he said.

My Interpretation

We are indeed living in perilous times. I am reminded of 2 Timothy 3:1: "But know this, in the last days perilous times will come . . ." Things are going to get worse and worse—not better. Prayer is a key factor individually and collectively, and we must pray now like never before. The word of God tells us that we should pray for one another, and that we should always pray and not give up. (James 5:16; Luke 18:1)

Regardless of how bad things get, or how things look in the natural, know that it is only temporary and you do have the victory in Christ Jesus. God promise us that if we keep our mind on Jesus, He would keep us in perfect peace (Isaiah 26:3); a peace that boggles the mind so that neither you nor the world can fully understand. Today is not the time for us to be playing church. It's time to be real with God, for your survival and eternal life depends upon it.

March 1, 1988

I was preaching, and the subject of my sermon was: "You Must Be Born Again." I was also pregnant, but the pregnancy wasn't noticeable. However, I felt the baby in my womb as it moved into a tight knot-like position. I thought to myself that it was impossible for me to be pregnant, because I had not been with a man sexually (or otherwise).

My Interpretation

Nicodemus was a little confused when Jesus told him that one must be born again, or they cannot enter the kingdom of God. (John 3:3) "How can one be born again? How can one enter into their mother's womb a second time?" Nicodemus asked Jesus. Jesus answered, "Most assuredly, I say to you, unless one is born of water and spirit, he cannot enter the kingdom of God. That which is born of the flesh is flesh, and that which is born of the Spirit is spirit. Do not marvel that I said to you, you must be born again" (John 3:4-7).

"Being born again, not of corruptible seed, but of incorruptible, by the word of God, which liveth and abideth forever" (1 Peter 1:23 KJV). We become born again when we invite Jesus Christ into our heart, and ask Him to forgive us of our sins. Our spiritual birth occurs through faith in Him, and we become a new creation spiritually.

"I will give you a new heart and put a new spirit within you; I will take the heart of stone out of your flesh and give you a heart of flesh. I will put My Spirit within you" (Ezekiel 36:26, 27).

March 3, 1988

In my dream I was pregnant. I felt the fetus (the size of a tiny ball) in my left fallopian tube. Again, I thought that it was impossible for me to be pregnant (because I wasn't sexually active); but if so, I would have an abortion. I am not ready for more children.

My Interpretation

Get ready for a supernatural invasion! Get ready for a spiritual revolution! I am spiritually pregnant with the word of God, and Satan wants me to abort God's word and the calling God has on my life. Satan knows that if I abort, many souls will not give their hearts to Jesus and they will be lost. These are souls that God has assigned for me to reach and perhaps only me. It may be only a handful of people, or it may be millions.

It is time for us to give birth, go forth, and tear Satan's kingdom down. Be impregnated with the word of God. God has planted a ministry in you, and it is now time for you to give birth to that ministry. It's a ministry that you did not think was possible. Yet God has made it possible, and has fully equipped you for such a ministry.

"Behold, I will do a new thing, Now it shall spring forth; Shall you not know it? I will even make a road in the wilderness, And rivers in the desert" (Isaiah 43:19).

March 4, 1988

I gave birth to a beautiful baby girl. As three women entered into my house and saw the baby lying on the bed, they spoke of how beautiful she was. The baby was lying on her tummy, and her head was turned (I never saw her face). As I got up to position her so we could see her face, I woke up.

My Interpretation

Please note that this is a continuation of the dream from March 3. Amazing isn't it? I did give birth. I will give birth to my ministry and the call of God on my life. I will deliver and bring forth the word of God to His people.

To give birth is to bring forth a new life into the world. I believe that God is telling me it is time for me to bring forth His word to His people. It is time for me (and you) to reap the end-time harvest of souls. This is the final countdown. This is a time where the people are in a stage to reap what they had not sown. It is a "whosoever will" (call upon the name of the Lord, shall be saved) time. It is a time to die to self and live unto the call of God on our life. It is time to get the light of God into the hearts of people. People are lost and without any sense of direction in their lives. They are hurting and dying without hope.

God is looking for someone He can use to bless His people. When we totally commit to His will and embrace His vision (and not our own); God will use us to plow His ground (the hearts of the people), and reap this end-time harvest of souls for Jesus Christ. The time is *ripe* and the time is *now*.

"As soon as the grain is ripe, he puts the sickle to it, because the harvest has come" (Mark 4:29). ". . . The harvest truly is great, but the laborers are few; therefore pray the Lord of the harvest, to send out laborers into His harvest. Go your way; behold, I send you out as lambs among wolves" (Luke 10:2, 3).

I have given birth. I am now responsible for taking care of what God has entrusted me with. Where He sends me I'll go. I'll say what He tells me to say, and I'll do what He tells me to do. I will not compromise the word of God. This is a great responsibility. But to whom much is given, much is required. (Luke 12:48) God has begun a good work in me and you; and He will finish what He has started. No devil can stop it. Satan may be able to hinder us in some way, but thank God he cannot stop us. I know that I have the victory through Jesus Christ, and I will go forth and declare the works of God.

"Being confident of this very thing, that He who has begun a good work in you will complete it until the day of Jesus Christ" (Philippians 1:6). "For He who gathers crops (souls) is wise, but he who sleeps during harvest is a disgraceful son" (Proverbs 10:5).

God loves us so very much. That is why He gave His Son, Jesus Christ, to die on the cross for our sins, and raised Him up on the third day for our justification. Jesus Christ loved us so much that He was obedient to His Father; suffered shame, beaten beyond recognition, sacrificed His life for us by dying on the cross bearing our sins (in His sinless body); so that we could be reconciled to God the Father, and have eternal life. Jesus rose from the grave on the third day with all power in His hand (Matthew 18:18); and He has the keys of hades and of death. (Revelation 1:18)

We are all His creation and He doesn't want any of us to perish. Jesus wants to give us eternal life, and we can reside in His Father's house; in the place that He has prepared for us. (John 14:2, 3) My desire is to live with Him all the days of my life and to behold His glory. I want to hear Him say to me one day, "Well done Sarah, my child, my good and faithful servant. Enter into My Kingdom and reign with Me forever!"

March 1988 (last two weeks)

I was preaching and speaking in tongues and the interpretation came through me also. In one of the dreams, I was in the church I attend and I began speaking in tongues. The interpretation came through a woman (Kat) in the church. God told us how we could be blessed like our brothers and sisters in Christ, and members of our family, so that we need not envy them. We must praise Him, He said.

Then she said that if our children would not obey, kick the hell out of them. That is when two ushers escorted the woman out. The pastor felt that this woman was not being led by God, because He would not say anything like that. Yet, as I looked around the church, I saw people shouting and praising God, being blessed by the interpretation. The pastor told one lady, who wasn't too far from where I was sitting, that she shouldn't shout off the interpretation. I asked, why not? I said it before I realized it (and I knew that I was out of order by asking the pastor this question in the midst of the service and congregation).

Two men to the right of me stood up (these men looked so distinguished, their skin was so beautiful and clear—without a blemish) and spoke in favor of the tongues and the interpretation; and as they looked at me, I nodded in agreement. One of these men continued saying, "If you put her (the woman) out of the church, then how would you be able to help her?" I looked at him and applauded them both in agreement.

My Interpretation

While some people do not believe in tongues, the gift of tongues, or the interpretation of tongues that the Bible speaks of: Apostle Paul, Christians in the New Testament, and Christians of today do believe; as so do I.

The distinguished looking men, whom I believe were angels of God, were saying: if everyone were put out of the church based on man's judgment, then more people would be getting hurt rather than getting helped and saved. The church would be putting people out rather than bringing them in, and winning souls for Christ.

As a matter of fact, I think that the very one or those who wish to put someone out of church, should perhaps put themselves out at the same time. We should first take the mote out of our eyes, so we can see clearly before trying to take the mote out of someone else's. Don't be so quick to judge; and you will not be judged.

So many of our children today are running wild, and they have no respect for their parents. As a matter of fact, the parents are afraid of them. The law does not allow us to discipline our children today—the old fashioned way, the way I was raised, and the way the Bible speaks of. We could go to jail simply because we discipline our children in love, because we want our children to do the right thing. It's no wonder so many of our young people end up in jail. My parents disciplined my brothers, sister, and me with switches, and it did not cause us any bodily injury. I believe it made us better individuals. We learn to respect our parents, each other, and other people. Our parents instilled good morals and mannerism in us.

"Do not withhold correction from a child, for if you beat him with a rod, he will not die. You shall beat him with a rod, and deliver his soul from hell" (Proverbs 23:13, 14). "He who spares his rod hates his son, but he who loves him disciplines him promptly (Proverbs 13:24). "Chasten your son (child) while there is still hope, and do not set your heart on his destruction" (Proverbs 19:18). "The rod of reproof give wisdom, but a child left to himself (or herself) brings shame to his (or her) mother" (Proverbs 22:15).

Jesus said in Revelations 3:19 to the church of Laodiceans: "As many as I love, I rebuke and chasten . . ." Paul again reminds us in Hebrew 12:5-7, that we should not despise the chastening of God. God does this because He loves us. Every parent who loves their children corrects them.

A word to the children: Do not think that your parents don't love you because they discipline you with a spanking. As long as they do no physical harm to you (and a loving parent will not), know that it is working for your good. They love you and just want you to grow up to be the kind of individual that they see, and know you can be. They see your potential better than you can, and they want you to strive to be the best that you can be, and to be happy in this life. And remember, God also disciplines us because we are His children, and because He loves us. He too wants us to be the best that we can be for ourselves, and desires for us to have all that He has plan and purpose for our lives.

True parents who discipline their child in love by spankings are not going to abuse or hurt their children. This is the way perhaps they were raised and they see that it made a difference in their lives. Therefore, they feel that this is the right way to train their child, hoping that it will keep him or her on a straight and narrow path. Admittedly, for some it works and for others it does not.

Hebrew 12:11: "No discipline (or chastening) seems pleasant at the time, but painful. Later on, however, it produces a harvest of righteousness and peace for those who have been trained by it." It worked for me, my siblings; and it worked for my children.

April 19, 1988

I plugged a lamp cord into an outlet and was shocked. Finally, I was able to somehow break loose from the hold of the shock. I hurried to the front porch to tell my mother what had just happened. As I was opening the screen door, I saw the most horrible looking sight—a herd of men riding on horses clothed in white garments with white masks over their faces. They were the Ku-Klux-Klansmen. (When I was a small child living in the south, I remember seeing these people riding on a horse with their head and body covered with a white sheet. I have also seen the KKK on television, and know what they represent.) They rode into our yard and began burning bushes.

Some children that were playing in the backyard ran to the front to see what was going on. I pointed towards the door, motioning for them to go inside the house. My mother and I stood on the porch unafraid. As they were doing their thing; I began doing mine. I began praying to God, my heavenly Father, and Jesus Christ, my Lord and Saviour. As I spoke in tongues (praying in the spirit); I thank God for rebuking the devil. Some of the Klansmen had left, but the leader was standing there with a few others watching me.

He said that I wasn't doing anything, insinuating that my prayer was ineffective. My mother replied, "Oh, yes she is!" I then spoke in tongues again, and in English saying, "Thank you Father for beginning to do the work right now."

My Interpretation

No matter how the devil (Satan) comes, no matter what he says, do not fear him. Stand on the word of God. Do not be intimidated by the individual (he's using); or by any of your surroundings. There is no weapon that Satan can form against us that can prosper. None! Just pray to God saying, "Thank you Father for beginning to do the work right now!" Believe what you say, and trust God to do.

Whenever I am afraid, I will trust in You. "In God I have put my trust; I will not fear. What can flesh do to me?" (Psalm 56:4). "The Lord is my light and my salvation; whom shall I fear? The Lord is the strength of my life; of whom shall I be afraid? When the wicked come against me to eat up my flesh, my enemies and foes will stumble and fall. Though any army should encamp against me, my heart will not fear. Though war should rise against me, even then I will be confident" (Psalm 27:1-3).

May 7, 1988

I was in a church in a place with a lot of people. A man was speaking against women preachers and women pastors. As the Spirit of God came upon me, I stood up and said, "Although it is not my desire to be a pastor of a church, I would if God told me to. Many women in the Bible contributed a great deal." Then in my mind I thought of doing a study on all the women in the Bible and what they did. Upon completing my study, I would then teach on the subject.

My Interpretation

God can, does, and will use anyone He so chooses (as long as your heart is right). He is not prejudice. He loves one no more than the other. He doesn't care about the color of your skin. We are all sons (and daughters) of God through faith in Christ Jesus. (Galatians 3:26) "For there is no distinction between Jew or Greek, for the same Lord over all is rich to all who call upon Him" (Romans 10:12). "There is neither Jew nor Greek, there is neither slave nor free, there is neither male nor female; for you are all one in Christ Jesus" (Galatians 3:28). ". . . In truth I perceive that God shows no partiality. But in every nation whoever fears Him and works righteousness is accepted by Him" (Acts 10:34, 35).

June 11, 1988

A co-worker (Shella), asked another co-worker (Buck) about the meaning of Psalm 51. Buck pointed to me and said, "She's the person to see."

My Interpretation

Let your light and your love for God shine in your work place. Psalm 51 is about repentance, and a plea for restoration. David prayed to God after he had committed adultery with Bathsheba (wife of Uriah). God sent Nathan, a prophet, to David with a message letting him know that He was aware of what he had done. Not only had David committed adultery with Bathsheba, but because she became pregnant by David, and he proceeded to have Uriah, her husband, killed so he could marry Bathsheba. David prayed for God's mercy, and forgiveness. (Read 2 Samuel Chapters 11 and 12).

David quickly acknowledges his sin, and realizes his broken relationship and fellowship with God. One must first acknowledge their sin, and confession to God of that sin brings forgiveness. God's forgiveness is always available (Psalm 86:5; 1 John 1:9), and it is complete (Psalm 103:12). He removes sin and remembers it no more. (Psalm 103:12) Hallelujah! Because of Jesus' death on the cross at Calvary over 2000 years ago, redemption is provided for all who will accept what He has done on their behalf. (Read Ephesians 1:7-14; Psalm 32:5; Colossians 1:14; Jeremiah 31:34).

Psalm 51 can be prayed by the believers who have fallen into sin, seek God for forgiveness and a restored relationship. It can also be prayed by unbelievers who want forgiveness of their sins; and give their life and heart to Jesus Christ. I was not going to write this Psalm because it is lengthy, but I feel that I must for those of you who may not go to your Bible and read it; or may not have a Bible.

Have mercy upon me, O God, According to Your lovingkindness; According to the multitude of Your tender mercies, Blot out my transgressions. Wash me thoroughly from my iniquity, And cleanse me from my sin. For I acknowledge my transgressions, And my sin is always before me. Against You, You only, have I sinned, And done this evil in Your sight—That You may be found just when You speak, And blameless when you judge.

Behold, I was brought forth in iniquity, And in sin my mother conceived me. Behold, You desire truth in the inward parts, And in the hidden part You will make me to know wisdom. Purge me with hyssop, and I shall be clean; Wash me, and I shall be whiter than snow. Make me hear joy and gladness, That the bones You have broken may rejoice. Hide your face from my sins,

And blot out all my iniquities. Create in me a pure heart, O God, And renew a steadfast spirit within me. Do not cast me from Your presence, And do not take Your Holy Spirit from me. Restore to me the joy of Your salvation, and uphold me by Your generous Spirit. Then will I teach transgressors Your ways, And sinners shall be converted to You.

Deliver me from the guilt of bloodshed, O God, The God of my salvation, And my tongue shall sing aloud of Your righteousness. O Lord, open my lips, And my mouth shall show forth Your praise. For You do not desire sacrifice, or else I would give it; You do not delight in burnt offering. The sacrifices of God are a broken spirit, A broken and a contrite heart—These O God, You will not despise. (Psalm 51:1-17)

September 17, 1988

A lady and I noticed that a small girl was missing. We spotted the child in a room and went to rescue her. As we were about to get the child out of a room (she was being held captive) a man walked in and right behind him, a young woman. We couldn't run out of the room because they were blocking the door. I said to the man, "Let us talk about this." He was trying to hypnotize the child so she would forget who she was. I was holding the child saying, "No! Don't listen, remember my daughters (as I called them by name in the order of their birth)." The child started smiling, and I knew she remembered my daughters.

The young woman that was with the man took out a knife. I started walking towards her saying something (I don't remember what) and took the knife out of her hand. I told the lady who was with me to run; and I ran behind her with the child saying, "Lord you have all power over the devil. I believe we are safe." The man then yelled to the young woman to seal the exit so we could not get out, but I quickly cut something; jumped into a tunnel, and slid down believing God would lead us to safety. And He did.

My Interpretation

This appears to have been a kidnapping for whatever reason. When it looks like there is no way out of a situation, know that God has already made a way of escape for you. And remember God has all power over Satan. Satan will try and bring fear upon you, and he will try to hypnotize you into believing something else. You stay focused on Jesus and begin to confess and thank God for deliverance (of your safety) out of that situation as you look for a way of escape. God will never allow us to be tunneled in with no way out. He can rescue you out of any trouble if you trust Him to do just that. For God is a personal deliverer of His people. Call upon Him in faith, and He will answer you.

"My loving kindness and my fortress, my high tower and my deliverer, my shield and the One in whom I take refuge, who subdues my people under me" (Psalm 144:2). "You are my help and my deliverer" (Psalm 70:5).

Read 2 Samuel 22. It is a beautiful song of David praising God for his deliverance from the hand of Saul and all his enemies. He exalts the God of his salvation, and sing praises to His name. "The LORD lives! Blessed be my Rock! (2 Samuel 22:47).

September 28, 1988

God was sending me to a place, a land where I should build a city to raise and teach a group of people (believers). The place would be called, *Faith City*. A small child was with me, and she pointed to the place or area where the city would begin. Then she said, "This is it!" I looked, the land was vast, and it needed attending—clearing and cultivating.

We (the child, one other person, and I) began walking viewing the land. I saw an old house that needed painting. I couldn't tell what it looked like on the inside. We continued walking, and as I looked to my left and saw a small snake. I was frightened and told the child to run. We ran towards the house. I looked back and the snake had become a very large anaconda. I continued to run as fast as I could.

My Interpretation

God may be calling you to build a church or building in a certain place. Perhaps He's already given you the name for this place. Upon going and viewing the land you may become a little discouraged at what you see. Perhaps it is not altogether what you expected. The land needs much work. The building needs complete renovation. Don't you be intimated by Satan, and do not let him run you away. This is where God wants you to be.

We can also apply the same principle to our lives. We must learn how to take care of our physical body by proper eating and exercising. There are many things in our lives that need attending to. There are some things that need to be chopped down, things that need to be fertilized, cultivated, and watered to enhance our personal and spiritual growth.

The enemy will magnify problems to make them appear much bigger than they really are. Don't run from your problems. You must face them head-on; eyeball to eyeball; or those very same problems will greet you again. Put your faith and trust in God.

"I will instruct and teach you in the way you should go; I will guide you with My eye" (Psalm 32:8). "The LORD is my light and my salvation; Whom shall I fear? The LORD is the strength of my life; Of whom shall I be afraid" (Psalm 27:1).

October 11, 1988

I was in a deli. I ordered a toasted corn muffin and decaffeinated coffee. When I started to pay for it, the young lady behind the counter put a white napkin on the counter and the tip of it was wet. She said that I had to take a mark before I could pay. I asked her who told her that, and she handed me a small booklet published by the owner of the store.

Quickly, I glanced through the booklet, and saw the most gruesome and disgusting pictures of robots; and people with parts of their bodies missing; either heads, arms or legs. I refused the mark and left the food on the counter. I then found myself telling everyone that the anti-christ was coming and that they should refuse to take a mark. If they didn't take a mark, they would have a chance to be saved. But, if they did take the mark, they would be doomed forever.

My Interpretation

Be watchful. Do not take the mark of the beast. Do not sell your soul to Satan just to satisfy your flesh (hunger and thirst). If I perish, let me perish, as long as I know I am going to my King Jesus. I would rather suffer hunger, pain, thirst, and hardship for a while by rejecting to take the mark of the beast; then to suffer in torment in hell forever.

"And causes all, both small and great, rich and poor, free and slave, to receive a mark on their right hand or on their foreheads, and that no one may buy or sell except one who has the mark or the name of the beast, or the number of his name" (Revelation 13:16-17). The man's number is 666 (verse 18). So you see dear people, your name, fame, or money won't be of any value. No matter what happens, you and your family may starve; may be tortured, and may be killed; but do not give in. Do not take the mark (666) of the beast. For if you do you will be destined to spend eternity in a place of torment with the very same man (beast and Satan) you took the mark 666 from. (Revelation 19:20; 20:10, 15)

Please read Revelation 14:9-11 which tells you what will happen to you if you receive the mark or worship the beast. Satan knows he is destined to spend eternity in the lake of fire, and there is nothing that he can do about it. However, you do have a choice; you can do something about it. Make the right choice—do not take the mark, and ask Jesus to forgive you of all your sins, and be your Lord and Saviour. I compel you to read the book of Revelation and allow God to reveal some amazing truths concerning current and final events that will take place (have already taken place; and are now taking place) on this earth; and where you (your spirit which never dies) will spend eternity.

October 14, 1988

I was in church and we were told to walk around and hug our neighbor. I obeyed, and when I hugged one lady, the spirit of God came over us heavily and I started speaking in tongues.

My Interpretation

Sometimes just a warm embrace may be all one needs. We don't know what they're going through. They simply need to feel loved and feel that someone cares. Only God knows what one is going through. Be obedient to the Spirit of God. "To everything there is a season, A time for every purpose under heaven: . . . A time to embrace, And a time to refrain from embracing" (Ecclesiastes 3:1, 5). Now is the time to embrace.

November 18, 1988

I was in a hospital praying for people. One lady told me how good she felt after I prayed for her. I said to her, "God uses me. He told me to come to the hospital and pray for the sick."

My Interpretation

God was telling me what He wanted me to do. There are so many sick people in the hospital who are thirsty and hungry for the word of God. People who are longing for someone to spend a little time with them to talk, laugh, or even cry. Many are reaching out for love, faith, and hope. Many are so afraid and lonely; they have no one to visit them. You have what they need. You have the medication that will heal their spirit, and mend their broken heart.

Has God been speaking to you about visiting the hospitals and praying for the sick? These are His children too and He loves them. These are your sisters and brothers if they are Christians. And if they are not Christians, if they have not given their hearts to Jesus, we should be concerned about them even the more. Love them, pray for them, and share the gospel of Jesus Christ with them. Let them feel and see Christ in you.

". . . with all lowliness and gentleness, with longsuffering, bearing with one another in love . . ." (Ephesians 4:2) "I was sick and you visited" (Matthew 25:36). ". . . they will lay hands on the sick, and they will recover" (Mark 16:18).

December 5, 1988

My younger brother was speaking in a church. He asked someone to read a scripture. As he spoke, a man stood up and interrupted him by questioning him about his level of education. He asked him if he had a college degree (insinuating that he didn't sound educated or not educated enough). I stood up and said to the man, "Excuse me, but whether he or anyone, for that matter, has a college education is not important. The Holy Spirit is the one who teaches. All the apostles had little or no education, except for Paul and Luke."

My Interpretation

If you are called by God to preach and teach the word of God, a college degree is not necessary, nor is it required. The Holy Spirit will lead, guide and teach you (as you study God's word) far better than man. Peter did not have a college education or degree but when he spoke people listened. What Peter did have was a personal relationship with Jesus Christ. They spent a lot of time with Him in fellowship, prayer, and listening to the word; while being taught the word by the Word. And, that my friend is necessary and required—not a college degree.

Do not allow Satan to embarrass you regarding your educational background. He will deceive you into thinking and feeling as though you are not qualified; or equipped to do the work God have called you to do, even though God has already told you that you are. So whom are you going to believe and trust? Remember, Satan is liar. You are a threat to him, and he doesn't want the Gospel of Jesus Christ preached; knowing that souls will be saved.

"But as for you, continue in the things which you have learned and been assured of, knowing from whom you have learned them . . ." (2 Timothy 4:14). All Scripture is given by inspiration of God . . . that the man of God may be complete, thoroughly equipped for every good work" (2 Timothy 4:16, 17). "But the anointing which you have received from

Him abides in you, and you do not need that anyone teach you; but as the same anointing teaches you concerning all things, and is true, and is not a lie, and just as it has taught you, you will abide in Him" (1 John 2:27). "For He instructs him in right judgment, His God teaches him" (Isaiah 28:26). "Commit your works to the LORD, And your thoughts will be established" (Psalm 16:3).

The Holy Spirit, whom the Father sent, is our helper and He will lead and guide us into all truth and He will tell you things to come. The Holy Spirit will also teach you all things, and will even bring things to your remembrance. (John 16:13; 14:26)

"Now when they saw the boldness of Peter and John, and perceived that they were uneducated and untrained men, they marveled. And they realized that they had been with Jesus" (Acts 4:13).

Please do not misunderstand me, nothing is wrong with a college education (I love to learn and challenge my mind, and I'm a firm believer in education). What I am saying is if God has given you an assignment, He has already given you a passing grade; and He has given you the ability and intellect to carry out that work assignment. If you need help with anything, just call on Him. But don't let anyone intimidate you regarding your level of education. They do not have that right. Who are they?

January 12, 1989

My younger brother said as he was speaking an evil spirit was trying to possess him. I jumped up from my chair, and laid my hand on his head speaking in tongues very powerfully. I rebuked the devil in the name of Jesus, telling him to come out of him and leave this house.

My Interpretation

As believers in Jesus Christ, Jesus has given us the authority and power to cast out demons. When dealing with evil spirits, make sure you know in whom you believe; know and use your authority given by Jesus; and speak boldly without fear in the name of Jesus. Satan may try to divert your attention in some manner or form, but don't fall into his trap. You must keep your mind focused on Jesus at all times.

". . . and to have power to heal sicknesses and to cast out demons . . ." (Mark 3:15). ". . . and the evil spirits went out of them" (Acts 19:12). ". . . he who had been demon-possessed was healed" (Luke 8:36).

February 1, 1989

I was in a large classroom. A woman was standing speaking about someone she said had turned "bad," and she wanted to blame Jesus for it. I said to her, "You can't believe everything you hear, and you should read the Bible for yourself. Ask Jesus to open your eyes and heart, and help you to understand His word. And I guarantee you that if you mean it from your heart, He will do it. I know because I did it. It's like you and your husband—you must have an intimate and personal relationship with Jesus. You have to know Him for yourself." The woman sat down beside me to hear more about Jesus, and she was no longer angry.

My Interpretation

Perhaps you need to ask God to open your eyes and heart, and help you to understand who He is. Make it a point not to believe everything someone tells you. Read God's word for yourself and pray. And if you haven't already done so, invite Jesus Christ into your life, ask Him to forgive you of your sins, and develop an intimate and personal relationship with Him.

"Behold, I stand at the door (of your heart) and knock. If anyone hears My voice and opens the door, I will come in to him and dine with him, and he with Me" (Revelation 3:20).

February 4, 1989

I was watching television. The discussion was about crime, drugs, and the death penalty. I began to mourn in my spirit very hard and said: "People must start praying in their community that is the only way to stop crime—prayer is the only answer."

My Interpretation

It is time to pray. We are fighting a war that is spiritual; not a war of flesh and blood. Therefore, prayer is the only answer. We must stand against the enemy and unite as one in God and pray. If you want to stop all type of crime in your community; the community must pray.

". . . helping together in prayer . . ." (2 Corinthians1:11). ". . . all continued with one accord in prayer and supplication . . ." (Acts 1:14).

March 18, 1989

A stranger looked at me and said, "Read the Bible."

My Interpretation

The Bible is the Word of God. God speaks to us through His Word. The Bible teaches us how to live. We learn of His ways and of His principles. We learn what He requires of us. We learn about His will and purpose for our lives. There is life in the Word of God. The word of God is spiritual food for our spirit man just as natural food is for our physical body. Do you know what will happen to our physical body if we do not feed it? Will it not become weak and eventually die? Even so, if we do not feed the word of God to our spirit man; the Holy Spirit, our spiritual life will feel deserted and lifeless. And it will eventually die spiritually.

"In the beginning was the Word, and the Word was with God, and the Word was God. He was in the beginning with God" (John 1:1, 2). "And the Word became flesh and dwelt among us, and we beheld His glory, the glory as of the only begotten of the Father, full of grace and truth" (John 1:14).

April 1, 1989

A lady prophesied to me regarding the church on Church Avenue between East 31st and 32nd Streets. It is a Hispanic Pentecostal church. The lady told me that I would speak in this church. I began to praise God, telling Him that I would go wherever He wants me to go. I then began speaking in tongues.

My Interpretation

We must be willing to go wherever God tells us to go—regardless of race, or their native tongue. God will arrange a way for us to communicate in their language.

"Commit your way to the LORD, Trust also in Him" (Psalm 37:5). "Trust in the LORD with all your heart, And lean not to your own understanding. In all your ways acknowledge Him, And He shall direct your paths" (Proverbs 3:5, 6).

May 6, 1989

I was on the subway train. A woman and I were engaged in a conversation about faith. I told her that I could pray for her and use my faith, but she would have to use her faith for her complete healing. I said, "Some people get prayer in church for a certain thing, they unite their faith with the pastors, elders, and other believers and they are healed. But what happens fifteen minutes later when they leave the church? They start complaining about the same problem, they begin to doubt. Why?—Because they did not use their faith from the beginning. You have to believe in God for yourself; you have to have faith to believe you have received what you asked God for.

My Interpretation

You have to "have faith in God." (Mark 11: 23) "Do not be afraid; only believe" (Mark 5:36) "He Himself took our infirmities And bore our sicknesses" (Matthew 8:17). "Therefore I say to you, whatever things you ask when you pray, believe that you receive them, and you will have them" (Mark 11:24). "This man heard Paul speaking. Paul, observing him intently and seeing that he had faith to be healed . . ." (Acts 14:9). And He (Jesus) said to her, "Daughter, your faith has made you well. Go in peace, and be healed of your affliction" (Mark 5:34).

May 18, 1989

Satan was after a group of us as we hurried up some high steps. I stopped and turned around facing Satan, and told the people not to run from him. Satan saw I was not afraid, but the people with me were—and they weren't praying people. I knew this as well and realized I needed help. I looked around and saw a big bus, loaded with praying believers of God.

My Interpretation

God have not given us a spirit of fear. (2 Timothy 1:3) If you stand up for God when the enemy is all around you, God will stand up for you. He will send angels to help and protect you. God will touch the heart of His people any place in this world to intercede in prayer for you. Yes, you! You are just that special to Him and He loves you so very much.

"Or do you think that I cannot now pray to My Father, and He will provide me with more than twelve legions of angels?" (Matthew 26:53).

August 17, 1989

I was with my mother and my sister, and I was combing my mother's hair. Mother said, "I want Jess (my sister) to go to church tomorrow because God will show her what to do, He has something for her to do." My sister was about to leave home to either join the military or travel to another city. Mother thought if she went to church first, God would speak to her and she would stay home. Jess said, "Well, I don't see why I should want God."

Hearing her say this really bothered me, so I stopped combing mother's hair and said, looking directly at her (she looked very lovely, her skin was so clear), "Because you are wretched, poor, lost, and filthy as rags. Without Christ you are nothing. Don't you know that your spirit will live forever? Only your flesh will die. Therefore, your spirit will have to dwell some place, and that place is either with God or with the devil. It's just that simple.

I'm surprised to hear you say this Jess. You know even before I accepted Jesus in my life, when someone approached me and talked to me about God, I would listen. Sometimes I had to tell them I had to go because they were talking too long. But thank God I had the sense to at least listen, and I didn't make fun of what they were saying" I said to her.

My Interpretation

We must pray for our unsaved loved ones and friends. Satan will do his best to keep their eyes blinded and ears deaf to the truth, because he doesn't want them to see and hear from God. We must remind them of who we are, what we are, where we were, and where we are going; with or without God our Father, and Jesus Christ our Saviour in our lives.

Please have an open mind when someone wishes to talk to you about God. Won't you at least listen—if only for a short while? It may very well be the wisest thing that you have ever done. Ask yourself a simple question. Where do I want to spend eternity? Your choices are: Eternal life in heaven with God and our heavenly family; or death in hell, an eternal place of torment (that burns with fire and brimstones) with Satan, demons, antichrist, all liars and pretenders—those who say that they love Jesus but don't; and everyone who rejects Jesus Christ. The choice is yours. I pray that you will choose eternal life.

". . . I have set before you life and death, blessing and cursing; therefore choose life, that both you and your descendants may live; that you may love the LORD your God, that you may obey His voice, and that you may cling to Him, for He is your life and the length of your days" . . . (Deuteronomy 30:10, 20). "But the cowardly, unbelieving, abominable, murderers, sexually immoral, sorcerers, idolaters, and all liars shall have their part in the lake which burns with fire and brimstone, which is the second death" (Revelation 21:8). Rev 20:10 "And anyone not found written in the Book of Life was cast into the lake of fire" (Revelation 20:15). (Also read 1 Corinthians 6:9-10; Revelation 20:10).

August 22, 1989

People were running towards this person. I was ahead, so I went back to see what was happening. I could sense something as I approached the people—they all looked at me. I looked on the pavement and saw my mother lying there, and someone said she was dead. I placed my body over her and gently touched her body; my arms and hands were placed under her head. Then I said, "Mother, wake up, open your eyes. God said you don't have to go yet, open your eyes." She then lifted her arms and put them around my neck and hugged me.

The people standing around us were amazed. Mother sat up, but now she was a small child around three or four years old. It was hard for her to keep her eyes open, for they were very heavy with sleep. So, I kept telling her to keep her eyes open. I gave her a toy and that made her keep her eyes open.

My Interpretation

You don't have to die in this life before your time. This also teaches how you should pray for someone who's asleep in death. Being led by the Spirit of God, speak in faith to the person as though they are just sleeping naturally. This should be done quickly as time is of the essence.

"The child is not dead, but sleeping" Jesus takes the child by the hand and said, "Little girl, I say to you arise" (March 5:39, 41).

August 23, 1989

A lady was telling me that a man was testifying to a lady about how someone stole his television, and God gave him two more televisions. Even if he got back the one that was stolen, he would not have any place to put it. Isn't God good?! She said. "Yes, God is good," I replied. And I began to rejoice with her.

My Interpretation

As long as we trust God, and continue to give Him praise, He will restore (with interest) all that Satan stole from us. God tells us that we are to rejoice in Him always, and to rejoice with those that do rejoice. (Philippians 4:4) Be happy for others when God blesses them with good things. It will enhance your blessing. "Rejoice with those who rejoice," (Romans 12:15).

September 18, 1989

I was reciting the 23rd Psalm.

In Real Life: As I woke up, I was still quoting the Psalm. I looked at my clock and the time was 5:23 a.m. I then went back to sleep and had the same dream again. I was still reciting the Psalm as though I had never stopped.

My Interpretation

Psalm 23 is a beautiful song of David—it has become my song. I know that:

The Lord is my shepherd; I shall not want. He makes me to lie down in green pastures; He leads me beside the still waters. He restores my soul; He leads me in the paths of righteousness for His name's sake. Yea, though I walk through the valley of the shadow of death, I will fear no evil; for You are with me; Your rod and Your staff, they comfort me. You prepare a table before me in the presence of my enemies; You anoint my head with oil; my cup runs over. Surely goodness and mercy shall follow me all the days of my life; and I will dwell in the house of the Lord forever.

God has always been by my side. He's always been my: comforter, protector, supplier, guide, and my God. The Lord is my Shepherd and I shall not want. Let Him be your Shepherd.

October 15, 1989

I went to inquire about a new job someone had referred me to because the pay was better. The area looked very bad. There were abandoned buildings, burned down houses, and trash everywhere. Homeless people were standing everywhere. The houses on one side of the street looked very bad, but on the opposite side the houses looked alright—and I wondered about this. I said to myself, "If I work in this area maybe I will be able to get better housing, and restore the old buildings for these homeless people, and others who need help" The building that I was in didn't look very good either. I would be working on the second floor, and a security guard was on the first floor. Seeing him standing there made me feel better.

My Interpretation

I hope someday that God will bless me so that I will be able to provide housing, counseling, clothing, jobs, and eventually permanent housing for people who are in need. This is one of my dreams and my heart desire. I just believe that He will open doors at the appointed time. "For the needy shall not always be forgotten; The expectation of the poor shall not perish forever" (Psalm 9:18).

November 10, 1989

I was singing a gospel song I made up. It was only a few words. The words I remember are: *I Am Saved*. It was a beautiful (slow) song.

My Interpretation

Jesus saves to the uttermost. (Hebrews 7:25) You are saved, I am saved, no matter what others and Satan may say. We have been forgiven and delivered from sin and its consequences.

". . . Save me, and I shall be saved, For You are my praise" (Jeremiah 17:14).

For those who are not saved, one might ask the question: What must I do to be saved? Believe on the Lord Jesus Christ, and you (and all in your household who believe) will be saved. (Acts 16:30-31) Ask God to forgive you of your sins, repent, and accept Jesus Christ into your life. ". . . if you confess with your mouth the Lord Jesus and believe in your heart that God has raised Him from the dead, you will be saved. For with the heart one believes unto righteousness, and with the mouth confession is made unto salvation" (Romans 10:9, 10). "For whoever calls on the name of the Lord shall be saved" (Romans 10:13). After you have invited Jesus into your heart, then you too can say with all joy, "I am saved!"

God is not prejudice, and is rich to all who call upon Him in truth for salvation no matter who you are: the color of your skin, what you have done, where you live, rich or poor; it doesn't matter.

December 1, 1989

Rhonda, my oldest daughter was visiting me. My daughter thought that she had left the alarm clock on. We went back to the house to turn it off, so that it would not wake my older brother. We crossed the road and came to our house (it was my special house), and I heard gospel singing. Then I noticed another door that led inside a church. There was a sign with the name of the church and a sign pointing the way to the church. It was a Baptist church but I cannot remember the name. Why is there a church in my house? I thought.

Then I heard my deceased father's voice he was preaching, so I hurried inside the church. I thought daddy said that he was reading from Acts 2:48. I told my daughter to remember the chapter and verse, not wanting to take my eyes off my dad. I then looked to the front row and saw my mother (whom is still alive). She looked so young and beautiful, and her face shone with a beautiful glow. I sat down quickly focusing my eyes back on my dad. He was young, tall, and extremely handsome.

Daddy's face had such a beautiful glow, and his hair was white and black, but mostly white. I sat in amazement, not wanting to take my eyes off of him, because I did not want him to disappear (knowing that he is deceased); it was such a delight to see him again. I told the person with me (it was no longer my daughter, but thought it was my friend May) to write down the scripture again that daddy was preaching from.

In Real Life: I woke up and got my Bible to look up the scripture daddy was preaching from. There were only 47 verses in Acts chapter 2. I laid back down hoping to fall asleep quickly, and dream about daddy again.

This is what I dreamt: I saw two hands scanning Acts chapter 2, and their fingers stopped at verse 38. I placed my finger beside theirs so that I would not lose it or forget the verse. I knew then that it was Acts chapter 2, verse 38 that my father had said and was preaching. I had been too busy noticing him and not focusing as much on the scripture; although I wanted to so that I could read it later.

In Real Life: Sunday morning I read Acts 2:38 and this is what it reads: Then Peter said to them, "Repent, and let every one of you be baptized in the name of Jesus Christ for the remissions of sins; and you shall receive the gift of the Holy Spirit."

My Interpretation

I believe God's message to every people, nation, and to the world is "Repent" and be baptized in the name of Jesus Christ for the remissions of your sins, and God will give you the gift of His Holy Spirit. Change the way you're living. Change the way you think. You may believe in God the Father, but you must also believe in Jesus Christ, His son. Make a U-turn to go in the right direction; invite Jesus in your life today, because the next second could be too late.

"Truly, these times of ignorance God overlooked, but now commands all men everywhere to repent, because He has appointed a day on which He will judge the world in righteousness by the Man whom He has ordained" (Acts 17:30, 31).

December 18, 1989

My sister-in-law and I got into a taxi. I realized the driver was going the wrong way. The road on which he was taking us looked very strange—like it was quicksand. The man then, of course, told us that if we were thinking about jumping out of the car, we would sink once we touched the ground. Yet, I saw two men riding their bikes on this same road. I knew then that the driver was not telling the truth. I began speaking in tongues. The man looked a little puzzled as to what was happening to me. No harm came to us.

My Interpretation

Satan is always trying to take us on a ride. Don't listen to him and believe nothing he says. He is a liar and deceiver, and he doesn't want us to see or hear the truth. Remember that God is with you even in the midst of trouble. Just start praising Him, and He will bring you out of any situation, and no harm will come to you (or your love ones).

"Watch and pray! (Matthew 26:41). "Deliver me out of the mire, and let me not sink" (Psalm 69:14). "For I am in trouble; . . . Deliver me because of my enemies" (Psalm 69:17, 18). "I will praise the name of God . . ." (Psalm 69:30).

January 12, 1990

I was in church taking communion. As I drank the grape juice, representing the shed blood of Jesus Christ, I began praising God like I never have before. I began speaking in tongues more powerfully than ever before. Then others in the church began praising the Lord. A young man began to prophesy. I heard someone say, "Come and see."

My Interpretation

There will be an outpouring of the Holy Spirit like never before. In these last days, I believe that we will see more of the gifts of the Spirit in operation, and a powerful anointing in the body of Christ. Get ready, come and see the wonderful working power of our God.

"As each one has received a gift, minister it to one another, as good stewards of the manifold grace of God. If anyone speaks, let him speak as the oracles of God. If anyone ministers, let him do it as with the ability which God supplies, that in all things God may be glorified through Jesus

Christ, to whom belong the glory and the dominion forever and ever. Amen" (1 Peter 4:10, 11).

January 31, 1990

There were a lot of people walking across a bridge. Suddenly, the bridge started breaking; some of the people made it across safely, others had to run back to their starting point. A man on a tractor-trailer and another man on foot began working on the bridge. There were still a lot of people to go across the bridge (including my child and me). Suddenly, I found myself looking down from a very tall place observing everything that was happening. I saw my child standing on the bridge but she was standing too close near the water. As I started down to get her (not wanting to yell because I did not want to frighten her), I looked again and she was not there. I screamed and said, "My child is in the water," pointing to place where she was standing. I looked into the water and saw bubbles and feared it was my child struggling to breathe, and then a seal appeared with something on its nose like a ball. I though the seal may have eaten my child or pulled her under the water.

Again, I was back at the bridge in this high place; it was a very large loft apartment; and I believe it belonged to Dervin and Deedee (some people that I know). Dervin was leaving as I arrived. Deedee and I walked over to a large open window, and I looked down and saw a small group of people floating on a raft. The raft had holes in it, and it really looked like a giant fish net. (It was dark outside, yet I saw the holes). It was getting darker as they floated slowly until the darkness covered them. I yelled out to them, "Wait, you left me!" (Thinking that my child was on the raft without me) "We've been out here a long time and now we are beginning to sink. The man said that Jesus would come and save us but Jesus didn't come yet," yelled a woman from the raft.

I began to call Jesus looking up toward heaven. I said, "Jesus, Jesus, Jesus, I believe." Then the people on the raft began calling Jesus as well. I prayed saying, "Jesus save these people. The man told them that You would come and save them." Then I motioned to my child (whom I now saw; she was not on the raft) not to come near the window, and to sit down quietly. I felt the power of God all over me very, very strong (even after I woke up).

My Interpretation

No matter how bad or how dark things look remember if you call upon the name of Jesus, He will save you. (Romans 10:13) He will lead you to safety. "I have called upon You, for You will hear me, O God. You who save those who trust in You" (Psalm 17:6, 7) "Stretch out your hand from above; Rescue me and deliver me out of great waters" (Psalm 144:7). "Behold, the LORD'S hand is not shortened, That it cannot save; Nor His ear heavy That it cannot hear" (Isaiah 59:1). "He will come and save you" (Isaiah 35:4). Just believe and call Him.

February 22, 1990

My friend (Ana) did not come to a birthday that dinner I invited her and her husband to. I planned the dinner on Sunday particularly for her (because she works on Saturdays), so that she would be able to come. She called me on the morning of the dinner and said that she could not come due to the weather. I was a little upset, disappointed, and surprised at the lack of consideration shown. After hanging up the telephone I told my daughters to invite everyone who lived in the building (we knew) that had not been invited. I was reminded of the parable of the great supper in Luke 14: 16-24.

In Real Life: On the day of the dinner, Sunday, February 25, my friend husband phoned to say that they could not make the dinner because of the weather and that he was not feeling very well. Needless to say, I was not surprised. I was a little upset and disappointed because I had just phoned my friend on that Friday, and told her about the dream. She assured me that they would be at the dinner since I had changed it from Saturday to Sunday for their convenience.

My Interpretation

As Christians our duty is to extend the invitation to others. It is entirely up to them to except and show up. God's divine and genuine invitation should take priority over anyone and anything leaving no room for an excuse. We all have an open invitation to come to God, and believe in His Son Jesus Christ accepting Him as our Lord and Saviour. Jesus said whosoever will let them come. Are you a—whosoever? Prostitutes, drug abusers, alcoholics, liars, gang members, gamblers, murders, adulterers, fornicators, homosexuals, lesbians, Seventh Day Adventists, Jehovah's Witnesses, Jewish, Hindus, Buddha's, Muslims, Protestants, Baptists, Pentecostals, Catholics, Lutherans, Methodists, all religions; and all people. Will you come to Jesus Christ, and invite Him into your life right now?

It does not matter who you are; or what you have done, so long as you sincerely and genuinely repent; ask God to forgive you of your sins, and accept Jesus Christ as your Lord and Saviour. After doing this you can now start anew. You are now a new creation in Jesus Christ, old things, your old life (way of doing things) will pass away, and now you have a new life in Jesus. (2 Corinthians 5:17) God no longer remembers your pass life. Jesus is saying to you right now:

"Behold, I stand at the door (of your heart) and knock. If anyone hears My voice and opens the door, I will come in to him and dine with him, and he with Me" (Revelation 3:20). ". . . and the one who comes to Me I will by no means cast out" (John 6:37). "For whoever calls on the name of the Lord shall be saved" (Romans 10:13).

March 8, 1990

I had on false eyelashes, though I had no idea where they came from or how they got on my eyes. I began to worry thinking someone was trying to put witchcraft on me. Two Scriptures came to mind: God has not given us a spirit of fear, but of love and of power and of a sound mind; and perfect love casts out all fear. (2 Timothy 2:17; 1 John 4:18)

My Interpretation

Satan will do anything to get attention, and to get us to take our eyes and mind off God. Do not let him distract you, or plant fear in your mind. God has not given us a spirit of fear, but of love and power, and a sound mind. Fear will paralyze you and will hinder you from walking into your full potential and destiny. Know that no weapon Satan forms against you can prosper (Isaiah 54:17), as long as you stay in the will of God. And just for the record—I don't think anything is wrong with wearing false eyelashes. I have worn them myself in my younger days.

March 27, 1990

I was singing a song God gave me: "I Want to Know What God Wants to Tell Me."

My Interpretation

Be in a state of readiness (mind and heart) to hear (receive and obey) what God is saying to you. "Whatever I tell you in the dark, speak in light; and what you hear in the ear, preach on the housetops" (Matthew 10:27). "And He said, Go, and tell this people:" (Isaiah 6:9). Speak Lord, speak to me.

April 20, 1990

I was singing the song: It's not by might, nor by power, but by my Spirit, says the Lord. I added my own words saying, "Lord send down your Holy Spirit and let Him live inside of me."

My Interpretation

Our God is always with us to help us and He will fight all of our battles. For, we can do nothing in our own strength. Without the Spirit of God, we can do nothing. Our ability, our authority outside of God is absolutely nothing. I want the Holy Spirit to abide in me and take total control of my life. "Not by might nor by power, but by My Spirit" says the Lord of hosts (Zechariah 4:6).

May 21, 1990

I was outside on a porch with a little girl, and saw small drops of rain. As the rain hit the ground I saw a little smoke. The child ran into the rain-fire, but it did not hurt her. I quickly told her to come back (while reaching my hand out to her). I looked at the rain-fire and said, "Jesus is coming!" Then we went inside the house and told everyone what was happening, and that they should put on a lot of clothing (hoping they would not be burned).

My Interpretation

Jesus is soon to come, and I believe that we will see more strange things happening as He approaches. I believe that one day God will rain down drops of fire. Are you ready?

June 12, 1990

I walked into my Grandma Sarah's (deceased) house and there were a lot of people. My first thought was that they were having a prayer meeting. As I walked into the house, starting at my right I shook each person's hand. One lady, as I shook her hand said smilingly, "I've heard a lot about you!" I came to a second room where most of my family was sitting. My uncle Rufus (a pastor) was the first person I saw as he motioned for me to get a chair and sit next to him. I took the chair that was near my grandmother's bed. (The third room was where my deceased grandfather laid). I believe that he died in1960. I was nine or years old). My mother and a lot of other people were singing Scriptures from the Bible. My uncle quickly shared his Bible with me. The scriptural songs were beautiful. My uncle read a Scripture and we sang it.

My Interpretation

When is the last time that you had prayer meeting or bible study at your house with family and friends? Have you heard a lot of talk about Jesus? Have you surrendered your life to Him? Have you shared the word of God with someone today? Have you sung scriptural songs today to God making melody in your spirit? Have you said something nice about someone, rather than something bad and negative?

August 28, 1990

I said, "Lord I just want to be found worthy to go back with you when you come."

My Interpretation

If we want to be found worthy when Jesus returns, then we must walk worthy of Him in full obedience, and fulfilling all the good pleasure of His goodness and work of faith with power. (2 Thessalonians 1:11) I want Him to find me worthy to go back home with Him.

". . . that you may walk worthy of the Lord, fully pleasing Him, being fruitful in every good work and increasing in the knowledge of God" (Colossians 1:10). ". . . that you may be counted worthy of the kingdom of God" (2 Thessalonians 1:5). Let us also hope and pray that our God will count us worthy to go back with Him.

August 29, 1990

I was being caught up in the rapture. As I was going up into heaven, I thought about the Bible scripture that tells us that we will be changed in a moment, in the twinkling of an eye. There were tiny drops of dew falling, and I thought to myself: "I will let dewdrops fall into my eyes. Then as fast as I could blink my eyes, I would be changed."

In the same dream, a woman was telling me about a dream she had. It was regarding a child but I do not remember the dream (although I dreamt this twice). I told the woman what the child represented, and what the dream meant which was: *You Must Be Born Again.*

My Interpretation

If you want to be caught up in the rapture and live eternally with Jesus, you must be born again. Jesus told Nicodemus (who was a ruler of the Jews): "Most assuredly, I say to you, unless one is born again, he cannot see the kingdom of God. Most assuredly, I say to you, unless one is born of water and the Spirit, he cannot enter the kingdom of God. That which is born of the flesh is flesh, and that which is born of the Spirit is spirit. Do not marvel that I said to you, 'you must be born again.'" (John 3:3, 5-7) Your spirit must be reborn.

"Now this I say, brethren, that flesh and blood cannot inherit the kingdom of God; nor does corruption inherit incorruption. Behold, I tell you a mystery: We shall not all sleep, but we shall all be changed—in a moment, in the twinkling of an eye, at the last trumpet" (1 Corinthians 15:50-52). Jesus is coming to take His people home. Will you be ready?

August 30, 1990

I was in church praising God in a dance and speaking in tongues.

My Interpretation

"Let the children of Zion be joyful in their King. Let them praise His name with the dance. Let them sing praises to Him with the timbrel and harp. Let the high praises of God be in their mouth" (Psalm 149:2, 3, 6).

November 17, 1990

I spoke in tongues and the interpretation came forth. God told me that a man was trying to destroy Washington, D.C., but he could not destroy it because He (God) built it; He made it; He is the creator of that city.

My Interpretation

Satan wants to steal, kill, and destroy. He may be trying to destroy: your city, your ministry, your church, your marriage, your relationship, your family, your job, and other things in your life. But know for certain; that which is built by God, no man or devil can destroy it. For God created it, established it, and made it so. He has already mapped out your destiny.

"He delivers me from my enemies. You also lift me up above those who rise against me; You have delivered me from the violent man" (Psalm 18:48). Pray for Washington, DC; the city where you live; the U.S.A., and the world.

We are living in trouble times, and it's going to get worse and worse. But don't worry and look up, because your redeemer Jesus Christ is coming.

November 18, 1990

I was speaking in tongues very heavily.

My Interpretation

This was a time of fellowship between God, the Holy Spirit, and me. "and truly our fellowship is with the Father and with His Son Jesus Christ" (1 John 1:3). "Surely the righteous shall give thanks to Your name; The upright shall dwell in Your presence" (Psalm 140:13). And in His presence there is fullness of joy. (Psalm 15: 11) "Let the words of my mouth and the meditation of my heart be acceptable in Your sight" (Psalm 19:14).

December 3, 1990

I was in a very large church and there were many people; musicians, several choirs, and including the choir from my church. The program started with a recital by about seven children.

The director signaled to the little girl to start first. The child silently said, "Who me?" The director said, "No, the oldest go first." The little girl was not prepared and was a bit nervous. Her clothing (a green sweater and plaid skirt), somehow got out of place and she was trying to fix them. Even her undergarments were showing a little, and I thought how embarrassing this must be for her and her mother. I reached over and helped the child fix her clothing, though she was neatly fixing each piece on her own.

Even after I assisted her, she still made sure that she arranged her skirt the way she wanted it; I apparently had it up too high on her waist. She then said a few words and decided to sing a song. The little girl ran to her mother, and pulled her up from the chair by the hand. Then she told her mother the song she wanted to sing. The mother said, "You want to sing that song?" The mother then told another lady, perhaps a relative or friend, the song her daughter wanted to sing.

The lady then got up, she was wearing yellow and she was a little heavy in size. As she approached the platform towards the organ, the musician got up and gave her the seat. As she was sitting, I whispered to my friend May, "This woman can play and sing." The woman started by praising God; saying how good He is; and then she prayed asking God to anoint her playing and singing. She continued to play and sing; the song was so beautiful. She spoke about God always being there even when we may have thought He wasn't. Regardless of how great or small our problems are. He knows and is always there. "What am I going to do?" she said. "I'm going to hold on to God's unchanging hand, hold on to His hand" (the choir joined in the chorus).

By now I was standing near her by the organ. Realizing that I might be blocking the view of others, I quickly sat down, but not far from her; listening to that lovely song. She continued singing, saying when she had something done to her lip (touching it), God was right there. She was speaking about all of her experiences, sicknesses, disappointments, and all that she had gone through. She said God was right there with her through it all.

In Real Life: I remembered (as I got out of bed to write down the dream) that my pastor had said in church the day before, that a prophecy came forth Saturday night (December 1st) while celebrating his 25th Pastoral Anniversary. God spoke (through the gift of prophecy) and said, "Hold on to His unchanging hand."

My Interpretation

And a little child shall lead them. (Isaiah 11:6) The message is in the song. Hold on to God's unchanging hand. No matter what you are going through, He will never leave you or forsake you. He is the same yesterday, today and forever. (Hebrew 13:5, 8) He never changes. He has already worked it all out for you. Just hold on to His hand and trust in Him.

"Behold, the Lord's hand is not shorten, That it cannot save; Nor His ear heavy, That it cannot hear" (Isaiah 59:1). "The Lord will guide you continually, And satisfy your soul in drought, And strengthen your bones; You shall be like a watered garden, And like a spring of water, whose waters do not fail" (Isaiah 58:11). And, "When the enemy comes in like a flood, The Spirit of the Lord will lift up a standard against him" (Isaiah 59:19). "For I am the Lord, I do not change" (Malachi 3:6).

Your family may change, your friends may change, your circumstances may change; but my God never ever changes. He is a present help when you're in trouble. (Psalm 46:1) Hold on to God's unchanging Hand, and don't you let go. Trust and believe His word.

January 7, 1991

Many people were possessed and were chasing me and a few other people. Demon-possessed people surrounded us, and they could not be hurt or killed. Somehow my younger brother and another person who had not been possessed were there. All the other people were taken by the demons. I jumped on one of them and drove my fingers into its eyes and face. It had no effect, except the face became very ugly. I prayed (while still holding the demon down) looking up towards heaven, saying, "Oh God, why are you letting this happen. Help us, deliver us, and we will do your will."

We were delivered immediately. I said to my younger brother, "We will have to teach these people because they have not realized what just happened to them. Therefore, we are responsible for teaching them about Jesus." I thought about being a pastor, but immediately said to myself, "No, I really don't go for women pastors being the head in the pulpit." Then I thought of my brother; but then thought he may mislead the people, and be more interested in the financial aspect of it. I had to be certain that these people hear the truth.

My Interpretation

There are some people who are waiting on you to deliver them from the claws of Satan. These are people whom God has assigned to you, and only you can deliver and make a spiritual change and impact in their lives through Jesus Christ. If you're going through something right now that you don't understand; it may be that your deliverance won't come until you say, "yes" to the will of God for your life. Do what God is calling you to do. Stop running! Satan doesn't want you to do the work God has ordained you to do. You are a threat to Satan; he knows that you will win souls for Jesus, and he does not want that to happen. Perhaps one day God will call me to pastor a church. If so, I will be ready and obedient to His call; and do His will.

"Where there is no counsel, the people fall; But in the multitude of counselors there is safety" (Proverbs 11:14). "And he who wins souls is wise" (Proverbs 11:30).

January 8, 1991

My telephone was ringing and I answered it. A man introduced himself as a reverend but I do not remember his name. He began telling me that I had two ministries and told me other things that God wanted me to do. I didn't take him very seriously in the beginning, thinking it was a crank call. By the time I realized that he was serious, I had missed or forgotten most of what he told me. I listened for the voice, but the man must have hung up.

My Interpretation

God has called you and me into ministry, and He is trying to tell us what He wants us to do; but we're not listening. It's time to get serious and listen for His voice; He's calling you, and wants to converse with you. Don't miss your call, don't miss your season. Don't let Satan trick you into not hearing, and obeying the voice of God.

"He who has an ear, let him hear, what the Spirit says . . ." (Revelation 2:7) "Today, if you will hear His voice: Do not harden your hearts," (Psalm 95:7, 8). Listen for God's voice.

January 13, 1991

My friend DuV (a minister), and I were in church. I got up to sing a song with the choir and began reciting various Psalms (23rd, 27th, 100th, and so on). In the church there seemed to be two different denominations and they spoke two different languages. From the position I was sitting, the larger congregation was on the right, and I thought they spoke French (which is my friend's native tongue). We were sitting on the left side of the church with the smaller congregation, and they spoke another language.

I was sitting in the back of him observing both sides. I noticed that all of the people on the right looked no different from the people on the left. The women were dressed in suits and wore lovely hats. Everyone were worshipping and praising God and all were on one accord. It was a beautiful sight. My friend asked a man for his camera and got up to take my picture; and snapped the picture before I was ready.

My Interpretation

God has no respect of persons. We are all His children if we believe in His son Jesus Christ. There is no language barrier in Him. Your denomination, the color of your skin, your native tongue; the way you dress, or whether you're rich or poor, none of these things matters to God; for His Son, Jesus Christ died for all people. What does matters is that we love Him with all of our heart and soul; we have no other before Him; we believe in Jesus Christ, His Son; we trust and obey Him, we love one another, and that we live according to His word. Be open to the things of God, and be led by the Holy Spirit.

"And above all things have fervent love for one another, for love will cover a multitude of sins. Be hospitable to one another without grumbling" (1 Peter 4:8, 9). "Let the peoples praise You, O God; Let all the peoples praise You" (Psalm 67:3, 5). "All the earth shall worship You And sing praises to You; They shall sing praises to Your name." Selah "Come and see the works of God; He is awesome in His doings towards the sons of men." (Psalm 66:4, 5).

February 8, 1991

My pastor showed a letter received from a radio listener who said they heard him speak about the rapture, but they didn't believe in it. He (the writer of the letter) said that he went to a theological seminary school—as though that made him right. I said to myself, "Well, maybe that is his problem, he's too theological."

My Interpretation

Some people will hear of nothing other than what they have been taught (by man) in a religious school or seminary. They are too wrapped up in their own theory or opinion. Some refuse to open their mind and heart to allow the Holy Spirit to teach and guide them. Some are just too theological for me. They won't listen to any other logic, theory or reasoning. They're right, and you and I are wrong—no further discussion. Please do not get me wrong, I attended a religious college and seminary school, and I learned a lot. But what I learned by spending personal quality time with God in prayer, and in His word (meditating on His word), and what I was taught by the Holy Spirit, could not have been learned or taught in a religious or seminary school.

I am a logical person, but I am also a person of faith. I believe in the word of God. I'm open to discussion, but I'm in tuned with the Holy Spirit. And yes, I do believe in the rapture. One day the believers in Jesus Christ will disappear from the face of this earth. We will be caught (lifted or go) up to meet our Saviour in the sky, and live with Him forever more.

February 12, 1991

I was on a bus with a group of people when I heard someone choking. Someone said a pill was stuck in a lady's throat. The bus driver replied, "Oh, she'll be all right." He was unconcerned as he stepped off of the bus. I turned and looked at the lady and indeed she could barely breathe. I rushed over to her and gently patted her on her back; as I said, "Jesus, Jesus, Jesus." The pill went down her throat; her breathing was now normal; and she was fine.

The woman asked me to pray for her left eye. It had something like a star growing on it and it bothered her. I prayed for her and returned to my seat. I heard the people in the front of the bus telling the lady's daughter, "Sarah Jones prayed for her." The daughter then said, "What if she gets sick with this same thing again; she thinks she is healed from it." Getting out of my seat, saying with boldness, (as I walked towards her): "If it does happen to her again, you pray for her!

Are you saved? Have you been born again? I see you (on the bus) throwing your hands up, saying, 'Praise the Lord!' Do you have the Holy Ghost? In the word of God, Jesus said that after the Holy Ghost has come upon you, you would have power—power to heal the sick, cast out devils, and raise the dead. God said that in the last days He would pour out His Spirit upon all flesh. Young men would see visions and old men would dream dreams."

My Interpretation

Are you saved? Have you been born again? Have you been baptized with the Holy Spirit? If so, you have the authority to pray for your children, yourself, and others. Stop depending on the pastors and others to pray for you. What if they are unavailable? If you pray with faith and doubt not, God will hear and answer your prayer. (Read John 3:3; Matthew 21:21, 22; 1 John 5:14, 15; Mark 3:15; Acts 1:5.8; Acts 2:17; 1 Peter 2:24; Isaiah 53:5).

February 26, 1991

I was visiting at a hospital. As I walked around, I saw a lady (I believe she was a nurse because she had on a white uniform, and by the conversation that she was having with another nurse). She was sitting in a wheelchair crying softly as she sang, *"Be not dismayed for the Lord God is with thee. He'll be by your side forever more. Be not dismayed for the Lord God will keep thee. He'll be by your side forever more."* I walked over to her and gently laid her head close to my waistline, as I embraced her to comfort her while crying with her. As she sang the song, I could sense that she was afraid to have an operation, thinking that she may not survive. I wanted to tell her not to have fear, and everything would be alright (regarding the operation), but she was comforting herself through this beautiful song. Still singing, she said *"No matter what, whether I live or die, God will be there where I am."*

My Interpretation

There are so many people in the hospitals that are hurting, lonely, and scared. They need someone like you to pray with them, or someone to just hold them. If you are scheduled to have an operation, know that God has not forsaken you. If He chooses to use the doctors to heal you, He will be right by your side in the operating room, supervising the whole staff. For God is the Great Physician and CEO. Do not fret yourself, and be not dismayed for God will take care of you, and He promised that He would never leave or forsake us. (Hebrews 13:5)

"I shall not die, but live, And declare the works of the Lord" (Psalm 118:17). "I go to prepare a place for you, that where I am, there you may be also." (John 14:2, 3)

Sing this song with your heart (in your own way) and be comforted, as you embrace yourself in God's wonderful everlasting love. Trust Him to do His will in your life.

"Be not dismayed for the Lord God is with me. He'll be by my side forever more. Be not dismayed for the Lord God will keep me. He'll be by my side forever more. No matter what, whether I live or die, God will be where I am."

April 14, 1991

I went into a Catholic church. It seemed as though it was a special time of year because many people were in line waiting for the door to open. I got on the line also and went inside the church. Once inside the church, I saw people standing on line as they knelt down before the priest as he ministered to them. One young man started talking about God's goodness, and a group of young men told him to be quiet or he would have to leave. The young man started to leave as the man who told him to leave walked behind him.

I stood up before I knew it; waved my hand to the group of young men to wait because I wanted them to hear what I had to say. "What the man said is true," I said. "However, I think that he picked the wrong time to say it. This is a place of worship, God's place, and should be respected as such. But those that worship God must worship Him in spirit and in truth. You must be careful."

Then the priest spoke and told me that I love God. I walked over to him looking directly into his eyes saying; "Even Satan knows God and trembles at His name." (I couldn't quote the scripture as clearly as I wanted to because he tried to cross me up. I knew Satan was using him. The Priest wasn't being sincere, and he knew not to mess with me. I stared him in the eyes and he could not look at me. He turned and walked away.

My Interpretation

There is a time to speak and a time to be quiet. Just because you dress or look holy does not mean that you are. Many church folk have a form of godliness but that is all; they deny God's power. Choose a church where the people worship and praise God in spirit, in truth, where you can testify (at the right time) of God's goodness, mercy, grace, and His love.

James 2:19 reads: "You believe that there is one God. You do well. Even the demons believe—and tremble." "Let all things be done decently and in order" (1 Corinthians 14:40).

April 18, 1991

A man was demon-possessed. I spoke to the demon but there was no response. I began speaking in tongues, and the demon departed from the man.

My Interpretation

Sometimes it may be necessary to speak in tongues in order to cast demons out of a possessed person. We don't always know precisely how to pray for certain situations, or the way God would have us to pray, so the Holy Spirit takes control of our vocal cords and prays to God (Our Heavenly Father) for us concerning the individual we are praying and seeking deliverance for. "Likewise the Spirit also helps in our weaknesses. For we do not know what we should pray for as we ought, but the Spirit Himself makes intercession for us with groaning which cannot be uttered. Now He who searches the hearts knows what the mind of the Spirit is, because He makes intercession for the saints according to the *will* of God" (Romans 8:26-28).

May 17, 1991

I was at a gospel concert singing a song God gave me: "There Are So Many Things We Ask of Him." It was a beautiful song.

My Interpretation

We are always asking God for so many things, yet He asks very little from us. We're so busy asking Him for things, that we can't hear what He's asking us to do. God daily loads us with precious benefits. It is time for us to think about what we can render to God for all He has done for us, be grateful, and show Him appreciation. Let's stop being so selfish. Go to our Father; and say what can I do for you? Jesus, what may I do for You? "What shall I render to the LORD for all His benefits towards me? (Psalm 116:12).

June 4, 1991

I was in church singing a hymn with the words, "We will wait till Jesus comes." Then I said why I would wait, but can't remember what I said. My mother was with me and she was also singing this song.

My Interpretation

My parents use to sing this hymn in church and at home. They both sung it so well; and it was one of my dad's favorite songs. The title is 'Land of Rest' and it can be found in the Primitive Baptist Hymn book.

"O land of rest for thee I sigh, When will the moment come, And dwell in peace at home? We will wait till Jesus comes, We'll wait till Jesus comes, We'll wait till Jesus comes, And we'll be gathered home." This is just a portion of the song. Wait on Jesus; be encouraged, for He is our salvation; our Hope, our King, and our Redeemer. Hold on, Jesus is coming to take us home to that land of rest; that place He prepared for us over 2000 years ago.

August 12, 1991

I was in church and started speaking in tongues. I believe it was the gift of tongues.

My Interpretation

The gift of tongues and the interpretation of tongues (and other spiritual gifts) are given by God for ministering to His people for the profit of all. I thank God for bestowing upon me the gifts of tongues, and the interpretation of tongues. (1 Corinthians 12:1-11)

August 21, 1991

I was at my late grandmother Sarah's house (it was the house that her husband, my grandfather, passed away in). Grandma was lying in bed, as she always does most of the time, and the color of the room was cream. (My grandma was blind and must have been a little sick because she rarely got out of the bed except to have it cleaned, and herself. Grandma asked my mother to name me after her, because she believed that she would not be able to see me. True enough she became blind before I was born).

Grandma was wearing a blue dress and she looked so beautiful. She recognized my voice as I bent over the bed to hug and kiss her. As she tried to lift up her head, I put my arm under her neck and head, and then kissed her. Grandma told me how glad she was to hear my voice, and I told her how glad I was to hear her voice and to see her. Then I woke up because my daughter was calling me to get up for work.

My Interpretation

My grandmother departed this life to live in her eternal home with God in the 1970's. I was so happy to see her again and I didn't want to let her go. I wanted to spend more time with her to look at her and talk with her. For, I knew that I may not see her for a long time again. She looked just like herself. I still miss my grandma Sarah. But I thank God for the good memories that I have of her.

If your grandmother or grandfather is stilling living on this side, please love them, respect, take care of them, and spend as much time as you can with them. Talk to them, go places with them; look at them, pray for them, and thank God for blessing you with them. I miss my grandma Sarah, and both of my grandfathers. I never knew my dad's mother because she died when he was fifteen years old. Good grandparents are special and they're a blessing.

August 26, 1991

I was traveling on a bus going south; a big tractor-trailer passed by as I glanced at the passenger in the truck. I could not see the driver. I sensed that they both were on drugs and as the truck passed by the bus, I knew it was going to turn over. (It was as if I was seeing all this happen on a TV screen). The truck was in the left lane, it passed the bus, then another tractor-trailer; and as the truck was turning into the right lane, it turned over. As we passed the truck, I cried aloud saying, "Jesus, I knew it! I knew that truck was going to turn over." I prayed that someone would stop and help them. However, I felt that both men were all right.

My Interpretation

Experiencing a gut feeling, intuition, or perhaps it's the gift of knowledge? (1 Corinthians 12:8) If you see someone who needs help along the highway in such a case; call 911, and pray.

November 29, 1991

I was being interviewed for a job. The man who was interviewing me said, "Do you think Paul is with us today? You have no doubt read about the apostle Paul." I replied, "Spiritually, Paul is with us, we have his writings. I think Paul can be one as a mentor for any Christian." Some of the people in the company then introduced themselves, and I felt as though I had already been chosen for the position. (I believe the interviewer was a Christian.)

My Interpretation

Paul was an Israelite (Hebrew) of the tribe of Benjamin (Philippians 3:5), and he was born in Tarsus (a city of Cilicia) and raised in Jerusalem. (Acts 22:3) The Apostle Paul wrote: Romans, 1& 2 Corinthians, Galatians, Ephesians, Philippians, Colossians, 1& 2 Thessalonians, 1& 2 Timothy, Titus, and Philemon; and some are led to think that Paul or his associates may have written Hebrews. However, a firm author is uncertain.

God used him mightily to preach the Gospel of Jesus Christ to all people, but especially to the Gentiles. Paul suffered much for preaching the Gospel of Jesus Christ, but was determined to let nothing separate him from the love of Christ. Paul learned how to be content in whatever state that he was in; and learned that God's grace was sufficient. He kept the faith, and he finished his course. From childhood Paul had both the Hebrew name Saul, and the Roman name Paul. He used his Roman name Paul after his conversion on the road to Damascus where he had an encounter with Jesus, which changed the rest of his life. (Acts 9:3-22)

December 30, 1991

I was speaking in tongues.

My Interpretation

It is a wonderful feeling when I speak in tongues. Knowing that only God and the Holy Spirit understands what I am saying. Satan cannot touch this!

"For he who speaks in a tongue does not speak to men but to God, for no one understands him; however, in the spirit he speaks mysteries" (1 Corinthians 14:2). "And it shall come to pass in the last days, says God, That I will pour out of My Spirit on all flesh;" (Acts 2:17). "And they were all filled with the Holy Spirit and began to speak with other tongues, as the Spirit gave them utterance" (Acts 2:4)

January 17, 1992

There was a man with at least two other people seemingly in a kitchen. I guess I was going to buy food. I did not remember what transpired but it must have been something bad. I looked and pointed my finger at this man and said with power and without doubt: "Within two months you will die and in hell will you open your eyes." The man must have believed me because he started murmuring something looking up, as if he was praying. As I left the place, I felt sorry for him. But because my word had already gone out of my mouth, I could not take it back.

My Interpretation

We must be careful what we say because our words have power. Your words (when spoken in faith and according to the word of God) can minister life or death to you or to someone else. You can have what you say, if what you say comes from faith in your heart, and is based on God's word. (Mark 11:23; James 3:5-10) The tongue is a small member, but it boasts great things. Control the words that come forth out of your mouth especially when spoken in anger.

"Have faith in God. For assuredly, I say to you, whoever says . . . and does not doubt in his heart, but believes those things he says will be done, he will have whatever he says" (Mark 11:22, 23) "Death and life are in the power of the tongue, And those who love it will eat its fruit" (Proverbs 18:21). ". . . I will guard my ways, Lest I sin with my tongue; I will restrain my mouth with a muzzle," (Psalm 39:1).

January 24, 1992

I was in church and the choir was singing, "I Can Do All Things Through Christ Who Strengthens Me." I whispered to the person sitting next to me, "That's my song." Pastor Ken had a note pad in his hand and spoke about people not giving offerings as they should. He read the amount of the church offering that was given the previous Sunday, and the offering just received. I was surprise to hear that it was such a small amount.

My Interpretation

At times we may feel overwhelmed with the cares of this life. Whether it has to do with our health, relationships, job, family, money, or whatever it may be. You need to believe and know that you can do all things through

Jesus Christ who will give you the strength and everything that you need. But we must trust and rely on Him; not on our feelings, or on man, or what we see, or what we hear. We must walk by faith in the word and promises of God, and not by what we see in the natural. Give to the work of God; don't be afraid (due to a lack of) to give and don't be stingy. As freely, as much, and as whole heartedly as you give your offering; you will receive. Remember, it can't come back to you—until you let it go. Have faith in God.

"I can do all things through Christ who strengthens me" (Philippians 4:13). "And my God shall supply all your need according to His riches in glory by Christ Jesus" (Philippians 4:19). "Give, and it will be given to you: good measure, pressed down, shaken together, and running over will be put into your bosom. For with the same measure that you use, it will be measured back to you" (Luke 6:38).

February 13, 1992

I was preaching and was telling people to pray for their enemies; and for people even when they talk about you and put you down; and they say, "God bless you" but don't really mean it. For an example, I use dressing well. When you try to look good in your appearance for Jesus: wear nice clothes, shoes, hats, and such, and when you try to have the best for yourself and your family; people will talk about you. They let jealousy and envy take control of them.

My Interpretation

Jesus tells us to love our enemies, bless those that who curse us, do good to those who hate us, and pray for those who spitefully use us and persecute us. (Matthew 5:44) "For if you love those who love you, what reward have you? Do not the tax collectors do the same?" (Matthew 5:46).

If we only love our families and friends, or only those who love us; then we are no different from the unbeliever (those who do not believe in Jesus Christ nor have not accepted Him as their Lord and Saviour). How can we say we are Christians; we love God, and do not have love for people who are of a different race, gender, denomination, and religion.

"He who loves his brother abides in the light, and there is no cause for stumbling in him. But he who hates his brother is in darkness and walks in darkness, and does not know where he is going, because the darkness has blinded his eyes" (1 John 2:10, 11).

April 4, 1992

I was at church and there were visitors from another church. I didn't quite know what was going on as the pastor and some of the visitors were near the pulpit conversing and looking over a paper, so it seemed. The service had now ended.

I went to the ladies room and saw a woman and man. The man was smoking a cigarette. He was in one of the bathrooms with a lot of bags, and he looked like he was homeless. Then I looked and saw someone else smoking and told them that smoking was not allowed in the church, not even in the bathrooms. I told them that they could not stay in the bathroom because people had to use it. The man acted as though he wasn't going to leave.

I left the bathroom and started to return to my seat when I noticed some of our visitors were in the kitchen. I heard gospel music and was about to peep inside (the door was slightly ajar) when someone closed the door. I wondered what was going on, and continued to my seat.

Inside the sanctuary I saw three men, one in each aisle coming from the front of the church cleaning the carpet. As they cleaned the carpet it became so white (although the carpet was a dark red). I stood there in total amazement.

The pastor and a couple of the visitors were still up front talking and looking at what seemed to have been a piece of paper. I thought I had better get to my seat before the man got up to where I was sitting, because I didn't want to step on that beautiful white carpet before it dried. As the three men cleaned the carpet, they were in unison in their work. This too, amazed me.

Approaching my seat, I decided that I was ready to leave, so I softly told my oldest daughter that I was leaving and asked if she was coming with me. She acted as if she wasn't ready to go. A lady in the next row, first seat, signaled for me to be quiet. Well, I really thought that I was being as quiet as I could and ignored her. I then thought about the two people I had seen in the ladies room, and wondered if they had left. Looking around for two particular deacons, but didn't see them. Then I looked for any male usher to inform them of the matter, and ask them to escort the two people outside, but I didn't see any ushers. As a matter of fact, the more I looked around now, the more new faces I saw. I did not see any of our members, though many people were still seated in the church. They had remained from the first service.

I left the sanctuary and noticed three visitors standing by the kitchen and second door entrance. I was about to open the bathroom door (as it was now closed) but was told by one of the visitors not to. I said, "Why not, what's going on?" "A Holy Convocation," the lady replied. At this time, I assume that they were not letting anyone in or out of the church, so I started to return to my seat.

My Interpretation

It's time for the church of God to have a Holy Convocation. Let the people of God assemble together for one purpose (having the same mind and be on one accord)—to blow the trumpets of praise unto our God, and worship Him for whom He is, and for all He has done for us. Let us confess our sins unto our God, re-dedicate ourselves unto Him, and renew our vows and commitments unto Him. Present your body a holy vessel to be used by Him.

"I beseech you therefore, brethren, by the mercies of God, that you present your bodies a living sacrifice, holy, acceptable to God, which is your reasonable service" (Romans 12:1). This is a holy calling. And God is calling for a holy and righteous people.

May 4, 1992

I was traveling with some others and we were confused as to which way to go because of heavy rains and flooding. I began praying in tongues. The interpretation came through me saying, "Go to the right." I knew now that we would be safe.

My Interpretation

Do you need some direction in your life? When you feel misguided, confused, lost, and life is weighing you down and you can hardly see your way clear; God is always available to guide you in the right direction. All you have to do is call on Him. The tongues described above are the gift of tongues and the interpretation of tongues. "to another different kinds of tongues, to another the interpretation of tongues" (1Corinthians 12:10). These are gifts that God gives to whoever He chooses.

May 11, 1992

Suddenly, I found myself with two women who had babies. I took one of the babies and held him in my arms. He was so beautiful. He began to cry, so I got up and walked around with him, hoping this would console him. The two women marveled at how I adored the child and took so much time with him.

One of the ladies said, "She acts as though it is her own child," (and she smiled). I then sat down and said to the little child, "What's your name?" The mother replied, "Joseph." Smiling, I said to the child "Do you know that your name is important? Joseph in the Bible became a great man." The mother of the child then began to preach about the Joseph in the Bible.

My Interpretation

Joseph was a very handsome young boy. He was a dreamer and he could interpret dreams. This was a gift from God. Joseph was loved by his father Jacob; sold into slavery for 20 shekels of silver (by his brothers because they were jealous and hated him); taken to Egypt, and was put in prison because Pharaoh's wife lied on him (because he would not sleep with her). But God was always with Joseph, and Joseph was always with God.

Pharaoh put Joseph in charge of all of Egypt, and he became a great man with power and great authority. When he saw his brothers again many years later he had no hatred in his heart. He cried tears of joy and blessed them. He was happy to see his family once again. Read Genesis Chapters 37, 39-45 for more information concerning Joseph's life.

May 24, 1992

I heard a voice say: "Hear O Israel, God is one, God is Holy." I heard another voice say, "The Holiness of God."

My Interpretation

There is only one true and living God, and His name is Jehovah. God is one, and He is Holy. "Hear, O Israel: The Lord our God, the Lord is one!" (Deuteronomy 6:4). "Who is like You, glorious in holiness," (Exodus 15:11). "You should love the Lord your God with all your heart, with all your soul, and with all your strength" (Deuteronomy 6:5). "You shall be holy, for I the Lord your God am holy" (Leviticus 19:2).

July 2, 1992

I saw a person in white apparel, lifted high up, and in a circle. As I was about to cross the street from my apartment, he called my name: "Sarah, Sarah Jones." He then began to tell me words from God saying that I should trust Him, and do the work He has called me to do, but do not commit fornication. (I don't remember all that was said).

My Interpretation

God knows you by your name. Stop being disobedient and do what God has called you to do before it is too late. Trust Him. Live a clean and holy life before God. If you're having sexual problems with your flesh, then you must speak to your flesh when these desires rise up. I am not saying that it will be easy, but I am saying that it can (by the power of God) be done, and it must be done if you want to be used by God and reign with Him. Do not entertain sexual thoughts combat them with the word immediately. Think on things that are lovely and are of a good report. Give the devil no place in your mind. He has no right and no authority, unless you choose to give it to him.

If you are single (not married), you should not be sexually active. God sees everything that you're doing, thinking of doing, and will do. Satan will do all that's in his power to block and stop you from doing what God has ordained you to do. But you must tell Satan where he can go; and rebuke him in the name of Jesus. God can keep you if you so choose to be kept.

"Trust in the Lord, and do good; Commit your way to the Lord" (Psalm 37:3, 5). "You did not choose Me; but I chose you and appointed you that you should go and bear fruit" (John 15:16). You can't bear fruit in sin.

"Now the body is not for sexual immorality but for the Lord, and the Lord for the body" (1 Corinthians 6:13). "For this is the will of God, your sanctification: that you should abstain from sexual immorality; that each of you should know how to possess his own vessel in sanctification and honor, not in passion of lust . . ." (1 Thessalonians 4:3-5). "For this you know, that no fornicator, unclean person, has any inheritance in the kingdom of Christ and God" (Ephesians 5:5. Also read 1 Corinthians 6:9). "Therefore put to death your members which are on the earth: fornication, uncleanness, passion, evil desire, and covetousness, which is idolatry" (Colossians 3:5).

We have been purchased by the blood of Jesus and are no longer our own. We now belong to God and should glorify Him in our body and spirit, which are His. Flee sexual sin.

July 3, 1992

Someone said to me: "Instead of branching, you should spread out."

My Interpretation

Branching means to grow out, to cover the limbs or smaller branches. Spread out is to stretch, to open wide or wider, to expand, to extend, to go, bring out, and deliver. God wants you to broaden your horizon. He wants to expand your territory. He wants you to extend your services. He wants you to go in places you've never been before, and preach the Gospel of Jesus Christ to bring out people out of darkness, and deliver the people of God. Instead of branching, it is time for you (and me) to spread out. "His branches shall spread." (Hosea 14:6)

July 20, 1992

I was in church when I was (reminded a second time) in my spirit to say to this person: "Learn how to give God the glory first, and then everything else will be taken care of."

My Interpretation

When we put God first and praise and worship Him wholeheartedly, He will bless us abundantly. "But seek first the kingdom of God and His righteousness, and all these things shall be added to you" (Matthew 6:33). Give God the glory first and you will reap your harvest.

October 4, 1992

I was talking to Juney on the telephone. I quoted a scripture to her saying, Jesus said, "Will I find faith when I return?"

My Interpretation

When Jesus returns to the earth, will He find trustworthiness, anyone reliable, anyone with confidence, anyone with expectations and hope, anyone who is faithful, and anyone who believes that Jesus Christ is the Son of God? Will He find anyone preaching the Gospel of Jesus Christ because they truly love Him, or are they doing it for their own greed and material gain?

". . . when the Son of Man comes, will He really find faith on the earth?" (Luke 18:8).

December 8, 1992

This dream was about peace. A man was telling someone about the man he sent to a certain place because he knew this man would preach about peace.

My Interpretation

We can talk about peace, but there will never be world peace on this earth until Jesus returns, and reigns. Jesus is the Prince of peace, and we are to preach the gospel of peace. (Romans 10:15) "For He Himself is our peace, who has made both one, and has broken down the middle wall of separation, having abolished in His flesh the enmity, that is, the law of commandments contained in ordinances, so as to create in Himself one new man from the two, thus making peace, that He might reconcile them both to God in one body through the cross, thereby putting to death the enmity. And He came and preached peace to you who were afar off and to those who were near" (Ephesians 2:14-17 "Depart from evil and do good; seek peace and pursue it" (Psalm 34:14).

Invite Jesus Christ into your life and except Him as your Lord and Saviour, and you will find peace in your spirit like you've never had before. A peace that passes all understanding, a peace words cannot explain. Jesus is the only One who can give us real peace.

December 18, 1992

I was singing a song God gave me in church saying: "How can I say no, how can I say no after all you've done for me; how you set me free. How can I say no?"

My Interpretation

I can't say "no" to God. For He has done (and still doing) so much for me, and my family. He saved my soul; He made me whole, He healed my body, He transform my mind, He filled me with the Holy Spirit, He has bestowed upon me spiritual gifts, He has anointed me, He has appointed me, and ordained me for such a time as this. He has taught me, He has bought me from a mighty long way, and He never left me alone. He has protected me, He visits me in dreams and visions, He honors me with His presence, He has given me authority and power, and He rescued me from the clutches of Satan. He saved, delivered, and protects me and my family.

For God gave His Son Jesus, and Jesus gave His life; suffered unbelievably, took on my sins, your sins, and the world; died on the cross, and shed His precious blood for me (and for you) so that we could have a chance to live forever with Him. Then He rose on the third day for our justification. Now, everyone who is a believer in Jesus Christ has become the righteousness of God; and we have been justified and declared "not guilty" before God. Jesus paid the price for our redemption by giving His life as a substitute for us. Hallelujah! Glory to God!

I am forgiven of all of my sin, and will reign with Jesus and be in the presence of God for the rest of my life. I will forever praise, honor, and worship Him. How can I say "no" after all that He has done for me (and my family)? I can't. And how can you say "no" after all that He's done, and is doing, for you and your family.

February 26, 1993

I heard someone say, "Well, let me ask you . . ."

My Interpretation

Well, let me ask you: Have you asked Jesus to forgive you of all your sins? Have you accepted Jesus as your Lord and Saviour? Do you believe that Jesus Christ is the Son of God? Do you believe He died on the cross for your sins, and the sins of the world? Do you believe He rose on the third day for our justification (and with all power in His hands)?

Have you been born again? Have you chosen where you will spend eternity? Do you think God is pleased with the way you're living your life? Are you living a holy life before God? Do you have love for everyone (regardless of race, gender, domination, or religion)? Do you help your neighbors? Do you give to those less fortunate than you? Do you pray? Do you read God's Holy Word (the Bible)? Do you truly love God, and Jesus, His Son? Are you obedient to His word, and doing His will? Are you ready to go back with Jesus when He comes? Are you sure?

December 9, 1993

I was talking to a lady (my oldest daughter was with me) and we were speaking about good gospel music. The lady said that people play gospel music too loud and she was tired of listening to it. I told her that I never get tired of listening to good gospel music, as long as it is not too contemporary.

The lady then replied that all that was not necessary, and all one needs is love. I replied, "You do need love, but have you been changed?" I began to tell her about how a person must be born again, and that there must be a change in their life. As I was about to leave, another young woman walked into the store to see this lady. I turned to the lady I was speaking to and pointed at her and said in a strong voice: "If you are still going to the same old friends, doing the same old things, something is wrong. I know there has got to be a change because I've been changed. You are not a Christian as you think."

My Interpretation

You must be born again. When I use the word "born again," I am speaking about a new birth spiritually. We believe that Jesus is the Christ; have accepted Him as Lord and Saviour, and asked for forgiveness of our sins. When born again, we receive a new heart transplant (by the Holy Spirit); we are transformed by renewing our mind with the word of God; and we have the Spirit of God living in us. There has got be a change in you (and your life style) when this new birth takes place. When we are born again of the incorruptible seed (of God), we then become children of God.

"who were born, not of blood, nor of the will of the flesh, nor of the will of man, but of God" (John 1:13). Human beings cannot reproduce divine life; only God can. Regeneration and the new birth is the work of God, and it is absolutely necessary if one wants to enter and live forever in His kingdom.

Jesus told Nicodemus, "Most assuredly, I say to you, unless one is born again, he cannot see the kingdom of God" (John 3:3). "Most assuredly, I say to you, unless one is born of water and the Spirit, he cannot enter the kingdom of God. That which is born of the flesh is flesh, and that which is born of the Spirit is spirit. Do not marvel that I said to you, You must be born again. The wind blows where it wishes, and you hear the sound of it, but cannot tell where it comes from and where it goes. So is everyone who is born of the Spirit." (John 3:5-8)

"Therefore, if anyone is in Christ, he is a new creation; old things have been passed away; behold, all things have become new" (2 Corinthians 5:17). "Beloved, now we are children of God; and it has not yet been revealed what we shall be, but we know that when He is revealed, we shall be like Him, for we shall see Him as He is" (1 John 3:2).

December 9, 1993

In this dream a young person was saying they would get saved one day. I said to the person, "Now is the time because Jesus is coming. I've been having dreams since I was 16 years old, I am now 43, and time as we know it is quickly winding down. Jesus is coming soon."

My Interpretation

Don't keep putting off God. If today you hear His voice, obey and invite Him into your heart. "One day" in this life may never come for you. Don't die in your sins and open your eyes in this place of eternal torment called hell. Please, do not wait until it's too late. Today is the accepted time. Do it now. Time is running out, life is short, and Jesus is coming soon!

""Behold, the Lord comes with ten thousands of His saints, to execute judgment on all, to convict all who are ungodly among them of all their ungodly deeds which they have committed in an ungodly way, and of all the harsh things which the ungodly sinners have spoken against Him" (Jude 1:14, 15).

January 1994

I spoke in tongues and I interpreted it. It was a wonderful feeling. The interpretation was, "Seek the Lord while He may be found."

My Interpretation

I thank God for the gifts of tongues and the interpretation of tongues. Seek the Lord while He may be found, call upon Him while He is near. This Scripture indicates that there will be a time when people will be hungry, and thirsty for God, they will seek Him with their whole heart, but they will not find Him. They will pray day and night calling upon him, but He will not answer. God will be silent.

"Seek the Lord while He may be found, Call upon Him while He is near. Let the wicked forsake his way, and the unrighteous man his thoughts; Let him return (or turn) to the LORD, and He will have mercy on him; And to our God, for He will abundantly pardon" (Isaiah 55:5,7).

"Break up your fallow ground, For it is time to seek the LORD, Till He comes and rains righteousness on you" (Hosea 10:12). "The LORD is with you while you are with Him. If you seek Him, He will be found by you; but if you forsake Him, He will forsake you" (2 Chronicles 15:2). Prepare your heart to seek the LORD your God.

My prayer for you: Father, Let all those who seek You rejoice and be glad in You. (Psalm 40:16) You will show them the path of life. For In Your presence is fullness of joy, and at Your right hand are pleasures forevermore. (Psalm 16:11). In Jesus name, I ask—Amen.

Seek God now, because there will come a time when He will close all communication. After all, He has tried many times to get your attention, but you just ignored Him, and continued having your own lustful and selfish way. God will not force you to love Him. You must choose to love Him of your own free will.

"Because you disdained all my counsel, And would have none of my rebuke, I will also laugh at your calamity; I will mock when your terror comes, When your terror comes like a storm, And your destruction comes like a whirlwind, When distress and anguish come upon you. Then they will call upon me, but I will not answer; They will seek me diligently, but they will not find me. Because they hated knowledge And did not choose the fear of the LORD. They would have none of my counsel, and despise my every rebuke" (Proverbs 1:25-30).

"Therefore they shall eat the fruit of their own way, And be filled to the full with their own fancies" (Proverbs 1:31). The Spirit of God will not always strive with man. (Genesis 6:3) God is now saying to you, "Okay, have it your way. I love you, but I will not force you do something that is against your will." So, please, if you hear His voice today open your heart and listen. Do not turn away from Him. Jesus Christ is coming soon to take His people home, and to judge the world. Be ready when He comes. Seek Him and call upon His name NOW!

March 13, 1994

In my dream I saw myself getting up for church. As I was getting on my knees to pray, a voice said, "Fast for obedience, as well as the other things you are fasting for."

In Real Life: I wasn't going to church that Sunday, but after seeing myself in the dream getting ready for church, putting on my black two-piece suit, I decided to go, wearing the same suit I saw in the dream. I arrived in church and the speaker was talking about obedience.

My Interpretation

God is calling for a people who will be obedient to His call, and do His will. We must obey the voice of God. Do what He tells you to do, say what He tells you to say, and go where He tells you to go. Go on a fast for obedience (to God), and other things you need and desire.

March 27, 1994

I heard these words, "Rejoice, despite the circumstances."

My Interpretation

No matter what you are going through, despite the circumstances—rejoice in the Lord always, and again I say rejoice. (Philippians 4:4) For the joy of the Lord brings strength and hope. Praise Him regardless of how bad the situation looks, and no matter what anyone says. Rejoice and put your faith and trust in Jesus Christ.

April 10, 1994

A voice said, "Do the works I called you to do or I will destroy you."

My Interpretation

Do the work God has called you to do, or you will be destroyed both spiritually and physically. I know this may sound harsh, but Spirit of God will not always strive with man. Yes, He is loving, merciful, longsuffering, kind, compassionate, and so much more; but He will not keep begging you to do what He's calling you to do. He will allow you to do those things that you desire to do. He will not force you nor go against your will. God is extremely patient with us become He does not want anyone to perish. "For the wages of sin is death, but the gift of God is eternal life in Christ Jesus our Lord" (Romans 6:23). The choice is yours.

April 27, 1994

In my spirit, I heard a voice saying, "Do the work I called you to do, or I will destroy you."

My Interpretation

This is my second time having this dream. I know that God is speaking to me personally. I have been running from God for several years now. I believe God's patience is running out for me, and He's saying: "Enough is enough; enough of being disobedient, enough of sitting and lounging in your comfort zone; enough of procrastinating, enough of listening to other voices, but not My voice, enough of pleasing self and others and not pleasing Me; enough of being slothful, and enough of your excuses. Be obedient and do the work I have called you to do, or I will destroy you both physically and spiritually."

I truly thank God for putting up with me, not giving up on me; and looking beyond my countless faults and seeing my needs. I thank Him for His longsuffering, love and compassion, patience, grace, and His mercy. He has been (and is) so faithful, gracious, and kind to me (and my family). Let us do what God is calling us to do NOW, and willingly.

"For if I preach the gospel, I have nothing to boast of, for necessity is laid upon me; yes, woe is me if I do not preach the gospel! For if I do it willingly, I have a reward" (1 Corinthians 9:16, 17). God has called and chosen me to preach the gospel of Jesus Christ. I did not choose myself. I will go forth and I will not misuse or abuse the authority God has given me. Do what God has called you to do, and live—now, and forever.

June 19, 1994

Someone said to me: When are you going to join the choir? I saw myself directing the choir as we sang a beautiful song. It was such a lovely arrangement.

My Interpretation

Is God calling you to join the choir in your church? Or perhaps He's calling you to direct the choir with one of your favorite songs. If so, just do it. Fear may tell you that you do not have the ability, but that is a lie from Satan. God will not tell you, or call you to do something He has not already equipped you to do. Believe in yourself; believe in God, trust, and rely on Him.

August 10, 1994

This was a very frightening dream. I looked out of my window and saw buildings that had burned—they appeared scorched, but not completely burned. The sky looked icy and very clear. Words can hardly explain the sight that I saw. I went to my door and then looked up at the building I was in, and it looked just like the others. I told my daughters to hurry and grab some clothes and then get out of the building; as I also started grabbing their clothing, anything that would keep them warm. As we were leaving the building, we ran into a lady who was also looking for a place to go for safety. She said, "There's a Catholic church not too far from here. Well, it looks like it's going to happen." I replied, "It's already happening." Then we both began to praise God.

My Interpretation

The second return of Jesus is coming, signs and wonders are everywhere. It's not going to happen, it is already happening; and expect Him to crack through the sky at any given time. Just stop for a minute, look around, and see what's going on all around you. The world is in a terrible, unfixable (by man) bad condition, and it will only get worse and worse.

These are some of the problems that will grow worse: people will hate God, the Bible, the name of Jesus, and anyone who believes and preach the Gospel more than they already do. There will be a law against reading a Bible in public, or even owning one; a law against preaching the word of God, and saying the name "Jesus." There will be lovers of money, more than lovers of God; discrimination (like never before); hatred; parents abusing and hurting their little children physically and verbally.

There will be more elderly abuse; mentally challenge abuse; old and young people killing each other heartlessly and senselessly. There will be more kidnapping, and physically abusing, hurting, and killing God's innocent children (you will pay to the utmost in hell fire forever, with no chance of pardon or parole); health care; housing; fierce storms, hurricanes, tornadoes, floods, mud slides, and cyclones all around the world; food shortage, starvation, crime (like you've never seen before), no jobs, unemployment, stealing, killing, earthquakes, fires, wars; and financial problems all around the world, just to name a few. No one will be exempt from this except the children of God; those who have believed and accepted Jesus Christ as Lord and Saviour; and trusted Him to take care of them. Today, people have no love or respect for God, themselves or for others, no regard for human life, and no morals. We are truly living in the final days—Jesus Christ is coming!

"But know this, that in the last days perilous times will come: For men will be lovers of themselves, lovers of money, boasters, proud, blasphemers, disobedient to parents, unthankful, unholy, unloving, unforgiving, slanderers, without self-control, brutal, despisers of good, traitors, headstrong, haughty, lovers of pleasure rather than lovers of God, having a form of godliness but denying its power" (2 Timothy 3:1-5).

People will grumble and complain more than ever before. They will walk according to their own lusts, and they will speak big and flattering words. (Jude 1:16) There will be mockers in the last days that will walk according to their own ungodly lusts, and many will have no desire to change. (Jude 1:18) They will out-right refuse to acknowledge Jesus Christ as Lord of Lord. Instead they will curse God, Jesus, and the children of God. They will try to turn the believers and non-believers against Jesus. (We are not to associate with such evil people, do not allow them to influence you, and do not support them.)

And Jesus answered and said to them: "Take heed that no one deceives you. For many will come in My name, saying, 'I am the Christ,' and will deceive many. And you will hear of wars and rumors of wars. See that you are not troubled; for all these things must come to pass, but the end (of this age) is not yet.

For nation will rise against nation, and kingdom against kingdom. And there will be famines, pestilences, and earthquakes in various places. All these are the beginning of sorrows. Then they will deliver you up to tribulation and kill you, and you will be hated by all nations for My name's sake. And then many will be offended, will betray one another, and will hate one another.

Then many false prophets will rise up and deceive many. And because lawlessness will abound, the love of many will grow cold. But he who endures to the end shall be saved. And this gospel of the kingdom will be preached in all the world as a witness to all the nations, and then the end will come" (Matthew 24:4-14).

Please read the entire chapter of Matthew 24, concerning things that are happening and will happen before Jesus Christ second return to this earth. Also read the book of Revelation which will inform you of what has, what is, and will happen. And it will also give you a view of your new home, regardless of where you decide to spend eternity (heaven or hell). The choice is yours.

August 15, 1994

I was on a bus with a group of people. A man was talking to me about a man named Dine (I don't know this man but I knew some of his children). The man on the bus was telling me how well Dine could pray (much to his surprise). I said, "Well, I've heard people pray, but the question is has he been born again? If a person is serious and really means it in their heart, and asks God for help, and say: 'I don't want to do this anymore; I'm tired of my life in this way, and I need your help.' If they mean it from their heart, God will answer. They will be a new creature in Christ. Hallelujah, praise God, thank you Jesus!" I shouted. By now, some of the people on the bus were agreeing with me.

My Interpretation

Be serious with God and He will be serious with you. Some people have a way with words; they can speak well and articulate. They think they will be heard for their many words. Yes, they can even sound like they are truly praying from their heart. They like to be seen and heard. Just remember, God sees the heart of a person. Many people have a form of godliness but deny the power of God. They do not truly believe the word of God. But, if you call on God and mean it with all of your heart, I guarantee He will answer you gladly and speedily.

"Call to Me, and I will answer you, and show you great and mighty things, which you do not know" (Jeremiah 33:3). "I cry out with my whole heart; Hear me, O Lord!" (Psalm 119:145) "Search me, O God, and know my heart" (Psalm 139:23).

November 9, 1994

I was among a select group of people, for some reason, and we were viewing a film. The lady who was showing the film began telling us about the man in the picture. She said, "This man saw a little of Jerusalem." Then I saw a bright glowing light coming from the movie projector, pointing towards heaven; and what I saw was so beautiful, words cannot describe it. I could not take my eyes off of it. Suddenly, I was seemingly, now in heaven in Jerusalem walking; yet not walking, perhaps I was flying. I saw trillions and trillions and trillions of people.

The streets were like clear gold, and the water was crystal clear. Everyone was at peace with one another as they strolled along taking their time, yet at a steady pace. I could only see that little bit and then the movie projection ended. I wanted to see more. It was the most beautiful sight one could ever see.

The lady said that the man was the only one who had the tape and it was 30 minutes long, and the cost was $50.00. I told her I wanted one, and she took a small piece of paper and asked for my name and phone number. I was about to give her my first name, phone number and street address, but she said she had to go pick up her child. She told me to write down the information and leave it on the desk. I began writing down the information but then changed my mind about leaving it for anyone to see. I would just call her back regarding the tape at some other time.

Suddenly, I saw myself sitting at a table with others. I was sitting in front of a Jewish man who was holding his baby, and he was having a meal. He had an egg shaped container but there were no eggs in it. I asked him if his baby drink milk. He said the baby drinks dry milk. The child looked very healthy. I turned and saw another Jewish man with a long black & white beard, and he had a large plate filled with pasta (long noodles), grapes, and what looked like a block-shaped piece of cake. I told others about the New Jerusalem, and I praised God every time I thought about it. Such a great joy over flood my soul, and I just couldn't restrain myself. This was a place where I wanted to be; the place where I must spend my eternal life.

My Interpretation

"Eye has not seen, nor ear heard, Nor have entered into the heart of man The things which God has prepared for those who love Him" (1 Corinthians 2:9).

"And He carried me away in the Spirit to a great and high mountain, and showed me the great city, the holy Jerusalem, descending out of heaven from God, having the glory of God" (Revelation 21:10). ". . . and the city was pure gold, like clear glass" (Revelation 21:18). "And he showed me a pure river of water of life, clear as crystal, proceeding from the throne of God, and of the Lamb" (Revelations 22:1).

"Now I saw a new heaven and a new earth, for the first heaven and the first earth had passed away. Then I, John, saw the holy city New Jerusalem, coming down out of heaven from God, prepared as a bride adorned for her husband" (Revelations 21:1, 2).

Our God has such a beautiful place prepared for His children to live forever. And it will be right here on a purified planet earth. Read Revelation chapters 21 and 22 for a glance of your new eternal home.

December 17, 1994

A voice said, "The condition of the world will get worse. The reason is because God is going to start calling his children home; so they will not be here to pray."

My Interpretation

The condition of this world will grow worse and worse. There will be more wars (and a third world war), famine, hate, great earthquakes, great floods, fires, tornadoes, hurricanes, and a rise in prices for everything. There will a lack of love, lack of jobs, and lack of money. There will be great disasters, unbelievable devastations, racial problems, rise in crime, and terrorists attacks in America. There will come a time when men will hate to hear the word of

God, and the name of Jesus. They will want to kill you or put you in jail if you preach the gospel, and Bibles will be forbidden to read—even right here in the United State of America. However these things must happen in order for the word of God to be fulfilled.

The effective fervent prayer of a righteous man avails much. (James 5:16) God hears answers, and honors the prayers of those who have a right relationship with Him. Watch and pray for perilous times are coming; a time of great sorrows for everyone, and for the nations.

December 30, 1994

I was singing a song titled: We Shall Behold Him, as I was walking over the Brooklyn Bridge in New York. I was singing to a great number of people.

My Interpretation

One day the trumpet of God will sound and Jesus will appear in the sky. Everyone in the world will see Him and behold His glory. What an awesome day this will be. For some it will be the day that they have long awaited, hoped, and prayed for. It will be a day of great rejoicing.

For some it will be a very sad and dreadful day. They will see the One that they rejected, the One they didn't believe in, and the One they refused to obey. They will see that Jesus is real and that He is alive. They will see that God is real, and is the One and only true God. They will try to run to a hiding place, but find none. They will try to kill themselves, but death will not come. They will then want to believe and repent, and ask Jesus for forgiveness of their sins, but then it will be too late.

"He who is unjust, let him be unjust still; he who is filthy, let him be filthy still; he who is righteous, let him be righteous still; he who is holy, let him be holy still" (Revelations 22:11). It is too late for you to repent, change, or ask for forgiveness.

". . . in a moment, in the twinkling of an eye, at the last trumpet. For the trumpet will sound . . ." (1 Corinthians 15:52). The trumpet will announce the second coming of Jesus.

"For the Lord Himself will descend from Heaven with a shout, with the voice of an archangel, and with the trumpet of God . . ." (1 Thessalonians 4:16). "Then we who are alive and remain shall be caught up together with them in the clouds to meet the Lord in the air. And thus we shall always be with the Lord" (1 Thessalonians 4:17).

We shall behold Him, face to face, and see Him as He really is in all of His glory.

FINAL WORDS

I pray that you have enjoyed reading **Volume 1**, and have been blessed. I pray that God our Father, Jesus Christ our Saviour, and the Holy Spirit have ministered to your spirit in a real, meaningful, and awesome way. I pray that He has revealed His will, plan, and purpose for your life. I pray that you had ears to hear, and you heard what the Spirit of God was saying to you. I pray that you had faith to believe, and a heart to receive what He was saying to you. I pray that you allowed God the opportunity to minister to you as He so desires. I pray that you did not allow Satan to steal your moment, time, season, and your blessing from you. I also pray that God will speak to you (if He hasn't already) through *your* dreams and visions.

Remember, when God speaks to you in a dream or vision, believe and receive whatever He says. And whatever He tells you to do—do it. Stay committed to what God has put in your spirit, to the dreams and visions He has given and shared with you, and don't let them die. God cannot lie and is true to His every word and promise. Once God tells you something, His word goes forth to do, perform, and accomplish that which He has spoken (and told it to do).

"Indeed I have spoken it; I will also bring it to pass. I have purposed it; I will also do it.

For as the rain comes down, and the snow from heaven, And do not return there, But water the earth, and make it bring forth and bud, That it may give seed to the sower and bread to the eater, So shall My word be that goes forth from my mouth; It shall not return to Me void, But it shall accomplish what I please, And it shall prosper in the thing for which I sent it" (Isaiah 46:11; 55:10-11).

If God said it—I believe it—His word settles it—no more discussion. May the grace of our Lord Jesus Christ be with you.

Remember, **Volume 1** and **Volume 2** goes hand in hand. Read them both and receive double blessings.

Prayer of Salvation

God, our Heavenly Father, loves us so much that He made us in His image. He loves us so much that He gave His only begotten Son, Jesus Christ, to die on the cross for our sins (settling the sin issue once and for all, and reconciled us back to Him so that we can have a chance for eternal life); that whoever believes in Jesus will not perish, but will have everlasting life.

Jesus Christ loves us so much that He gave His life for us and the world. He suffered, bled, died on the cross for our sins, and God raised Him from the grave on the third day for our justification. It is through His shed blood at the cross that we have been purchased and reconciled back to God. We can once again have fellowship and a personal relationship with God the Father. God can once again call us His children, and we can call Him "our Father." Once again we have a chance to live with Him forever in that place that Jesus has prepared for us, and we can have His best and live a victorious life while living here on earth.

If you would like to invite Jesus Christ into your life, and have a personal relationship with Him; please say out loud the following prayer. (And, if you mean it with all of your heart, I promise you that your life will change; and you will never be the same. You will become a new born creation in Him. You will feel His love, joy, and peace as you have never in your life experienced or felt before). Let us pray:

Lord Jesus, Forgive me of my sins and have mercy upon me. I repent and invite You to come into my heart, and into my life. Wash me in your blood, and baptize me with Your Holy Spirit. I confess with my mouth and I believe in my heart that You are the Son of God; that You died on the cross for my sins; and that God the Father, raised You from the dead on third day for my justification. I surrender my life to You, and I accept You as my Lord and Saviour. Thank you Jesus for salvation! Amen

If you said this prayer in all sincerity, let me be the first to say: "Welcome to the Family of God." I rejoice along with the angels and your enormous family in heaven.

"Behold what manner of love the Father has bestowed upon us, that we should be called the children of God! Therefore the world does not know us, because it did not know Him. Beloved, now we are the children of God; and it has not yet been revealed what we shall be, but we know that when He is revealed, we shall be like Him, for we shall see Him as He is. And everyone who has this hope in Him purifies himself, just as He is pure" (1 John 3:1-3).

Now that you are a born-again child of God, find a church where the pastor teaches the Bible, and will not compromise the Word. Go to bible study and Sunday school as often as you can, and if possible attend a bible college, where you can learn and grow in the word of God. Read your Bible daily as well as pray. Jesus Christ, our Lord and Saviour, is coming for us very soon. For God, our Heavenly Father awaits us, and yearns for us to be where He is.

May the grace of Jesus, our Lord and Saviour; the love of God, our Heavenly Father; and the communion of the Holy Spirit; be with you and all those who love Him. Amen

Author's Note

Due to the large size (number of pages) of my book and the high retail price it would cost for a single book, we have made a **Volume 1** and **Volume 2** (each sold separately). I want these books to be available to everyone at the lowest price possible. In expressing this to my publisher they have diligently worked with me to make this happen, and I thank them for doing so. I know that God wants you to have this book.

I pray that you will read both volumes of
My Dreams, My Interpretations: Night Visions in My Head,
and receive a double blessing.

Volume 1:
My Dreams and My Interpretations:
Summer 1966—December 1994

Volume 2:
My Dreams and My Interpretations:
February 1995—December 2008

Volume 2 comes with a brief preview of some of my dreams
and a few of my interpretations from January 2009—April
2011, to be published in my forthcoming edition Volume 3.

Scriptures On Dreams
And Interpretations

Genesis 20: 3, 6, 7; 28:12-16

(God had a discussion with Abimelech concerning another man's wife. Jacob and God conversed in his dream. God assuring Jacob that He would be with him wherever he went. God promised that He would never leave nor forsake us. Will you make that same promise to God?)

Genesis 31:10, 13, 24

(God spoke to Jacob and acknowledged that He was aware of what Laban was doing to him, and to leave and return to the land of his family in Canaan. God warned Laban to be careful how he approached and spoke to Jacob whether it was good or bad. God is listening so be careful how you speak and what you say to a child of God.)

Genesis 37:5-10

(Joseph, son of Jacob and Rachel, was seventeen years old when he had this dream. His father had trouble believing and accepting the interpretations of his dreams, but he did not dismiss them totally and kept them in mind. However his brothers (except perhaps Benjamin) hated him because of his dreams; and because they felt that their father favored him more.

Joseph brothers called him the "dreamer." Little did his father or brothers knew that their interpretation of Joseph's dream would actually come to pass twenty one years later. God blessed Joseph mightily and used him to be a great blessing to his family, and countless others. Read about it in Genesis chapters 42-47.

God can take a bad situation and turn it into something good for you. For all things work together for good to those who love God, to those who are called according to His purpose. (Romans 8:28) No matter what anyone says, especially those who may dislike you, jealous of you, and think more highly of themselves than they should; you just keep on dreaming and stay in the will of God. Our God will bless you abundantly, and you will also be a blessing to others.)

Genesis 40:5-22

(Pharaoh's chief butler and baker were put in the same prison with Joseph. Both the butler and baker had a dream in the same night. God gave Joseph the interpretation of their dreams, and it came to pass just as he had interpreted. You have been in prison with some things in your life and you just can't break loose from them. Well, get ready because Jesus Christ is about to make you free. And when He makes you free you are free for certain. Call upon Him in faith. Ask Him to forgive you of your sins (if you haven't already done so), and be your Lord and Saviour.

Also, some interpretations may not be what you want to hear.)

Genesis 41:1-7; 14-36

(Pharaoh had two dreams following each other and no one in all of Egypt could interpret it except Joseph. God warns us, prepares, and gives us solutions to famines in our lives.)

Daniel 2:1-47; 1:1, 3, 5-7

(Nebuchadnezzar, the king of Babylon, had a dream that troubled him so much he could not sleep. However he could not remember what he dreamt. He called his magicians, sorcerers, the Chaldeans, and the astrologers to tell him what he dreamt, and the interpretation of his dream. But they could not make known the dream to him, and told the king that only gods whose dwelling was not with flesh could do what he asked. Because of this Nebuchadnezzar sent out a decree to kill all the wise men which would have included Daniel (Belteshazzar), Hananiah (Shadrach), Mishael (Meshach), and Azariah (Abed-Nego), his companions. (The four of them had been carried to Babylon from Jerusalem as captives, and were being trained to serve in the king's palace and in government—at the king's request).

Daniel asked Nebuchadnezzar to give him time, that he might tell him the dream and the interpretation. Daniel and his companions sought God concerning the dream, and God revealed the dream to Daniel in a night vision, and gave him the interpretation. This revelation made a believer out of Nebuchadnezzar. He said to Daniel: "Truly your God is the God of gods, the Lord of kings, and a revealer of secrets, since you could reveal this secret" (v 47).

Jehovah God of heaven is the only God who can reveal deep and secret things. Our God can do what no other gods can do. Trust Him with your future for Jesus is coming and will set up His kingdom here on earth. A kingdom that will not be destroyed, but it will stand forever.)

Scriptures On Visions

Genesis 15:1; Genesis 46:2
Micah 3:6; Psalm 89:19; Job 4:13
Job 7:14; Ezekiel 1:1; Ezekiel 7:26; 8:3
Ezekiel 12:23; Ezekiel 40:2; 43:3
Daniel 1:17 (God gifted Daniel with understanding in all visions and
    dreams)
Daniel 2:28; Daniel 4:5, 9-10, 13
Daniel 7:1-2, 7, 13, 15; Daniel 8:1-27
Daniel 9:21-24; Daniel 10:4-10
Obadiah 1; Numbers 12:6; Numbers 24:4

Some visions (and dreams) may not be meant for us to understand now. It may be appointed for a later time, however God wants us to be aware of things before it happens, and before He brings it to pass.

"Write the vision and make it plain on tablets, That he may run who reads it. For the vision is yet for an appointed time; But at the end it will speak, and it will not lie. Though it tarries, wait for it; Because it will surely come, It will not tarry" (Habakkuk 2:2, 3).